Teach Yourself
Red Hat® Linux

VISUALLY™

IDG's **3-D Visual**™ Series

IDG BOOKS *From* **maranGraphics**™

IDG Books Worldwide, Inc.
An International Data Group Company
Foster City, CA • Indianapolis • Chicago • New York

Teach Yourself Red Hat® Linux VISUALLY™

Published by
IDG Books Worldwide, Inc.
An International Data Group Company
919 E. Hillsdale Blvd., Suite 400
Foster City, CA 94404

Copyright©   1999 by maranGraphics Inc.
5755 Coopers Avenue
Mississauga, Ontario, Canada
L4Z 1R9

Library of Congress Catalog Card No.: 99-068241

ISBN: 0-7645-3430-0

Printed in the United States of America

10 9 8 7 6 5 4 3 2 1

Distributed in the United States by IDG Books Worldwide, Inc.

Distributed by CDG Books Canada Inc. for Canada; by Transworld Publishers Limited in the United Kingdom; by IDG Norge Books for Norway; by IDG Sweden Books for Sweden; by IDG Books Australia Publishing Corporation Pty. Ltd. for Australia and New Zealand; by TransQuest Publishers Pte Ltd. for Singapore, Malaysia, Thailand, Indonesia, and Hong Kong; by Gotop Information Inc. for Taiwan; by ICG Muse, Inc. for Japan; by Intersoft for South Africa; by Eyrolles for France; by International Thomson Publishing for Germany, Austria and Switzerland; by Distribuidora Cuspide for Argentina; by LR International for Brazil; by Galileo Libros for Chile; by Ediciones ZETA S.C.R. Ltda. for Peru; by WS Computer Publishing Corporation, Inc. for the Philippines; by Contemporanea de Ediciones for Venezuela; by Express Computer Distributors for the Caribbean and West Indies; by Micronesia Media Distributor, Inc. for Micronesia; by Chips Computadoras S.A. de C.V. for Mexico; by Editorial Norma de Panama S.A. for Panama; by American Bookshops for Finland.
For corporate orders, please call maranGraphics at 800-469-6616.
For general information on IDG Books Worldwide's books in the U.S., please call our Consumer Customer Service department at 800-762-2974.
For reseller information, including discounts and premium sales, please call our Reseller Customer Service department at 800-434-3422.
For information on where to purchase IDG Books Worldwide's books outside the U.S., please contact our International Sales department at 317-596-5530 or fax 317-596-5692.
For consumer information on foreign language translations, please contact our Customer Service department at 1-800-434-3422, fax 317-596-5692, or e-mail rights@idgbooks.com.
For information on licensing foreign or domestic rights, please phone 1-650-655-3109.
For sales inquiries and special prices for bulk quantities, please contact our Sales department at 650-655-3200.
For information on using IDG Books Worldwide's books in the classroom or for ordering examination copies, please contact our Educational Sales department at 800-434-2086 or fax 317-596-5499.
For press review copies, author interviews, or other publicity information, please contact our Public Relations department at 650-653-7000 or fax 650-655-7500.
For authorization to photocopy items for corporate, personal, or educational use, please contact maranGraphics at 800-469-6616.
Screen shots displayed in this book are based on pre-release software and are subject to change.

© 1999 maranGraphics, Inc.

The 3-D illustrations are the copyright of maranGraphics, Inc.

ABOUT IDG BOOKS WORLDWIDE

Welcome to the world of IDG Books Worldwide.

IDG Books Worldwide, Inc., is a subsidiary of International Data Group, the world's largest publisher of computer-related information and the leading global provider of information services on information technology. IDG was founded more than 30 years ago by Patrick J. McGovern and now employs more than 9,000 people worldwide. IDG publishes more than 290 computer publications in over 75 countries. More than 90 million people read one or more IDG publications each month.

Launched in 1990, IDG Books Worldwide is today the #1 publisher of best-selling computer books in the United States. We are proud to have received eight awards from the Computer Press Association in recognition of editorial excellence and three from Computer Currents' First Annual Readers' Choice Awards. Our best-selling ...*For Dummies*® series has more than 50 million copies in print with translations in 31 languages. IDG Books Worldwide, through a joint venture with IDG's Hi-Tech Beijing, became the first U.S. publisher to publish a computer book in the People's Republic of China. In record time, IDG Books Worldwide has become the first choice for millions of readers around the world who want to learn how to better manage their businesses.

Our mission is simple: Every one of our books is designed to bring extra value and skill-building instructions to the reader. Our books are written by experts who understand and care about our readers. The knowledge base of our editorial staff comes from years of experience in publishing, education, and journalism — experience we use to produce books to carry us into the new millennium. In short, we care about books, so we attract the best people. We devote special attention to details such as audience, interior design, use of icons, and illustrations. And because we use an efficient process of authoring, editing, and desktop publishing our books electronically, we can spend more time ensuring superior content and less time on the technicalities of making books.

You can count on our commitment to deliver high-quality books at competitive prices on topics you want to read about. At IDG Books Worldwide, we continue in the IDG tradition of delivering quality for more than 30 years. You'll find no better book on a subject than one from IDG Books Worldwide.

John Kilcullen
Chairman and CEO
IDG Books Worldwide, Inc.

Steven Berkowitz
President and Publisher
IDG Books Worldwide, Inc.

*Eighth Annual
Computer Press
Awards ➤1992*

*Ninth Annual
Computer Press
Awards ➤1993*

*Tenth Annual
Computer Press
Awards ➤1994*

*Eleventh Annual
Computer Press
Awards ➤1995*

IDG is the world's leading IT media, research and exposition company. Founded in 1964, IDG had 1997 revenues of $2.05 billion and has more than 9,000 employees worldwide. IDG offers the widest range of media options that reach IT buyers in 75 countries representing 95% of worldwide IT spending. IDG's diverse product and services portfolio spans six key areas including print publishing, online publishing, expositions and conferences, market research, education and training, and global marketing services. More than 90 million people read one or more of IDG's 290 magazines and newspapers, including IDG's leading global brands — Computerworld, PC World, Network World, Macworld and the Channel World family of publications. IDG Books Worldwide is one of the fastest-growing computer book publishers in the world, with more than 700 titles in 36 languages. The "...For Dummies®" series alone has more than 50 million copies in print. IDG offers online users the largest network of technology-specific Web sites around the world through IDG.net (http://www.idg.net), which comprises more than 225 targeted Web sites in 55 countries worldwide. International Data Corporation (IDC) is the world's largest provider of information technology data, analysis and consulting, with research centers in over 41 countries and more than 400 research analysts worldwide. IDG World Expo is a leading producer of more than 168 globally branded conferences and expositions in 35 countries including E3 (Electronic Entertainment Expo), Macworld Expo, ComNet, Windows World Expo, ICE (Internet Commerce Expo), Agenda, DEMO, and Spotlight. IDG's training subsidiary, ExecuTrain, is the world's largest computer training company, with more than 230 locations worldwide and 785 training courses. IDG Marketing Services helps industry-leading IT companies build international brand recognition by developing global integrated marketing programs via IDG's print, online and exposition products worldwide. Further information about the company can be found at www.idg.com.   1/24/99

maranGraphics is a family-run business
located near Toronto, Canada.

At **maranGraphics**, we believe in producing great computer books–one book at a time.

Each maranGraphics book uses the award-winning communication process that we have been developing over the last 25 years. Using this process, we organize screen shots, text and illustrations in a way that makes it easy for you to learn new concepts and tasks.

We spend hours deciding the best way to perform each task, so you don't have to! Our clear, easy-to-follow screen shots and instructions walk you through each task from beginning to end.

Our detailed illustrations go hand-in-hand with the text to help reinforce the information. Each illustration is a labor of love–some take up to a week to draw!

We want to thank you for purchasing what we feel are the best computer books money can buy. We hope you enjoy using this book as much as we enjoyed creating it!

Sincerely,
The Maran Family

Please visit us on the Web at:
www.maran.com

CREDITS

Author:
Ruth Maran

Technical Consultants:
Eric Kramer
Paul Whitehead

Copy Editors:
Cathy Benn
Jill Maran
Frances Lea

Project Manager:
Judy Maran

Editors:
Raquel Scott
Janice Boyer
Stacey Morrison

Screen Captures & Editing:
James Menzies

Layout Design & Illustrations:
Treena Lees
Sean Johannesen
Jamie Bell

Illustrators:
Russ Marini
Peter Grecco
Steven Schaerer

Screen Artist:
Jimmy Tam

Indexer:
Raquel Scott

Permissions Coordinator:
Jenn Reid

Post Production:
Robert Maran

**Senior Vice President,
Technology Publishing
IDG Books Worldwide:**
Richard Swadley

**Editorial Support
IDG Books Worldwide:**
Barry Pruett
Martine Edwards

ACKNOWLEDGMENTS

Thanks to the dedicated staff of maranGraphics, including
Cathy Benn, Janice Boyer, Peter Grecco, Sean Johannesen,
Eric Kramer, Wanda Lawrie, Frances Lea, Treena Lees,
Jill Maran, Judy Maran, Robert Maran, Sherry Maran,
Russ Marini, James Menzies, Stacey Morrison, Jenn Reid,
Steven Schaerer, Raquel Scott, Jimmy Tam, Roxanne Van Damme,
Paul Whitehead and Kelleigh Wing.

Finally, to Richard Maran who originated the easy-to-use
graphic format of this guide. Thank you for your
inspiration and guidance.

TABLE OF CONTENTS

Chapter 1

INSTALL LINUX

Chapter 2

LINUX BASICS

Chapter 3

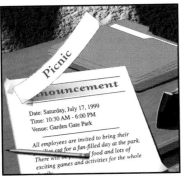

Chapter 4

TABLE OF CONTENTS

Chapter 5

CUSTOMIZE LINUX

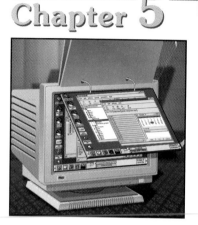

Chapter 6

CUSTOMIZE THE GNOME PANEL

Chapter 7

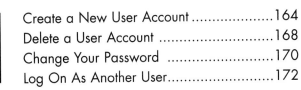

WORK WITH ACCOUNTS

Chapter 8

WORK WITH FLOPPY AND CD-ROM DRIVES

Chapter 9

WORK WITH HARDWARE AND SOFTWARE

TABLE OF CONTENTS

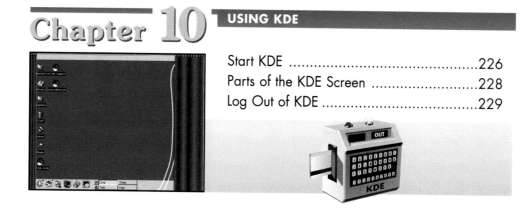

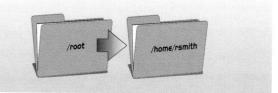

Chapter 13

BROWSE THE WEB

Chapter 14

EXCHANGE ELECTRONIC MAIL

Chapter 15

JOIN NEWSGROUPS

CHAPTER 1

Install Linux

In this chapter you will learn how to install the Linux operating system on your computer.

PREPARE TO INSTALL LINUX

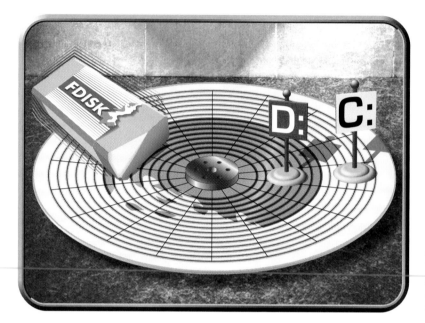

Before you can install Linux on your computer, you need to use FDISK to delete all existing partitions on your computer.

A partition is a part of the hard drive that acts as a separate drive. Most hard drives have only one partition.

PREPARE TO INSTALL LINUX

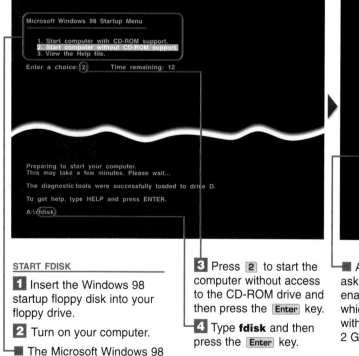

START FDISK

1 Insert the Windows 98 startup floppy disk into your floppy drive.

2 Turn on your computer.

■ The Microsoft Windows 98 Startup Menu appears.

3 Press **2** to start the computer without access to the CD-ROM drive and then press the **Enter** key.

4 Type **fdisk** and then press the **Enter** key.

■ A message appears, asking if you want to enable large disk support, which allows you to work with partitions larger than 2 GB.

5 To enable large disk support, press **Y** (for Yes) and then press the **Enter** key.

4

? **What should I do before preparing to install Linux?**

▶ You should back up the information on your computer. Deleting partitions will permanently remove all the information on your computer.

▶ Obtain a Windows 98 startup floppy disk. If you do not have a Windows 98 startup floppy disk, you can create a startup disk using any Windows 98 computer.

▶ Make sure your computer will start from the floppy drive when you turn on your computer. If your computer does not start from the floppy drive, consult your computer's manual to determine how to change the BIOS settings.

```
                    Microsoft  Windows  98
                    Fixed  Disk  Setup  Program
              (C)Copyright  Microsoft  Corp.  1983  –  1998

                          FDISK Options

   Current  fixed  disk  drive:  1

   Choose  one  of  the  following:

     1.  Create  DOS  partition  or  Logical  DOS  Drive
     2.  Set  active  partition
     3.  Delete  partition  or  Logical  DOS  Drive
     4.  Display  partition  information


   Enter  choice: [4]




   Press  Esc  to  exit  FDISK
```

```
                     Display  Partition  Information

   Current  fixed  disk  drive:  1

   Partition   Status   Type    Volume Label   Mbytes   System   Usage
   C:  1          A     PRI DOS    WIN 98        4088    FAT32    100%


   Total  disk  space  is  4088  Mbytes  (1  Mbyte  =  1048576  bytes)




   Press  Esc  to  continue_
```

VIEW PARTITION INFORMATION

■ This area displays a list of FDISK options that you can choose from.

1 Press **4** to display information about the partitions on your hard drive and then press the **Enter** key.

■ This area displays information about each partition on your hard drive.

■ This area displays the total amount of space on the hard drive.

2 Press the **Esc** key to return to the list of FDISK options.

PREPARE TO INSTALL LINUX

You must delete all the partitions on your computer before you can install Linux. Deleting the partitions will permanently erase all the information on your computer.

PREPARE TO INSTALL LINUX (CONTINUED)

```
                    FDISK Options

Current fixed disk drive: 1

Choose one of the following:

  1. Create DOS partition or Logical DOS Drive
  2. Set active partition
  3. Delete partition or Logical DOS Drive
  4. Display partition information


Enter choice: [3]



Press Esc to exit FDISK
```

```
        Delete DOS Partition or Logical DOS Drive

Current fixed disk drive: 1

Choose one of the following:

  1. Delete Primary DOS Partition
  2. Delete Extended DOS Partition
  3. Delete Logical DOS Drive(s) in the Extended DOS Partition
  4. Delete Non-DOS Partition


Enter choice: [1]



Press Esc to return to FDISK Options
```

DELETE A PARTITION

■ This area displays a list of FDISK options that you can choose from.

1 Press ③ to delete a partition and then press the Enter key.

■ This area displays the types of partitions that you can delete.

2 Press ① to delete the primary partition and then press the Enter key.

■ A warning message appears, stating that you will lose the data in the partition.

I have more than one partition.
How do I delete all the partitions?

Primary Partition

Each hard drive has a primary partition, which is usually known as drive C. You can delete the primary partition by performing the steps below.

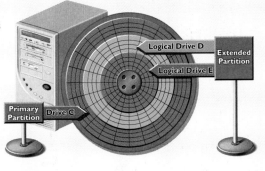

Extended Partition

A hard drive can also have an extended partition. An extended partition contains one or more drives, called logical drives, that are usually known as drives D, E and so on. You must remove all logical drives before you can delete an extended partition. To delete a logical drive, press ③ in step 2 below. To delete an extended partition, press ② in step 2 below.

```
                    Delete Primary DOS Partition
Current fixed disk drive: 1

Partition   Status   Type      Volume Label   Mbytes   System   Usage
C: 1          A     PRI DOS     WIN 98         4088     FAT32    100%


Total disk space is 4088 Mbytes (1 Mbyte = 1048576 bytes)


WARNING! Data in the deleted Primary DOS Partition will be lost.
What primary partition do you want to delete...? [1]
Enter Volume Label................................? [WIN 98]
Are you sure (Y/N)................................? [Y]

Press Esc to return to FDISK Options
```

```
                    Delete Primary DOS Partition
Current fixed disk drive: 1




Total disk space is 4088 Mbytes (1 Mbyte = 1048576 bytes)



Primary DOS Partition deleted

Press Esc to continue_
```

■ This area displays information about existing partitions such as the number and label of each partition.

3 Press the number of the partition you want to delete and then press the Enter key.

4 Type the label of the partition and then press the Enter key.

5 To delete the partition, press Y (for Yes) and then press the Enter key.

■ The partition is deleted.

6 Press the Esc key to return to the list of FDISK options.

■ If you want to install only Linux on your computer, you can now install Linux as shown on page 12. If you want to set up your computer to run both Linux and Windows, see page 8.

PREPARE TO INSTALL LINUX

If you want to set up your computer to run both Linux and Windows, you must create a partition that will store Windows.

A computer that can run two operating systems, such as Linux and Windows, is known as a dual-boot setup.

PREPARE TO INSTALL LINUX (CONTINUED)

```
                        FDISK Options

Current fixed disk drive: 1

Choose one of the following:

  1. Create DOS partition or Logical DOS Drive
  2. Set active partition
  3. Delete partition or Logical DOS Drive
  4. Display partition information


Enter choice: [1]




Press Esc to exit FDISK
```

```
            Create DOS Partition or Logical DOS Drive

Current fixed disk drive: 1

Choose one of the following:

  1. Create Primary DOS Partition
  2. Create Extended DOS Partition
  3. Create Logical DOS Drive(s) in the Extended DOS Partition


Enter choice: [1]




Press Esc to return to FDISK Options
```

CREATE A PARTITION

■ This area displays a list of FDISK options that you can choose from.

1 Press [1] to create a partition and then press the [Enter] key.

■ This area displays the types of partitions that you can create.

2 Press [1] to create a primary partition and then press the [Enter] key.

■ FDISK checks the integrity of the drive.

8

What size should I use for a partition that will store Windows?

Before determining the size for a partition that will store Windows, consider the following:

▶ The total amount of hard drive space on your computer.

▶ The amount of hard drive space required to install Windows 98 and Linux. Windows 98 requires about 260 MB of hard drive space. Linux requires about 600 MB of hard drive space.

▶ How often you will use Windows 98 compared to Linux. If you will use Windows 98 more often than Linux, devote more hard drive space to the Windows partition.

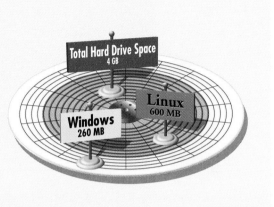

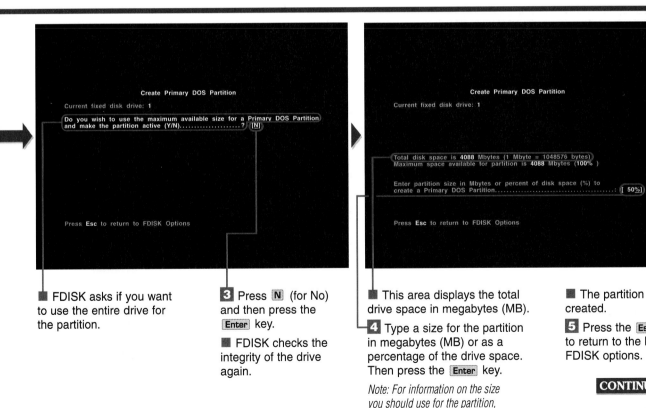

■ FDISK asks if you want to use the entire drive for the partition.

3 Press [N] (for No) and then press the [Enter] key.

■ FDISK checks the integrity of the drive again.

■ This area displays the total drive space in megabytes (MB).

4 Type a size for the partition in megabytes (MB) or as a percentage of the drive space. Then press the [Enter] key.

Note: For information on the size you should use for the partition, see the top of this page.

■ The partition is created.

5 Press the [Esc] key to return to the list of FDISK options.

CONTINUED

PREPARE TO INSTALL LINUX

After you create a partition that will store Windows, you must set the partition as the active partition. This gives your computer the ability to start Windows.

FDISK Options

Current fixed disk drive: 1

Choose one of the following:

1. Create DOS partition or Logical DOS Drive
2. Set active partition
3. Delete partition or Logical DOS Drive
4. Display partition information

Enter choice: [2]

WARNING! No partitions are set active – disk 1 is not startable unless a partition is set active

Press **Esc** to exit FDISK

Set Active Partition

Current fixed disk drive: 1

Partition	Status	Type	Volume Label	Mbytes	System	Usage
C: 1		PRI DOS		2047	UNKNOWN	50%

Total disk space is **4088** Mbytes (1 Mbyte = 1048576 bytes)

Enter the number of the partition you want to make active.............: [1]

Press **Esc** to return to FDISK Options

SET THE ACTIVE PARTITION

■ This area displays a list of FDISK options that you can choose from.

1 Press **2** to set the active partition and then press the **Enter** key.

■ This area displays information about each partition.

2 Press **1** to set the partition that will store Windows as the active partition and then press the **Enter** key.

■ The partition is made the active partition.

3 Press the **Esc** key to return to the list of FDISK options.

Is there anything else I need to do before installing Linux and Windows?

If you set up your computer to run both Linux and Windows, you need to format the partition that will store Windows. After you format the partition, you can install Windows and Linux.

```
A:: format c: /s

WARNING, ALL DATA ON NON-REMOVABLE DISK
DRIVE C: WILL BE LOST!
Proceed with Format (Y/N) y

Formatting 1, 000. 09M
Format complete.
Writing out file allocation table
Complete.
Calculating free space (this may take several minutes)...
Complete.
System transferred

Volume label (11 characters, ENTER for none)? WIN 98
```

To format the partition that will store Windows:

1 Perform steps **1** to **3** on page 4.

2 Type **format c: /s** and then press the **Enter** key.

3 Press **y** (for Yes) to format the drive and then press the **Enter** key.

4 Type a label for the drive and then press the **Enter** key.

```
                    FDISK Options

Current fixed disk drive: 1

Choose one of the following:

1. Create DOS partition or Logical DOS Drive
2. Set active partition
3. Delete partition or Logical DOS Drive
4. Display partition information

Enter choice: [1]



Press Esc to exit FDISK
```

```
You MUST restart your system for your changes to take effect.
Any drives you have created or changed must be formatted
AFTER you restart.

Shut down Windows before restarting.



Press Esc to exit FDISK_
```

■ This area displays a list of FDISK options.

4 Press the **Esc** key to exit FDISK.

■ A message appears, stating that you must restart your computer for your changes to take effect.

5 Press the **Esc** key to exit FDISK.

6 To restart your computer, press and hold down the **Ctrl** and **Alt** keys as you press the **Delete** key.

Linux comes with an installation program that takes you step by step through the process of installing Linux.

You can complete the installation of Linux in about half an hour.

INSTALL LINUX

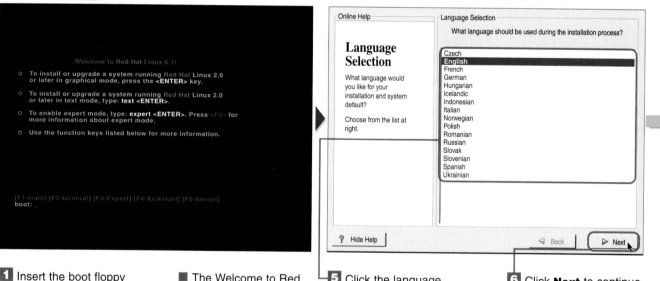

1 Insert the boot floppy disk that came with Linux into your floppy drive.

2 Turn on your computer.

3 When your computer begins to start, insert the CD-ROM disc 1 that came with Linux into your CD-ROM drive.

■ The Welcome to Red Hat Linux 6.1 screen appears.

Note: If this screen does not appear, restart your computer.

4 To install Linux using a graphical mode, press the Enter key.

5 Click the language you want to use for Linux.

6 Click **Next** to continue.

Where can I get help information on installing Linux?

The Official Red Hat Linux box set comes with an Installation Guide and Reference Guide that provide help information on installing Linux. If you have misplaced the guides or do not own the box set, you can view the guides at the following Web page.

www.redhat.com/corp/support/manuals

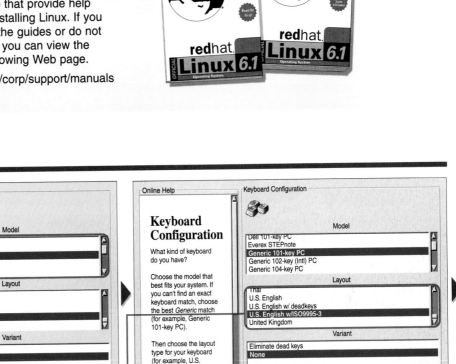

7 Click the model of the keyboard you use.

Note: If the model of your keyboard does not appear in the list, click the Generic keyboard option that best matches your keyboard.

8 Click the layout of your keyboard.

9 Click **Next** to continue.

CONTINUED

Linux asks you to specify the type of mouse you use. Linux can work with a variety of mouse types.

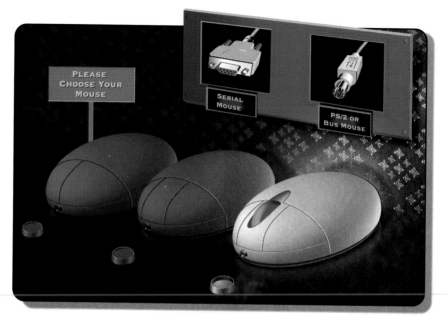

If the connector on your mouse is rectangular, you have a serial mouse. If the connector on your mouse is round, you have a PS/2 or a Bus mouse.

INSTALL LINUX (CONTINUED)

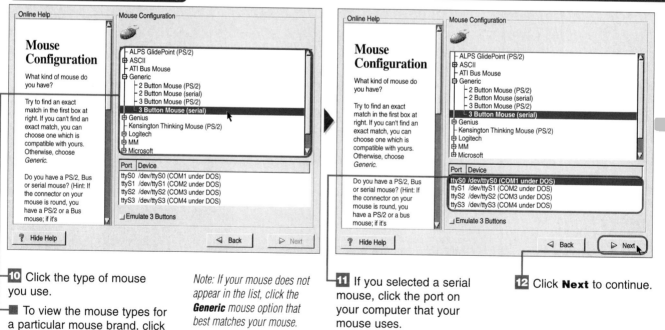

10 Click the type of mouse you use.

■ To view the mouse types for a particular mouse brand, click the plus sign (⊞) beside the brand (⊞ changes to ⊟).

*Note: If your mouse does not appear in the list, click the **Generic** mouse option that best matches your mouse.*

11 If you selected a serial mouse, click the port on your computer that your mouse uses.

*Note: A port connects your mouse to the computer. In most cases, you will select the **ttyS0** port.*

12 Click **Next** to continue.

What other ways can I install Linux?

KDE Workstation

Installs the KDE desktop environment. KDE is an alternative to the GNOME desktop environment that is shown throughout this book.

Server

Sets up your computer as a server on a network. A server is the control center of a network.

Custom

Gives you complete flexibility when installing Linux. For example, you can choose exactly what software you want to install.

Upgrade

Allows you to install the newest version of Linux without erasing existing Linux data on your computer.

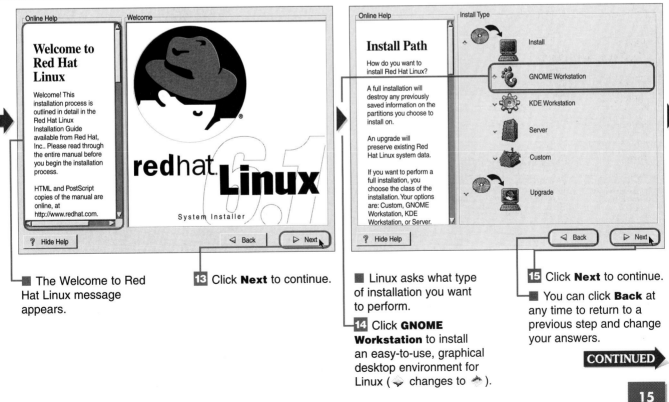

■ The Welcome to Red Hat Linux message appears.

13 Click **Next** to continue.

■ Linux asks what type of installation you want to perform.

14 Click **GNOME Workstation** to install an easy-to-use, graphical desktop environment for Linux (changes to).

15 Click **Next** to continue.

■ You can click **Back** at any time to return to a previous step and change your answers.

CONTINUED

Installing Linux will erase any existing Linux information on your computer. Make sure your computer does not contain information you want to keep before installing Linux.

INSTALL LINUX (CONTINUED)

■ Linux states that you are about to erase any existing Linux data on your computer.

16 Click **Remove data** to erase any existing Linux data (⬦ changes to ⬥).

17 Click **Next** to continue.

■ A message may appear, stating that you do not have much memory on your computer.

Note: If this message does not appear, skip to step 19.

18 Click **OK** to allow your computer to use space on your hard drive to act as memory.

What information do I need to set up my network card?

If your network does not have a DHCP server, you will need some or all of the following information from your network administrator. A DHCP server automatically assigns an IP address to each computer on a network.

IP Address	Identifies your computer on the network.
Netmask	Number that determines how many computers can be on the network.
Network	Basic IP address of the network.
Broadcast	Address used to communicate with all computers on the network.
Hostname	Name of your computer.
Gateway	Address of the device that connects your network to the Internet.
DNS	Address of the computer that changes Web page addresses you type into IP numbers. IP numbers uniquely identify each computer that stores Web pages.

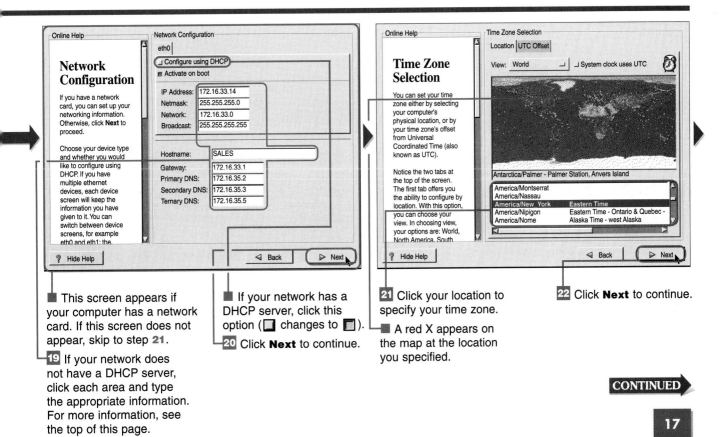

■ This screen appears if your computer has a network card. If this screen does not appear, skip to step 21.

19 If your network does not have a DHCP server, click each area and type the appropriate information. For more information, see the top of this page.

■ If your network has a DHCP server, click this option (☐ changes to ☑).

20 Click **Next** to continue.

21 Click your location to specify your time zone.

■ A red X appears on the map at the location you specified.

22 Click **Next** to continue.

CONTINUED

INSTALL LINUX

Linux automatically sets up an administrative account, called the root account. You can enter the password you want to use for the root account.

You will use the root account to perform administrative and maintenance tasks on your computer.

INSTALL LINUX (CONTINUED)

23 Click this area and type a password for the root account. The password must be at least six characters long.

Note: A symbol (x) appears for each character you type to prevent others from seeing the password.

24 Click this area and type the password again to confirm the password.

25 To create a user account, click this area and type a name for the account.

26 Click this area and type a password for the account.

27 Click this area and type the password again to confirm the password.

28 Click this area and type the full name of the user who will use the account.

18

Why should I create a user account?

You should create a user account to perform daily tasks. The root account should only be used for performing administrative and maintenance tasks, since you can damage your computer when using the root account.

If you plan to share your computer with family members or colleagues, you can create a user account for each person so they will each have their own personalized settings.

Online Help

Account Configuration

Enter a root password. The password must be at least six characters in length. Confirm the password. The "Next" button will become enabled once both entry fields match.

Now create a user account.

Enter a user account name. Then, create a password for that user account and confirm it. Finally, enter the full name of the account

? Hide Help

Account Configuration

Root Password:	××××××
Confirm:	××××××
Account Name:	
Password:	Password (confirm):
Full Name:	

Add · Edit · Delete · New

Account Name	Full Name
tsmith	Tom Smith

◁ Back · ▷ Next

Online Help

X Configuration

The installation program will now probe for your video card and monitor to determine your machine's best display settings. If successful, your hardware will be listed. If the program cannot determine your video hardware, you will be presented with a list of video cards and monitors to choose from.

After your hardware is set, you can test the configuration settings. When you test your

? Hide Help

X Configuration

In most cases your video hardware can be probed to automatically determine the best settings for your display.

Autoprobe results:

> Video Card: 3D Rage Pro AGP 1X/2X
> Video Ram: 4096 kb
> X server: Mach 64

Your monitor could not be autodetected. Please choose it from the list below:

- TAXAN 875
- Tandberg ErgoScan 21c
- **Tatung CM14UHE**
- Tatung CM14UHR
- Tatung CM14UHS
- Unisys-19
- ViewSonic 1
- ViewSonic 14E

Test this configuration

☐ Customize X Configuration
☐ Use Graphical Login
☐ Skip X Configuration

◁ Back · ▷ Next

---

29 Click **Add**.

■ This area displays the user account information.

■ To create additional user accounts, repeat steps **25** to **29** for each user.

30 Click **Next** to continue.

■ If Linux automatically detects your video card, this area displays the video card information.

■ If Linux could not detect your monitor, this area displays a list of monitors.

31 Click the monitor you use.

*Note: If your monitor does not appear in the list, click the **Generic** monitor option that best matches your monitor.*

CONTINUED

INSTALL LINUX

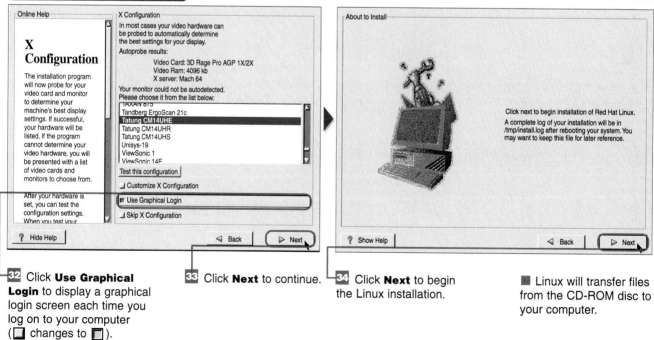

You can choose to display a graphical login screen each time you log on to your computer.

If you do not choose to display a graphical login screen, a text-based login screen will appear instead.

INSTALL LINUX (CONTINUED)

32 Click **Use Graphical Login** to display a graphical login screen each time you log on to your computer (☐ changes to ☑).

33 Click **Next** to continue.

34 Click **Next** to begin the Linux installation.

■ Linux will transfer files from the CD-ROM disc to your computer.

What can I do after I install Linux?

Register Linux

If you purchased the Official Red Hat Linux box set, you can register your product at the www.redhat.com/now Web page. Registering Linux will give you additional support.

Update Linux

You can obtain updates that will solve Linux problems at the support.redhat.com/errata Web page.

Install Packages

You can install packages on your computer that will add new capabilities to Linux. Packages can contain programs and files. To install a package, see page 214.

Online Help

Installing Packages

Please wait while the installer compiles the completed information and begins installing your packages.

Installing Packages

Package: XFree86-devel-3.3.5-3
Size: 7,897 KBytes
Summary: X11R6 static libraries, headers and programming man pages.

Status	Packages	Size	Time
Total	396	561 M	1:29.38
Completed	41	63 M	0:10.09
Remaining	355	497 M	1:19.29

? Hide Help   ◁ Back   ▷ Next

Congratulations

Congratulations, installation is complete.

Remove the boot media and press return to reboot. For information on fixes which are available for this release of Red Hat Linux, consult the Errata available from http://www.redhat.com.

Information on configuring your system is available in the post install chapter of the Official Red Hat Linux User's Guide.

? Show Help   ◁ Back   ◄̶ Exit

■ This area displays information about the package Linux is currently installing. A package can contain programs and files.

■ This area displays the progress of the installation for the current package.

■ This area displays information about the installation, including the total number of packages and the time required for the installation.

■ This area displays the progress of the entire installation.

■ A message appears, stating that the installation is complete.

35 Remove the floppy disk from your floppy drive.

36 Click **Exit** or press the Enter key.

■ Your computer restarts.

37 When your computer begins to restart, remove the CD-ROM disc from your CD-ROM drive.

■ Linux is now installed on your computer.

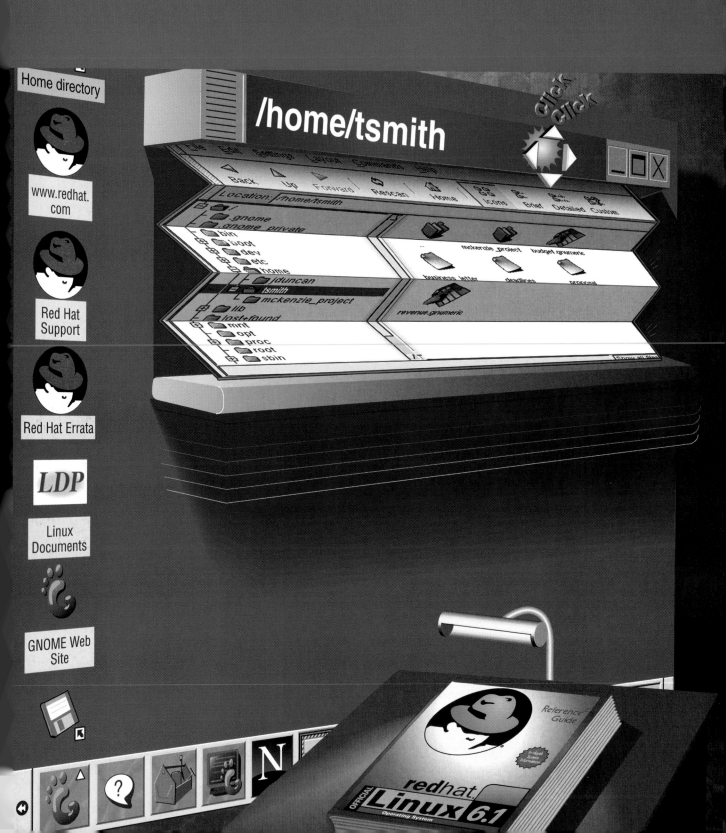

CHAPTER 2

Linux Basics

This chapter teaches you the basic skills you will need to use Linux.

INTRODUCTION TO LINUX

Red Hat Linux is an operating system that controls the overall activity of your computer and ensures that all parts of your computer work together smoothly and efficiently.

Red Hat is the company that distributes Red Hat Linux.

HISTORY OF LINUX

A student from Finland named Linus Torvalds created Linux in 1991. With the help of hundreds of volunteer programmers around the world, Linux grew from a simple hobby project to a complete, fully functional operating system. Today, millions of people worldwide use Linux.

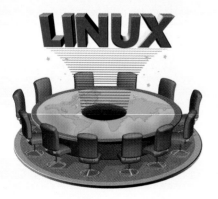

OBTAIN LINUX

You can download Red Hat Linux for free from the www.redhat.com Web site. If you do not want to transfer Linux over the Internet, you can purchase the Red Hat Linux box set at the Web site and have Red Hat send you the program. You can also buy Red Hat Linux at many computer stores and bookstores.

GNOME

Linux comes with the GNOME desktop environment, which offers an easy-to-use, graphical display for accomplishing tasks in Linux. The GNOME desktop environment is shown throughout this book.

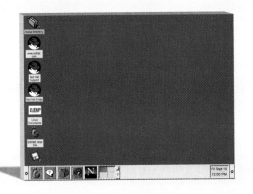

WORK WITH FILES

Linux provides ways to organize and manage the files stored on your computer. You can open, sort, rename, move, print, find and delete files.

WORK WITH LINUX APPLICATIONS

Linux includes a drawing program, spreadsheet program, calendar program and a simple text editor. You will also find an on-screen calculator, an address book and many games that you can play.

CUSTOMIZE LINUX

You can customize Linux in many ways. You can add a colorful design to your desktop, set up a screen saver, change the way your mouse works and have Linux play sounds for certain program events, such as when an error message appears.

INTRODUCTION TO LINUX

WORK WITH ACCOUNTS

When you installed Linux, the root account and one or more user accounts were created. You should only use the root account to perform administrative and maintenance tasks, since you can damage your computer when using the root account. When performing daily tasks, you should work in a user account.

WORK WITH FLOPPY AND CD-ROM DRIVES

You can view the contents of floppy disks and CD-ROM discs. You can also copy files to a floppy disk, format a floppy disk to prepare the disk for use and play music CDs on your computer.

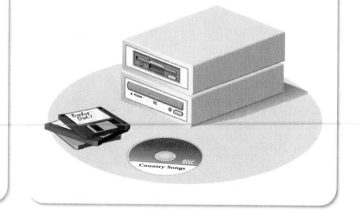

SET UP HARDWARE AND SOFTWARE

Linux helps you set up hardware, such as a printer, sound card and network card. Linux also helps you install packages that contain programs and files that add new capabilities to Linux.

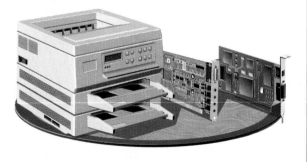

CONNECT TO THE INTERNET

Linux comes with Netscape Communicator, which allows you to browse the Web, exchange electronic mail with people around the world and join newsgroups to communicate with people who have common interests.

A mouse is a handheld device that lets you select and move items on your screen.

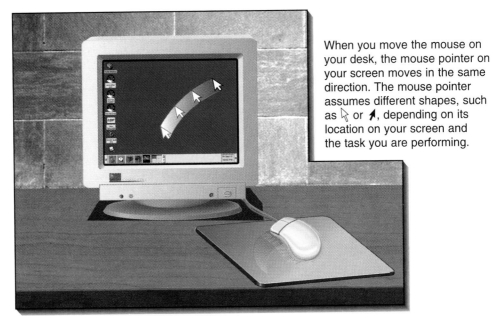

When you move the mouse on your desk, the mouse pointer on your screen moves in the same direction. The mouse pointer assumes different shapes, such as ⌖ or ↖, depending on its location on your screen and the task you are performing.

MOUSE ACTIONS

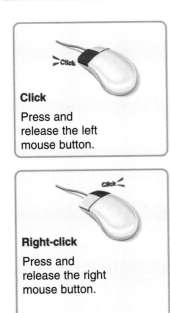

Click

Press and release the left mouse button.

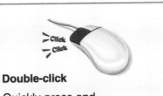

Double-click

Quickly press and release the left mouse button twice.

Right-click

Press and release the right mouse button.

Drag

Position the mouse pointer over an object on your screen and then press and hold down the left mouse button as you move the mouse to where you want to place the object. Then release the button.

THREE-BUTTON MOUSE

If you have a mouse with three buttons, you can use the middle mouse button to perform certain tasks. If you have a mouse with two buttons, you can imitate a third button by pressing the left and right mouse buttons at the same time.

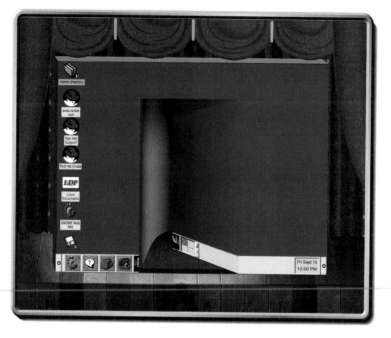

When you turn on your computer, you can start using Linux to perform tasks.

When you installed Linux, the root account and one or more user accounts were created. You should only use the root account to perform administrative tasks. When performing daily tasks, you should use a user account. To create a user account after you install Linux, see page 164.

START LINUX

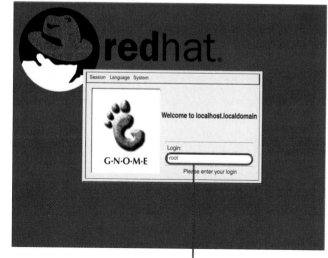

1 Turn on your computer.

■ A dialog box appears, asking for your user name.

Note: If the dialog box does not appear, see the top of page 29.

2 Type your user name and then press the `Enter` key.

3 Type your password and then press the `Enter` key.

Note: A symbol (ˣ) appears for each character you type to prevent others from seeing the password.

Why does this screen appear when I start Linux?

This screen appears if you did not choose to use a graphical login screen when Linux was installed on your computer. To start the GNOME desktop environment, perform the following steps.

```
Red Hat Linux release 6.1 (Cartman)
Kernel 2.2.12-20 on an i686

localhost login: tsmith
Password:
Last login: Thu Nov 4 14:45:50 on localhost
[tsmith@localhost tsmith]$ startx
```

Note: When changing your display settings using the Xconfigurator program, you can choose to use a graphical login screen. To change your display settings using Xconfigurator, see page 142.

1 Type your user name and then press the `Enter` key.

2 Type your password and then press the `Enter` key.

Note: The password does not appear on the screen to prevent others from seeing the password.

3 Type **startx** and then press the `Enter` key.

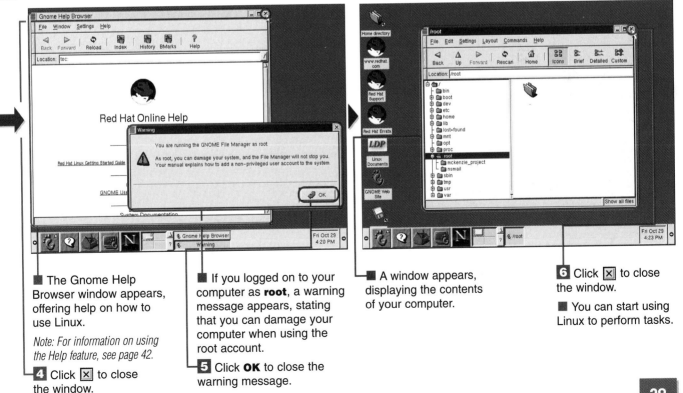

■ The Gnome Help Browser window appears, offering help on how to use Linux.

Note: For information on using the Help feature, see page 42.

4 Click ⊠ to close the window.

■ If you logged on to your computer as **root**, a warning message appears, stating that you can damage your computer when using the root account.

5 Click **OK** to close the warning message.

■ A window appears, displaying the contents of your computer.

6 Click ⊠ to close the window.

■ You can start using Linux to perform tasks.

PARTS OF THE SCREEN

Home directory

Allows you to display the contents of the directory that stores your personal files.

Help Web Pages

Allows you to quickly display pages on the Web that offer help on using Linux.

Floppy Icon

Allows you to display the contents of a floppy disk.

GNOME Panel

Desktop

The background area of your screen.

Clock

Displays the current date and time.

Hide Button

Hides the GNOME Panel.

Main Menu Button

Gives you quick access to programs.

Application Launchers

❶ Help System

Provides help on using Linux.

❷ GNOME Control Center

Allows you to view and change settings such as the color of your desktop.

❸ Terminal

Allows you to display the Terminal window where you can type Linux commands.

❹ Netscape Communicator

Allows you to browse the Web, exchange electronic mail and join newsgroups.

GNOME Pager

❶ Desktop View

Allows you to switch between different desktops.

❷ Task List Button

Allows you to display a list of all open windows.

❸ Applications View

Displays a button for each open window on the current desktop.

You can use the Main
Menu button to start
your programs.

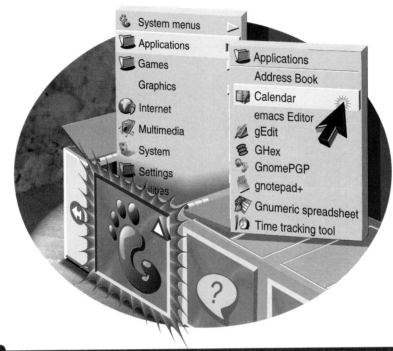

START A PROGRAM

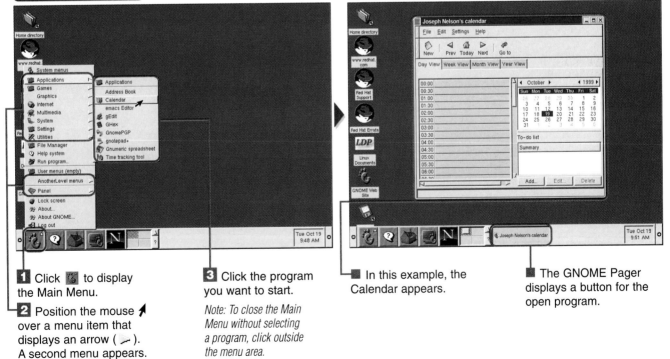

1 Click to display
the Main Menu.

2 Position the mouse ↑
over a menu item that
displays an arrow (▸).
A second menu appears.

3 Click the program
you want to start.

*Note: To close the Main
Menu without selecting
a program, click outside
the menu area.*

■ In this example, the
Calendar appears.

■ The GNOME Pager
displays a button for the
open program.

If a window covers items
on your screen, you can
move the window to a
different location.

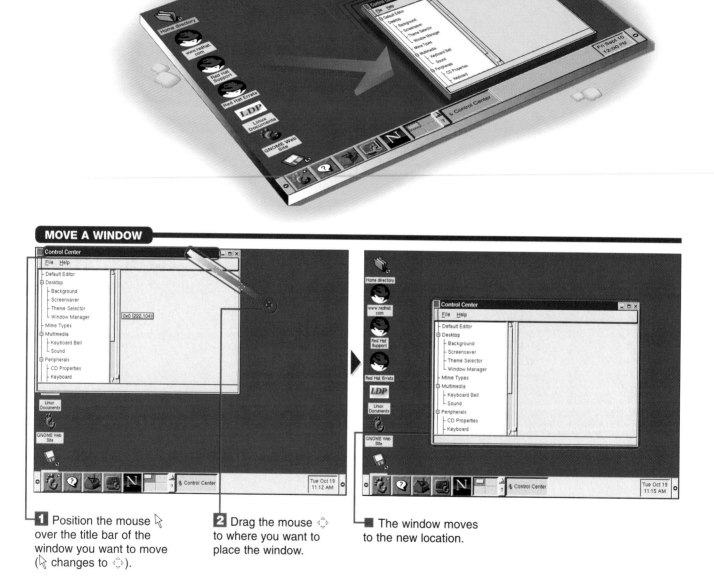

MOVE A WINDOW

1 Position the mouse ⌖
over the title bar of the
window you want to move
(⌖ changes to ✥).

2 Drag the mouse ✥
to where you want to
place the window.

■ The window moves
to the new location.

RESIZE A WINDOW

You can change the size
of a window displayed
on your screen.

Enlarging a window lets
you view more of its contents.
Reducing a window lets
you view items covered
by the window.

RESIZE A WINDOW

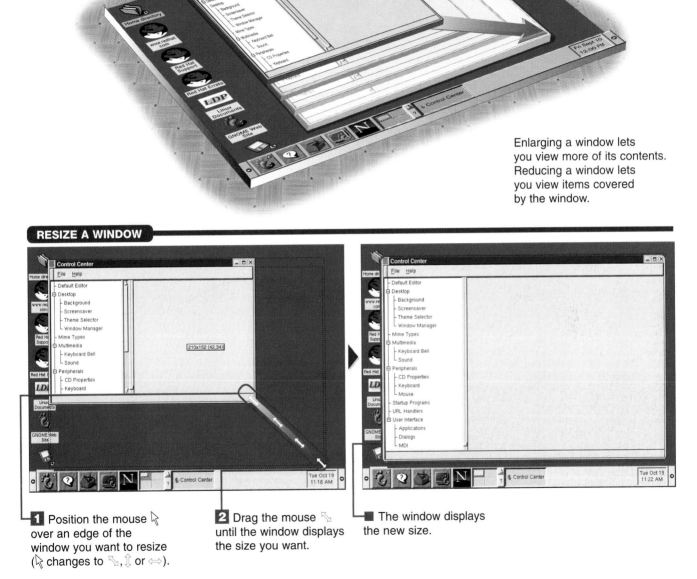

1 Position the mouse ▷
over an edge of the
window you want to resize
(▷ changes to ⬉, ⬍ or ⬌).

2 Drag the mouse ⬉
until the window displays
the size you want.

■ The window displays
the new size.

MAXIMIZE A WINDOW

You can enlarge a
window to fill your
screen. This lets you
view more of the
window's contents.

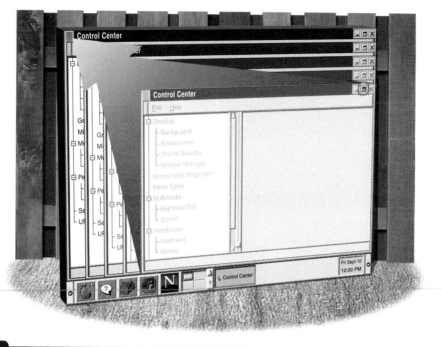

MAXIMIZE A WINDOW

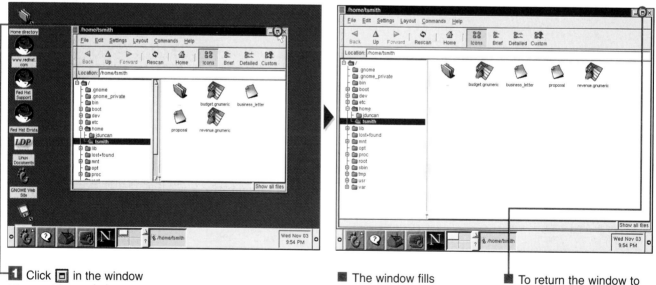

1 Click 🔲 in the window
you want to maximize.

■ The window fills
your screen.

■ To return the window to
its previous size, click 🔲.

If you are not using a window, you can minimize the window to temporarily remove it from your screen. You can redisplay the window at any time.

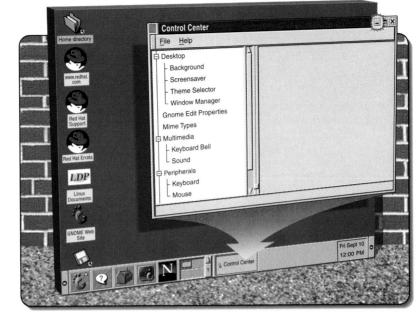

MINIMIZE A WINDOW

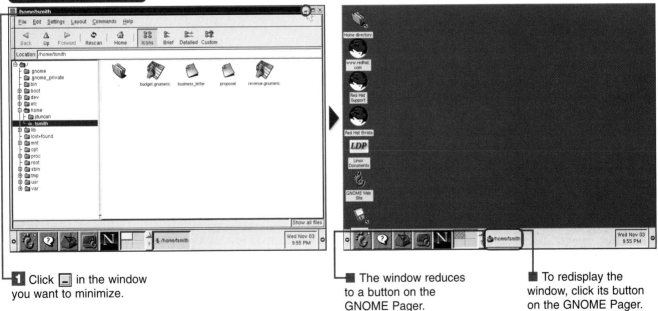

1 Click ▬ in the window you want to minimize.

■ The window reduces to a button on the GNOME Pager.

■ To redisplay the window, click its button on the GNOME Pager.

SCROLL THROUGH A WINDOW

You can use a scroll bar to browse through the information in a window. This is useful when a window is not large enough to display all the information it contains.

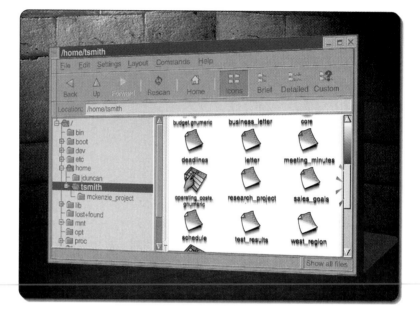

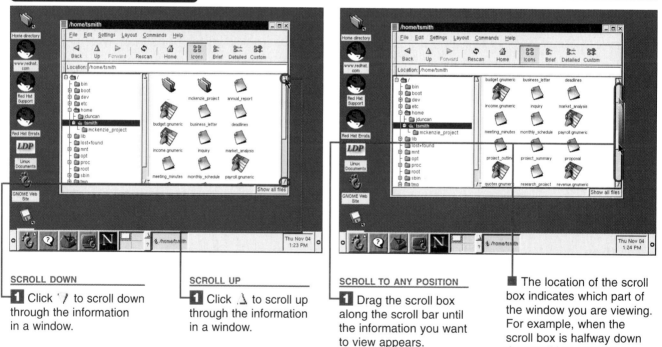

SCROLL DOWN

1 Click ' / to scroll down through the information in a window.

SCROLL UP

1 Click ⌃ to scroll up through the information in a window.

SCROLL TO ANY POSITION

1 Drag the scroll box along the scroll bar until the information you want to view appears.

■ The location of the scroll box indicates which part of the window you are viewing. For example, when the scroll box is halfway down the scroll bar, you are viewing information from the middle of the window.

If you have more
than one window
open, you can
easily switch
between the
windows.

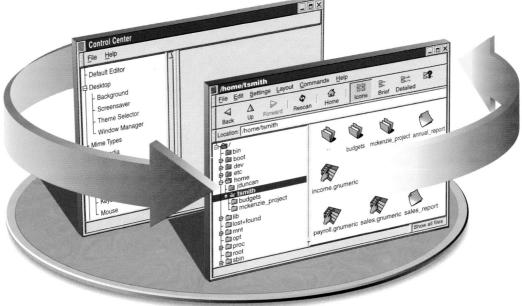

SWITCH BETWEEN WINDOWS

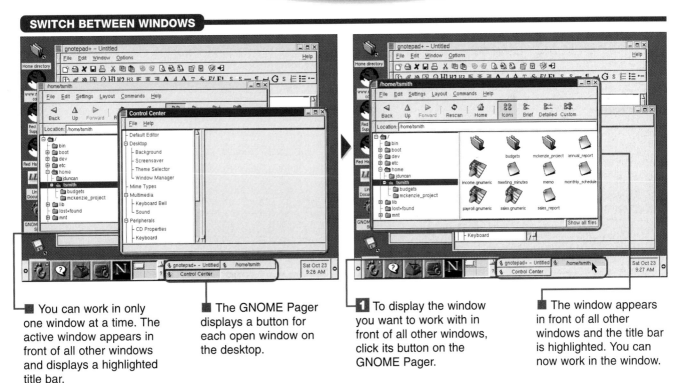

■ You can work in only
one window at a time. The
active window appears in
front of all other windows
and displays a highlighted
title bar.

■ The GNOME Pager
displays a button for
each open window on
the desktop.

1 To display the window
you want to work with in
front of all other windows,
click its button on the
GNOME Pager.

■ The window appears
in front of all other
windows and the title bar
is highlighted. You can
now work in the window.

SHADE A WINDOW

You can shade a
window to temporarily
hide the contents of
the window. This can
help reduce clutter
on your desktop.

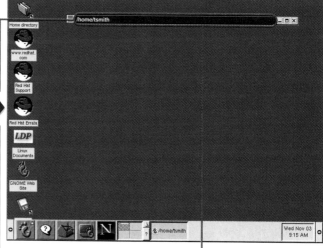

1 Double-click the title
bar of the window you
want to shade.

■ The contents of the
window are temporarily
hidden. The title bar
remains on the desktop.

■ To redisplay the
contents of the window,
double-click the title bar
of the window.

When you finish
working with a
window, you can
close the window
to remove it from
your screen.

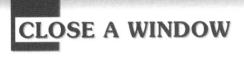

CLOSE A WINDOW

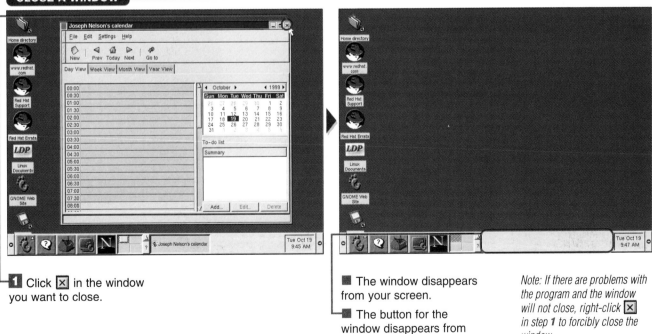

1 Click ⊠ in the window
you want to close.

■ The window disappears
from your screen.

■ The button for the
window disappears from
the GNOME Pager.

*Note: If there are problems with
the program and the window
will not close, right-click ⊠
in step 1 to forcibly close the
window.*

If you are experiencing problems with Linux, you can restart your computer to try to fix the problem.

RESTART YOUR COMPUTER

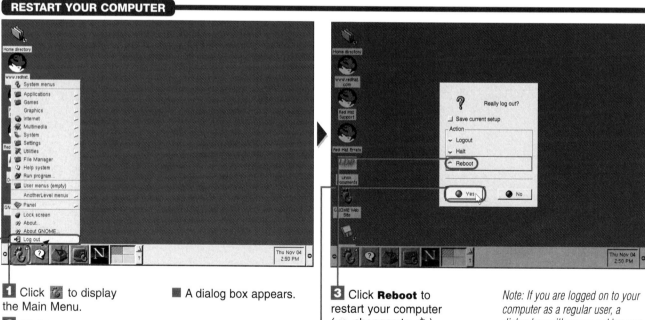

1 Click ![icon] to display the Main Menu.

2 Click **Log out**.

■ A dialog box appears.

3 Click **Reboot** to restart your computer (↩ changes to ↪).

4 Click **Yes**.

Note: If you are logged on to your computer as a regular user, a dialog box will appear, asking you to enter your password. Click the dialog box and type your password. Then press the **Enter** *key.*

■ Linux restarts your computer.

When you finish using Linux, you can exit Linux to shut down your computer.

Unmounting proc file system
The system is halted
stopping all md devices.
Power down.

■ When this message appears, you can turn off your computer. Many new computers will turn off automatically.

EXIT LINUX

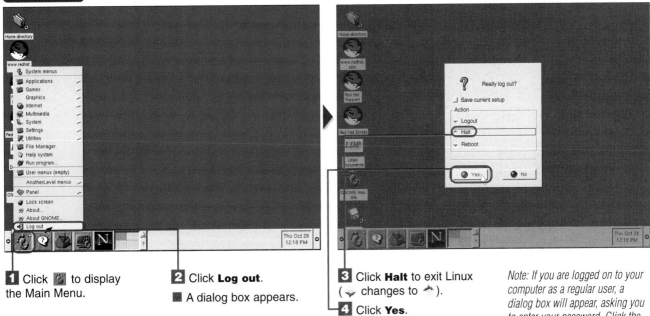

1 Click 📁 to display the Main Menu.

2 Click **Log out**.

■ A dialog box appears.

3 Click **Halt** to exit Linux (🔽 changes to 🔼).

4 Click **Yes**.

Note: If you are logged on to your computer as a regular user, a dialog box will appear, asking you to enter your password. Click the dialog box and type your password. Then press the [Enter] key.

■ Linux shuts down your computer.

GETTING HELP

If you do not know how to perform a task in Linux, you can use the Help feature to get information.

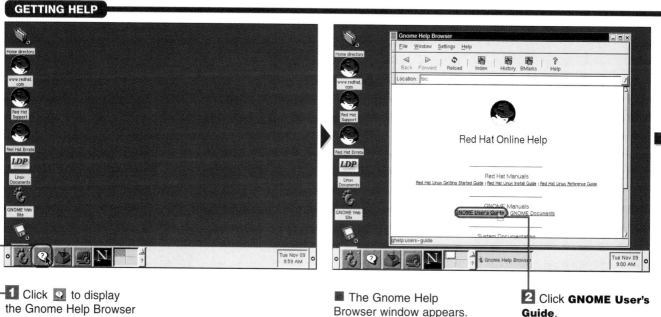

1 Click ? to display the Gnome Help Browser window.

■ The Gnome Help Browser window appears.

2 Click **GNOME User's Guide**.

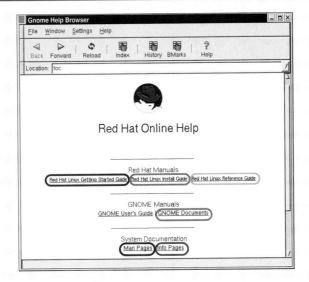

What other types of help information does the Help feature offer?

In the Gnome Help Browser window, you can click one of the following options to get help information.

Red Hat Linux Getting Started Guide
Provides basic help on using Linux.

Red Hat Linux Install Guide
Provides help on installing Linux.

Red Hat Linux Reference Guide
Provides detailed help on installing and using Linux.

GNOME Documents
Provides help on GNOME programs.

Man Pages
Provides basic help on Linux commands.

Info Pages
Provides detailed help on Linux commands.

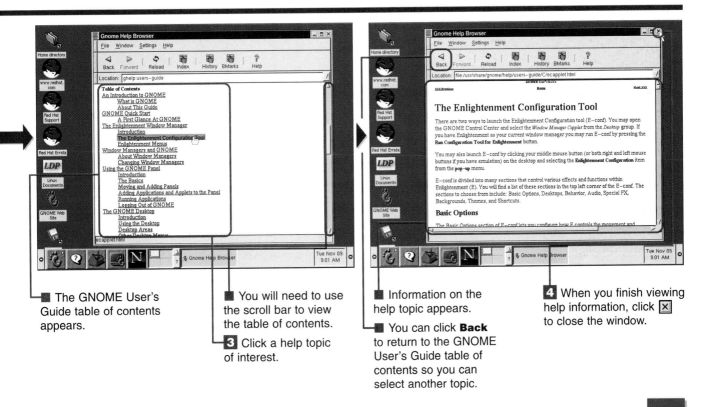

■ The GNOME User's Guide table of contents appears.

■ You will need to use the scroll bar to view the table of contents.

3 Click a help topic of interest.

■ Information on the help topic appears.

■ You can click **Back** to return to the GNOME User's Guide table of contents so you can select another topic.

4 When you finish viewing help information, click ⊠ to close the window.

When you find a help topic that contains useful information, you can bookmark the topic so you can quickly return to the topic at a later time.

BOOKMARK A HELP TOPIC

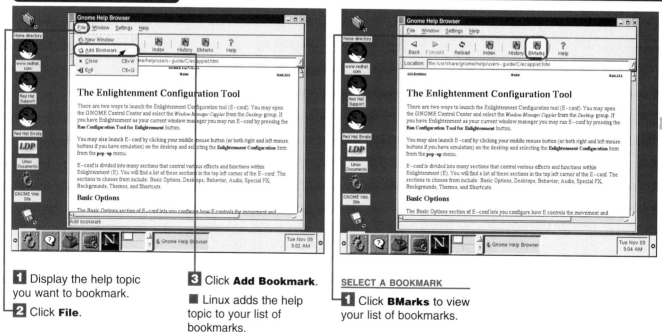

1 Display the help topic you want to bookmark.

2 Click **File**.

3 Click **Add Bookmark**.

■ Linux adds the help topic to your list of bookmarks.

SELECT A BOOKMARK

1 Click **BMarks** to view your list of bookmarks.

How do I delete a bookmark?

You can perform the following
steps to delete a bookmark
you no longer need.

1 In the Gnome Help
Bookmarks window,
click the bookmark
you want to delete.

2 Click **Remove**.

■ The bookmark
disappears from
the list.

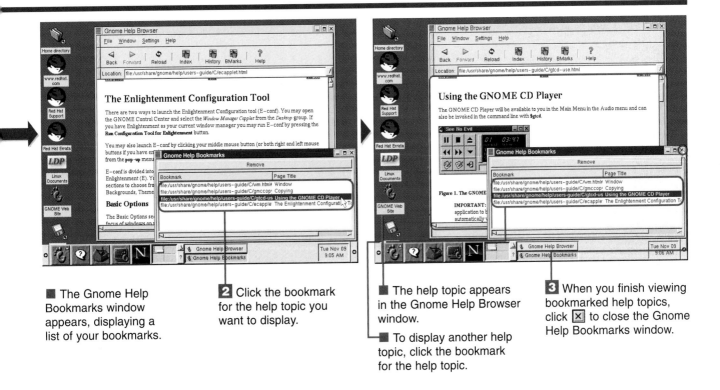

■ The Gnome Help
Bookmarks window
appears, displaying a
list of your bookmarks.

2 Click the bookmark
for the help topic you
want to display.

■ The help topic appears
in the Gnome Help Browser
window.

■ To display another help
topic, click the bookmark
for the help topic.

3 When you finish viewing
bookmarked help topics,
click ⊠ to close the Gnome
Help Bookmarks window.

GETTING HELP

If you are having problems with Linux, there are many resources available where you can get help.

MANUALS

The Official Red Hat Linux 6.1 box set comes with three manuals that can help you install and use Linux.

If you have misplaced the manuals or do not own the box set, you can view the manuals at the following Web page.

www.redhat.com/corp/support/manuals

Installation Guide

Provides detailed instructions on how to install Linux.

Getting Started Guide

Provides general information on how to use Linux.

Reference Guide

Provides detailed information on how to install and use Linux.

WEB PAGES

You can use the icons on your desktop to quickly access help information on the Web. To display a Web page, double-click the icon for the Web page.

www.redhat.com

Provides general information about Red Hat, the company that distributes Red Hat Linux.

Red Hat Support

support.redhat.com

Provides help on how to install and use Linux and how to fix Linux problems. You can also access the Hardware Compatibility Lists to determine whether your hardware will work with Linux.

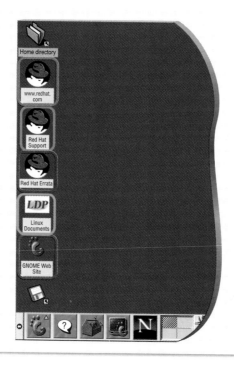

Red Hat Errata

support.redhat.com/errata

Provides information about updates, fixes and corrections for Linux.

Linux Documents

www.redhat.com/mirrors/LDP

Provides a collection of documents containing the most up-to-date information about Linux.

GNOME Web Site

www.gnome.org

Provides information and support on GNOME, a graphical desktop environment in Linux.

MAILING LISTS

You can join a mailing list to get Linux help through e-mail. A mailing list is a discussion group that uses e-mail to communicate.

linux-list

A mailing list offering general discussions about Linux. To join the list, send an e-mail message to linux-list-request@ssc.com with the word "subscribe" in the body of the message.

linux-newbie

A mailing list for new Linux users. To join the list, send an e-mail message to majordomo@vger.rutgers.edu with the words "subscribe linux-newbie" in the body of the message.

NEWSGROUPS

You can join newsgroups to find out more about Linux. A newsgroup is a discussion group that allows people with common interests to communicate.

Newsgroup messages are stored on computers called news servers. You can connect to the news.redhat.com news server to join newsgroups dedicated to Linux topics. For more information on newsgroups, see pages 286 to 293.

Here are some newsgroups you will find on the news.redhat.com news server.

redhat.config

Discussions about setting up hardware and software and fixing hardware and software problems.

redhat.general

General information discussions about Linux.

redhat.hardware.arch.intel

Discussions about hardware, including how to set up hardware and fix hardware problems.

CHAPTER 3

Work With Files

Linux allows you to organize and manage your files efficiently. In this chapter you will learn how to view the files stored on your computer, sort files, print files and much more.

HOW FILES ARE STORED

DIRECTORIES

Directory

Like folders in a filing cabinet, directories organize the files stored on your computer. Each directory usually stores related files.

Root directory

The **/** symbol represents the root directory on your computer. All other directories are located below this directory.

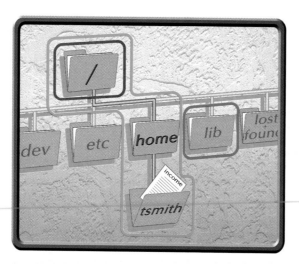

Path

A path specifies the location of a file on your computer. A path is a list of each directory you must open to access a file, followed by the file name. The directories and the file name are separated by slashes (/). For example, to specify the location of the income file, you would use the **/home/tsmith/income** path.

SAVING AND OPENING FILES

When you save or open files, Linux displays this window.

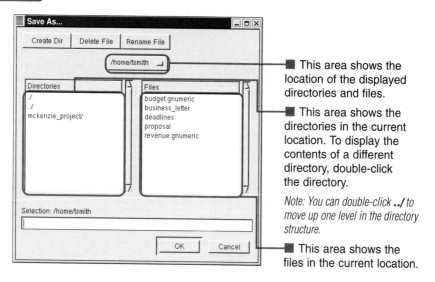

■ This area shows the location of the displayed directories and files.

■ This area shows the directories in the current location. To display the contents of a different directory, double-click the directory.

Note: You can double-click ../ to move up one level in the directory structure.

■ This area shows the files in the current location.

You will find the following directories on your computer.

/

This is the main directory that stores all the directories and files on your computer.

bin

This directory contains programs that are essential to the operation of Linux.

dev

This directory contains a file for each hardware device used by Linux, such as a monitor or printer.

etc

This directory stores files that specify Linux settings, such as the settings for your monitor resolution.

home

This directory contains a directory for each user set up on your computer. Each directory stores the personal files and settings for one user.

lost+found

This directory stores damaged or lost files.

mnt

This directory displays the contents of a floppy or CD-ROM drive.

root

This directory stores the personal files and settings for the root account. The root account is the administrative account set up when Linux was installed on your computer.

sbin

This directory stores programs used for performing administrative tasks in Linux.

usr

This directory contains programs and information that people often access, such as games and help files.

VIEW CONTENTS OF YOUR COMPUTER

You can use the GNOME File Manager to view the directories and files on your computer.

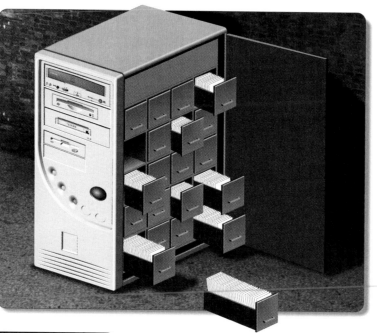

The GNOME File Manager allows you to perform tasks such as moving, deleting and sorting files.

VIEW CONTENTS OF YOUR COMPUTER

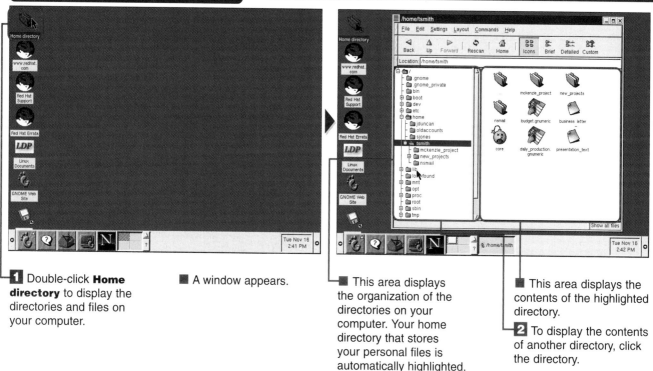

■1 Double-click **Home directory** to display the directories and files on your computer.

■ A window appears.

■ This area displays the organization of the directories on your computer. Your home directory that stores your personal files is automatically highlighted.

■ This area displays the contents of the highlighted directory.

■2 To display the contents of another directory, click the directory.

What do the icons in the GNOME File Manager represent?

Each directory and file displays an icon to help you distinguish between the different types of items. Common types of items include:

Directory	Image file	Program file	Sound file	Text file	Video file

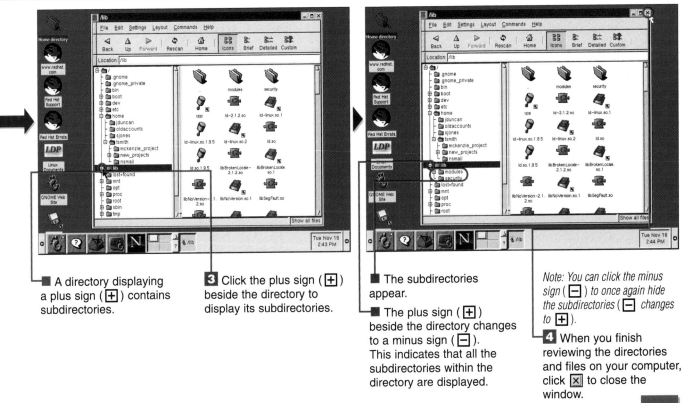

■ A directory displaying a plus sign (⊞) contains subdirectories.

3 Click the plus sign (⊞) beside the directory to display its subdirectories.

■ The subdirectories appear.

■ The plus sign (⊞) beside the directory changes to a minus sign (⊟). This indicates that all the subdirectories within the directory are displayed.

Note: You can click the minus sign (⊟) to once again hide the subdirectories (⊟ changes to ⊞).

4 When you finish reviewing the directories and files on your computer, click ✕ to close the window.

DISPLAY YOUR HOME DIRECTORY

You can quickly display the contents of your home directory. Your home directory stores your personal files and settings.

DISPLAY YOUR HOME DIRECTORY

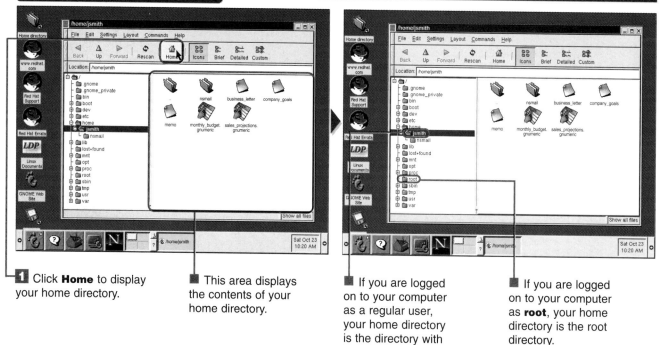

1 Click **Home** to display your home directory.

■ This area displays the contents of your home directory.

■ If you are logged on to your computer as a regular user, your home directory is the directory with your user name.

■ If you are logged on to your computer as **root**, your home directory is the root directory.

DISPLAY FILE PROPERTIES

You can display information about a file, such as the size of the file and the date the file was last changed.

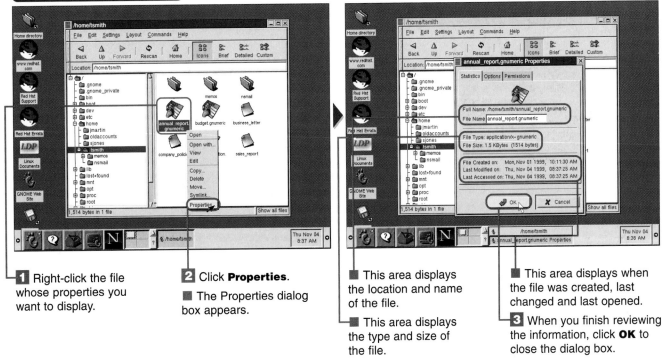

DISPLAY FILE PROPERTIES

1 Right-click the file whose properties you want to display.

2 Click **Properties**.

■ The Properties dialog box appears.

■ This area displays the location and name of the file.

■ This area displays the type and size of the file.

■ This area displays when the file was created, last changed and last opened.

3 When you finish reviewing the information, click **OK** to close the dialog box.

CHANGE VIEW OF ITEMS

You can change the
way items appear
in directories.

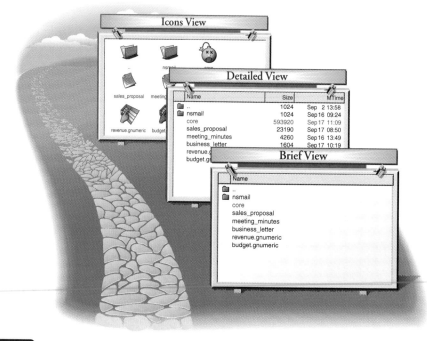

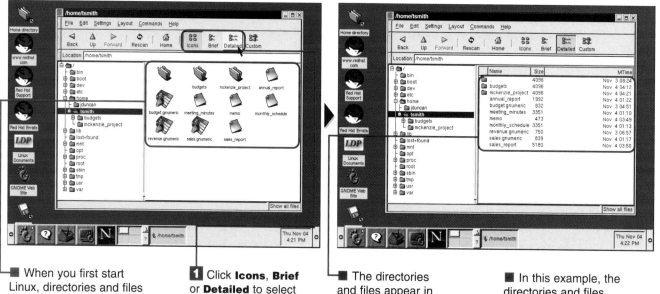

■ When you first start
Linux, directories and files
appear in the Icons view.

1 Click **Icons**, **Brief**
or **Detailed** to select
the way you want to
view the directories
and files.

■ The directories
and files appear in
the new view.

■ In this example, the
directories and files
appear in the Detailed
view. This view displays
information about each
directory and file.

You can sort
the items in a
directory to help
you find items
of interest.

You can sort items
by name, size or
the date the item
was last changed.

SORT ITEMS

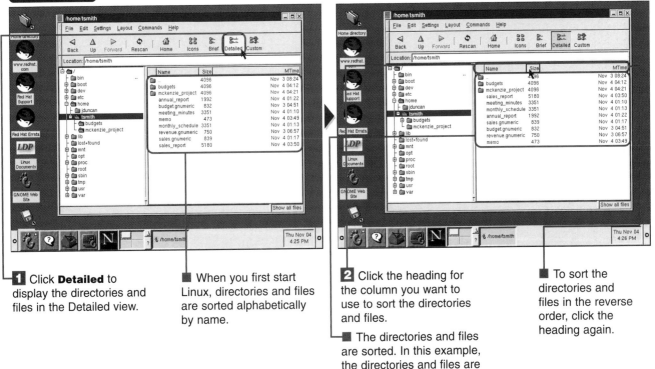

1 Click **Detailed** to display the directories and files in the Detailed view.

■ When you first start Linux, directories and files are sorted alphabetically by name.

2 Click the heading for the column you want to use to sort the directories and files.

■ The directories and files are sorted. In this example, the directories and files are sorted by size.

■ To sort the directories and files in the reverse order, click the heading again.

CUSTOMIZE DISPLAY OF FILE INFORMATION

You can change the type of information that Linux displays about the files on your computer.

CUSTOMIZE DISPLAY OF FILE INFORMATION

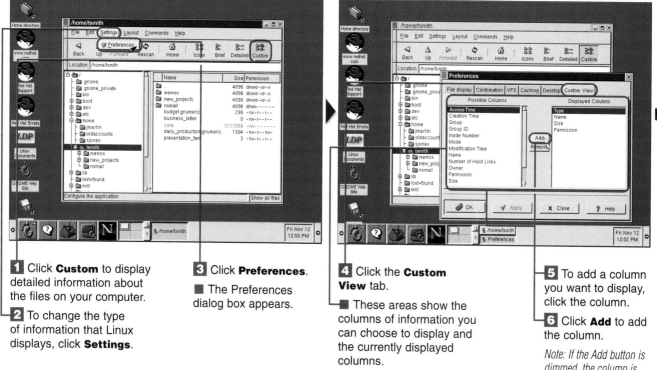

1 Click **Custom** to display detailed information about the files on your computer.

2 To change the type of information that Linux displays, click **Settings**.

3 Click **Preferences**.

■ The Preferences dialog box appears.

4 Click the **Custom View** tab.

■ These areas show the columns of information you can choose to display and the currently displayed columns.

5 To add a column you want to display, click the column.

6 Click **Add** to add the column.

Note: If the Add button is dimmed, the column is already displayed.

What type of information can I display about the files on my computer?

Here are some columns of information that you may want to display.

Column	Description
Access Time	Displays the date and time each file was last accessed.
Creation Time	Displays the date and time each file was created.
Modification Time	Displays the date and time each file was last changed.
Name	Displays the name of each file.
Owner	Displays the user name of the person who owns each file.
Permission	Displays the read (r), write (w) and execute (x) permissions for each file.
Size	Displays the size of each file in bytes.
Type	Displays an icon that represents the type of each file.

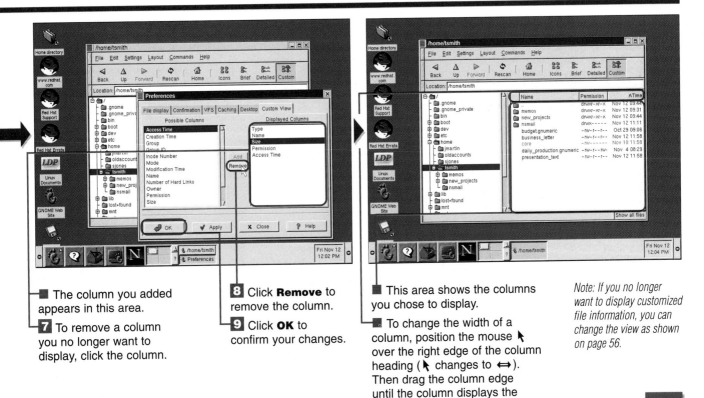

■ The column you added appears in this area.

7 To remove a column you no longer want to display, click the column.

8 Click **Remove** to remove the column.

9 Click **OK** to confirm your changes.

■ This area shows the columns you chose to display.

■ To change the width of a column, position the mouse ▶ over the right edge of the column heading (▶ changes to ⟷). Then drag the column edge until the column displays the width you want.

Note: If you no longer want to display customized file information, you can change the view as shown on page 56.

SELECT FILES

Before working with files, you often need to select the files you want to work with. The names of selected files appear highlighted on your screen.

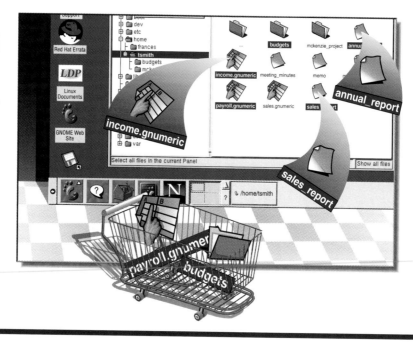

You can select directories the same way you select files. Selecting a directory will select all the files in the directory.

SELECT FILES

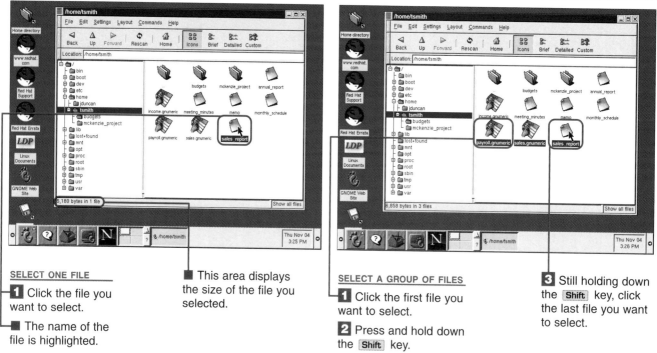

SELECT ONE FILE

1 Click the file you want to select.

■ The name of the file is highlighted.

■ This area displays the size of the file you selected.

SELECT A GROUP OF FILES

1 Click the first file you want to select.

2 Press and hold down the Shift key.

3 Still holding down the Shift key, click the last file you want to select.

How do I deselect files?

To deselect all files, click a blank area on the right side of the window.

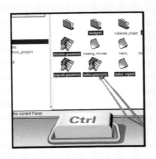

To deselect one file from a group of selected files, press and hold down the **Ctrl** key while you click the file you want to deselect.

Note: You can deselect directories the same way you deselect files.

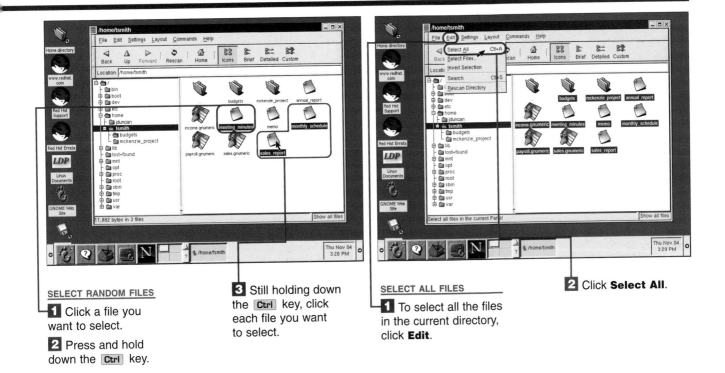

SELECT RANDOM FILES

1 Click a file you want to select.

2 Press and hold down the **Ctrl** key.

3 Still holding down the **Ctrl** key, click each file you want to select.

SELECT ALL FILES

1 To select all the files in the current directory, click **Edit**.

2 Click **Select All**.

OPEN A FILE

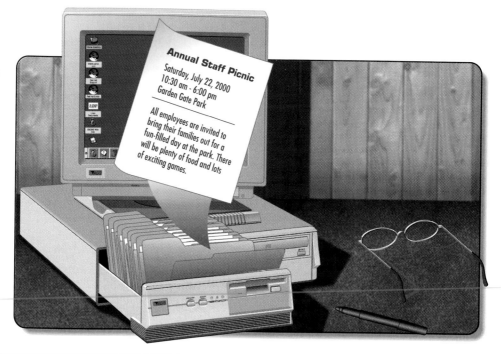

You can open a file to display its contents on your screen. This lets you review and make changes to the file.

OPEN A FILE

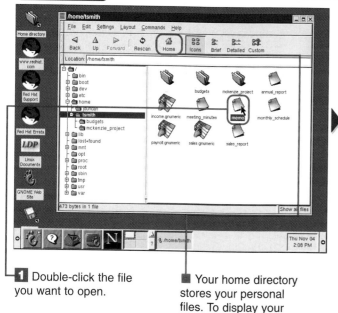

1 Double-click the file you want to open.

■ Your home directory stores your personal files. To display your home directory, click **Home**.

■ A dialog box may appear, asking you to select the program you want to use to open the file.

2 Click the program you want to use to open the file.

?

How did Linux open my file without asking which program to use?

If the name of the file you are opening contains a file extension, Linux may automatically open the file. Linux uses the file extension to determine which program to use to open the file. A file extension appears at the end of a file name and is separated from the name by a period (example: manual.txt).

Here are some common file extensions.

Type of File	File Extensions
Audio	au, mp3, ram, snd, wav
Image	bmp, gif, jpeg, jpg, png
Text	asc, txt
Video	avi, mpeg, mpg, mov

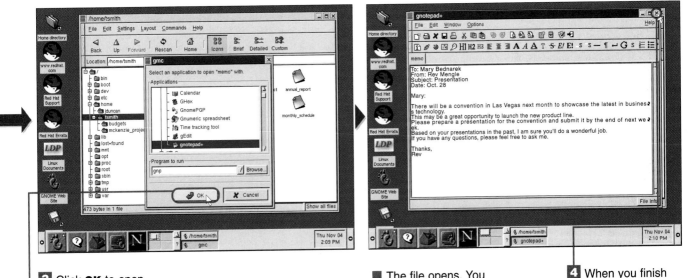

3 Click **OK** to open the file.

■ The file opens. You can now review and make changes to the file.

4 When you finish working with the file, click ⊠ to close the file.

RENAME A FILE

You can give a
file a new name
to better describe
the contents of
the file.

Date: Saturday, July 17, 1999
Time: 10:30 AM - 6:00 PM
Venue: Garden Gate Park

All employees are invited to bring their
families out for a fun-filled day at the park.
There will be plenty of food and lots of
exciting games and activities for the whole
family.

If you are logged on
to your computer as
a regular user, you can
usually only rename
files that you have
created. If you are
logged on as **root**,
you can rename most
files on your computer.

RENAME A FILE

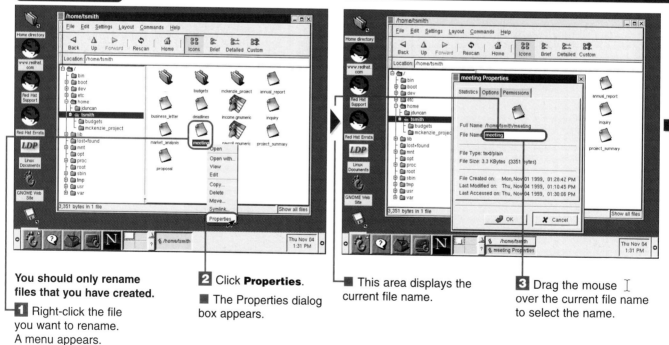

You should only rename
files that you have created.

1 Right-click the file
you want to rename.
A menu appears.

2 Click **Properties**.

■ The Properties dialog
box appears.

■ This area displays the
current file name.

3 Drag the mouse
over the current file name
to select the name.

Can I rename a directory?

Yes. To rename a directory, perform the steps below, except right-click the directory you want to rename in step **1**. You should only rename directories that you have created.

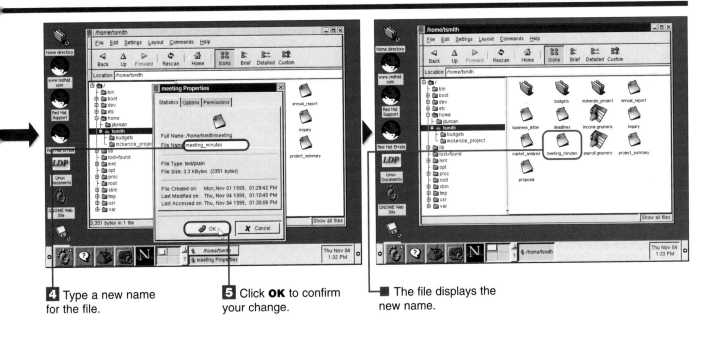

4 Type a new name for the file.

5 Click **OK** to confirm your change.

■ The file displays the new name.

You can delete a file you no longer need. Linux will permanently delete the file from your computer.

If you are logged on to your computer as a regular user, you can usually only delete files that you have created. If you are logged on as **root**, you can delete any file on your computer.

DELETE A FILE

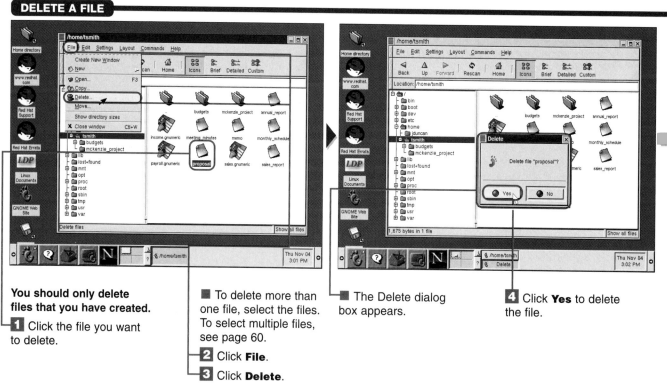

You should only delete files that you have created.

1 Click the file you want to delete.

■ To delete more than one file, select the files. To select multiple files, see page 60.

2 Click **File**.

3 Click **Delete**.

■ The Delete dialog box appears.

4 Click **Yes** to delete the file.

How do I delete a file located on my desktop?

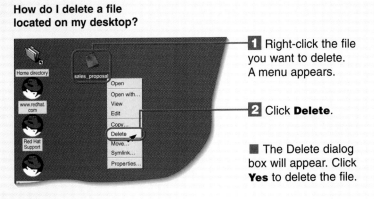

1 Right-click the file you want to delete. A menu appears.

2 Click **Delete**.

■ The Delete dialog box will appear. Click **Yes** to delete the file.

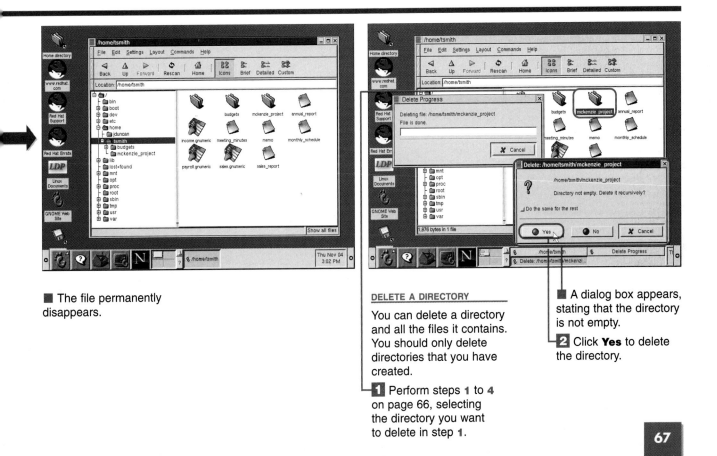

■ The file permanently disappears.

DELETE A DIRECTORY

You can delete a directory and all the files it contains. You should only delete directories that you have created.

1 Perform steps **1** to **4** on page 66, selecting the directory you want to delete in step **1**.

■ A dialog box appears, stating that the directory is not empty.

2 Click **Yes** to delete the directory.

You can organize the files stored on your computer by moving or copying them to new locations.

If you are logged on to your computer as a regular user, you can usually move and copy files only within your home directory. If you are logged on as **root**, you can move and copy files to any location on your computer.

MOVE FILES

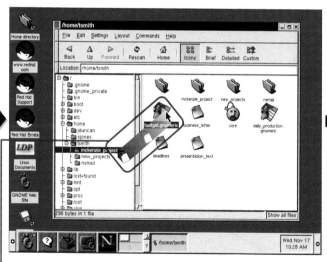

1 Position the mouse ▶ over the file you want to move.

■ To move multiple files at the same time, select the files. Then position the mouse ▶ over one of the files. To select multiple files, see page 60.

2 Drag the file to the directory where you want to place the file.

■ The file moves to the directory you specified.

What is the difference between moving and copying a file?

Move a File

When you move a file, you place the file in a new location on your computer.

Copy a File

When you copy a file, you make an exact copy of the file and then place the copy in a new location. This lets you store the file in two locations.

COPY FILES

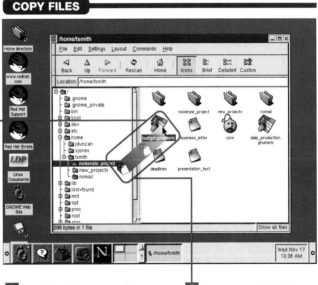

3 To view the file in the new location, click the directory you moved the file to.

■ This area displays the contents of the directory, including the file you moved.

Note: You can move directories the same way you move files. When you move a directory, all the files in the directory also move.

1 Position the mouse ▶ over the file you want to copy.

■ To copy multiple files at the same time, select the files. Then position the mouse ▶ over one of the files. To select multiple files, see page 60.

2 Press and hold down the **Ctrl** key as you drag the file to the directory where you want to place a copy of the file.

You can produce
a paper copy of
a file stored on
your computer.

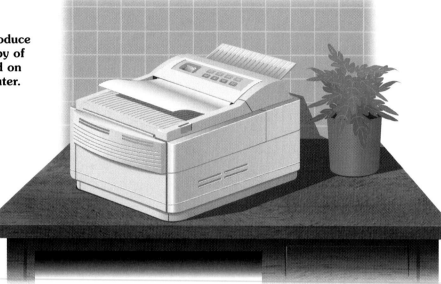

Before you can
print files, you must
set up a printer as
shown on page 198.

PRINT A FILE

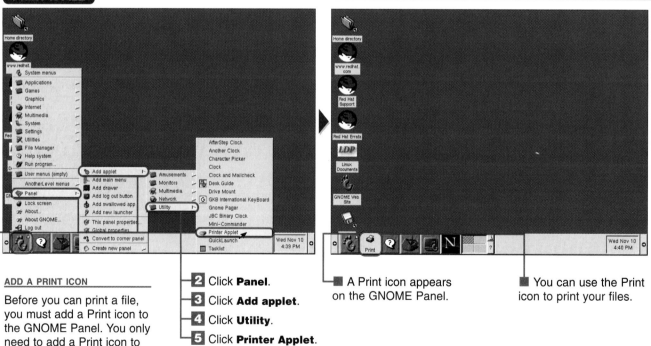

ADD A PRINT ICON

Before you can print a file,
you must add a Print icon to
the GNOME Panel. You only
need to add a Print icon to
the GNOME Panel once.

1 Click 🐾 to display the
Main Menu.

2 Click **Panel**.

3 Click **Add applet**.

4 Click **Utility**.

5 Click **Printer Applet**.

■ A Print icon appears
on the GNOME Panel.

■ You can use the Print
icon to print your files.

Can I print several files at the same time?

You can print several files at the same time by performing the following steps.

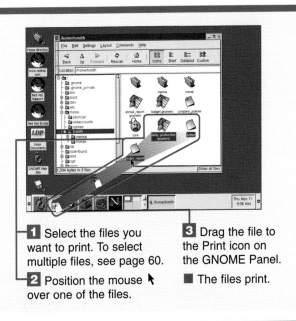

1 Select the files you want to print. To select multiple files, see page 60.

2 Position the mouse over one of the files.

3 Drag the file to the Print icon on the GNOME Panel.

■ The files print.

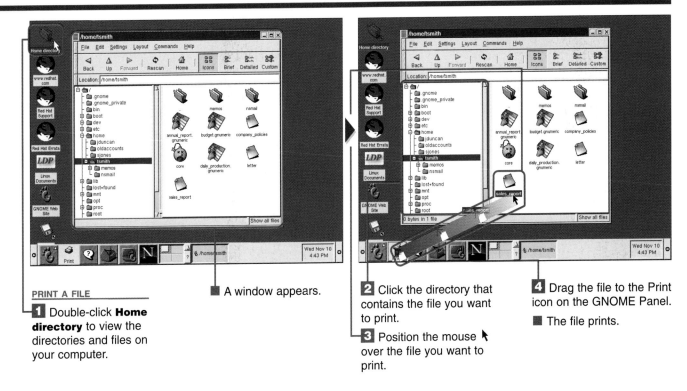

PRINT A FILE

1 Double-click **Home directory** to view the directories and files on your computer.

■ A window appears.

2 Click the directory that contains the file you want to print.

3 Position the mouse over the file you want to print.

4 Drag the file to the Print icon on the GNOME Panel.

■ The file prints.

FIND A FILE

If you cannot remember the location of a file you want to work with, you can have Linux search for the file.

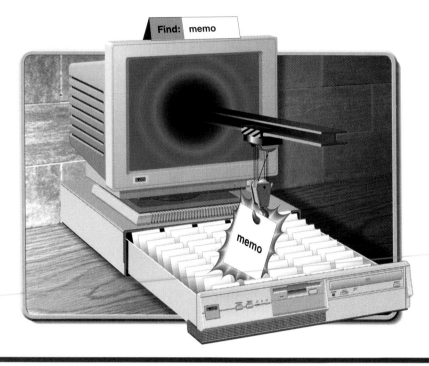

Find: memo

memo

FIND A FILE

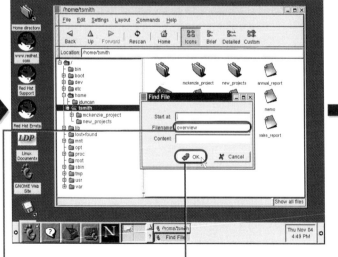

1 Click the directory where you want to search for the file. If the directory contains other directories, Linux will also search these directories.

2 Click **Commands**.

3 Click **Find File**.

■ The Find File window appears.

4 Double-click this area and type the name of the file you want to find. Make sure you type the correct upper and lower case letters.

Note: If you do not know the exact name of the file, you can use an asterisk (*) or question mark (?) to help you find the file. For more information, see the top of page 73.

5 Click **OK** to start the search.

How can I search for a file if I know only part of the file name?

You can use the asterisk (*) or a question mark (?) to help you find the file.

The asterisk (*) represents many characters. For example, type **report*** to find files beginning with **report**.

The question mark (?) represents a single character. For example, type **199?report** to find files beginning with **199** followed by a single character and ending with **report**.

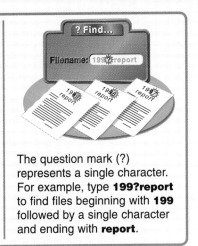

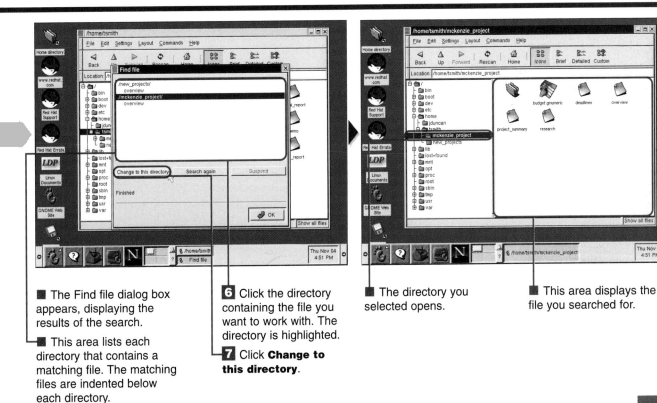

■ The Find file dialog box appears, displaying the results of the search.

■ This area lists each directory that contains a matching file. The matching files are indented below each directory.

6 Click the directory containing the file you want to work with. The directory is highlighted.

7 Click **Change to this directory**.

■ The directory you selected opens.

■ This area displays the file you searched for.

CHANGE FILE PERMISSIONS

You can change the permissions for a file to control the type of access users have to the file.

income.gnumeric

	January	February	March
REVENUE	$ 230,700	$ 435,900	$ 425,650
Payroll	$ 50,000	$ 62,000	$ 62,000
Rent	$ 5,000	$ 5,000	$ 5,000
Supplies	$ 1,920	$ 1,980	$ 2,030
TOTAL EXP.	$ 56,920	$ 68,980	$ 69,030
INCOME	$ 173,780	$ 366,920	$ 356,620

If you are logged on to your computer as a regular user, you can usually only change the permissions for files that you have created. If you are logged on as **root**, you can change the permissions for any file on your computer.

CHANGE FILE PERMISSIONS

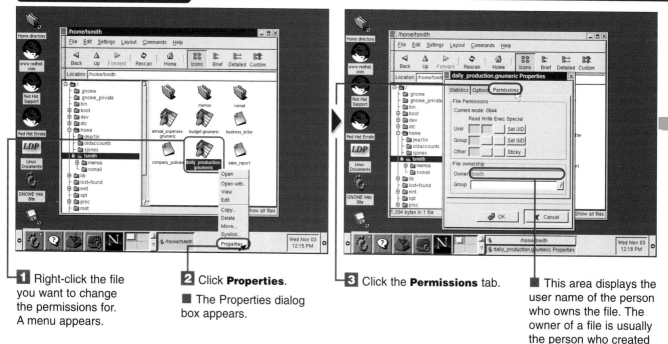

1 Right-click the file you want to change the permissions for. A menu appears.

2 Click **Properties**.

■ The Properties dialog box appears.

3 Click the **Permissions** tab.

■ This area displays the user name of the person who owns the file. The owner of a file is usually the person who created the file.

I changed the permissions for a file, but other users cannot access the file. What is wrong?

You must change the permissions for your home directory before other users can access a file in the directory. You can change the permissions for a directory the same way you change the permissions for a file. Turning on the execute (Exec) permission will allow users to open the directory. Turning on the read permission will allow users to view the files in the directory.

SARAH'S HOME DIRECTORY

☑ READ
☑ EXEC

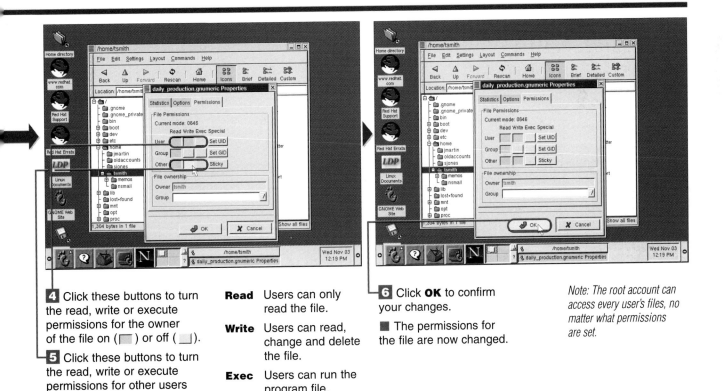

4 Click these buttons to turn the read, write or execute permissions for the owner of the file on (▢) or off (▢).

5 Click these buttons to turn the read, write or execute permissions for other users on (▢) or off (▢).

Read Users can only read the file.

Write Users can read, change and delete the file.

Exec Users can run the program file.

6 Click **OK** to confirm your changes.

■ The permissions for the file are now changed.

Note: The root account can access every user's files, no matter what permissions are set.

CREATE A LINK ON THE DESKTOP

You can create a link on the desktop that will provide a quick way of opening a file you use regularly.

CREATE A LINK ON THE DESKTOP

1 Position the mouse ▶ over the file you want to create a link to.

2 Press and hold down the left and right mouse buttons at the same time as you drag the file to a blank area on the desktop.

Note: If your mouse has a middle mouse button, press and hold down the middle mouse button as you drag the file.

**How do I rename or delete
a link on the desktop?**

You can rename or delete a
link on the desktop the same
way you would rename or
delete a file. Renaming or
deleting a link does not affect
the original file. To rename a
file, see page 64. To delete
a file, see page 66.

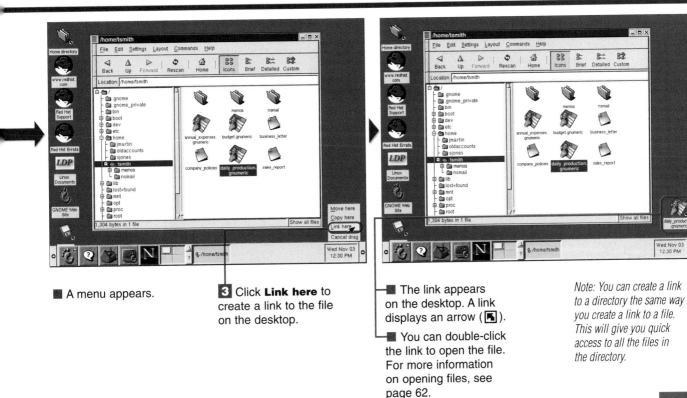

■ A menu appears.

3 Click **Link here** to
create a link to the file
on the desktop.

■ The link appears
on the desktop. A link
displays an arrow ().

■ You can double-click
the link to open the file.
For more information
on opening files, see
page 62.

*Note: You can create a link
to a directory the same way
you create a link to a file.
This will give you quick
access to all the files in
the directory.*

CREATE A NEW DIRECTORY

You can create a new directory to help you better organize the files stored on your computer.

If you are logged on to your computer as a regular user, you can create directories in your home directory and on your desktop. If you are logged on as **root**, you can create directories anywhere on your computer.

CREATE A NEW DIRECTORY

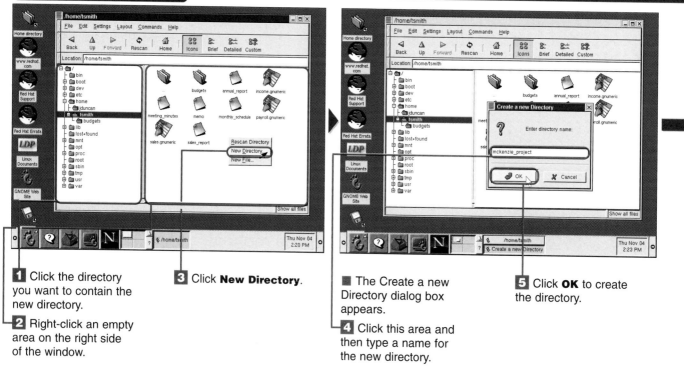

1 Click the directory you want to contain the new directory.

2 Right-click an empty area on the right side of the window.

3 Click **New Directory**.

■ The Create a new Directory dialog box appears.

4 Click this area and then type a name for the new directory.

5 Click **OK** to create the directory.

How can creating a new directory help me organize the files on my computer?

Creating a new directory is like placing a new folder in a filing cabinet. You can create a directory to store files you want to keep together, such as files for a particular project or files created during a specific time period. You can create as many directories as you need to organize files using a system that makes sense to you.

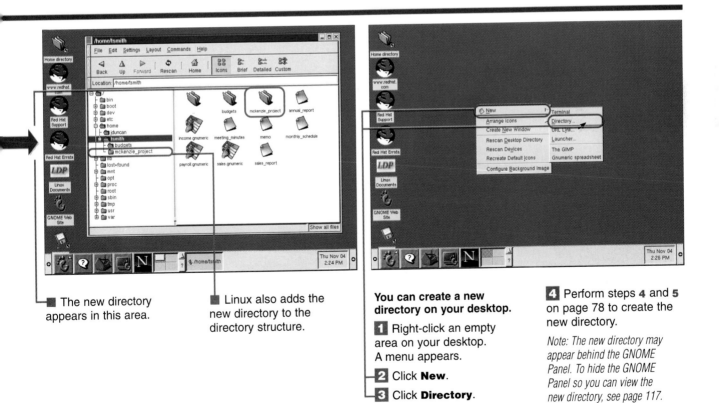

■ The new directory appears in this area.

■ Linux also adds the new directory to the directory structure.

You can create a new directory on your desktop.

1 Right-click an empty area on your desktop. A menu appears.

2 Click **New**.

3 Click **Directory**.

4 Perform steps 4 and 5 on page 78 to create the new directory.

Note: The new directory may appear behind the GNOME Panel. To hide the GNOME Panel so you can view the new directory, see page 117.

CHAPTER 4

Using Linux Applications

Linux offers many applications that you can use to perform tasks. Find out how to schedule appointments using Calendar, create simple documents using gnotepad+ and more in this chapter.

Memo:
There will be an important staff meeting on Monday, October 5. Questions regarding the upcoming Halloween party will be addressed. There will be coffee and donuts, so don't be late!

GNOTEPAD+

INCOME STATEMENT, Houston Office

First Quarter, 1999

	January	February	March
REVENUE	230,700	435,900	425,650
Payroll	9,850	10,850	10,250
Rent	1,750	1,750	1,750
Supplies	1,920	1,980	2,030
TOTAL EXP.	13,520	14,580	14,030
INCOME	217,180	421,320	411,620

GNUMERIC

John Smith

E-MAIL:

jsmith@abc.com

MAILING ADDRESS:

50 Tree Lane
Boston, MA
02117

GNOMECARD

USING GNOME CALCULATOR

Linux provides a calculator you can use to perform calculations.

USING GNOME CALCULATOR

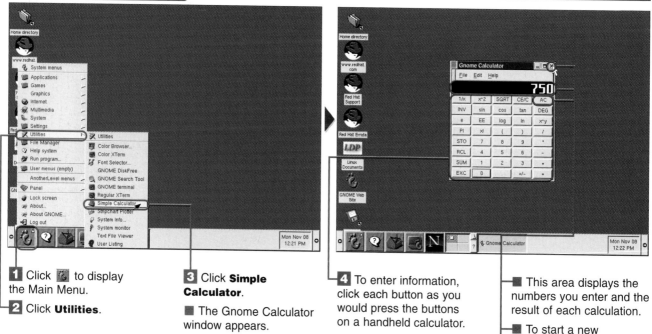

1 Click 🐾 to display the Main Menu.

2 Click **Utilities**.

3 Click **Simple Calculator**.

■ The Gnome Calculator window appears.

4 To enter information, click each button as you would press the buttons on a handheld calculator.

Note: You can make the buttons larger by increasing the size of the window. To resize a window, see page 33.

■ This area displays the numbers you enter and the result of each calculation.

■ To start a new calculation, click **AC**.

5 To close the Gnome Calculator window, click ⊠.

Linux includes several games you can play on your computer. Games are a fun way to improve your mouse skills and hand-eye coordination.

PLAY GAMES

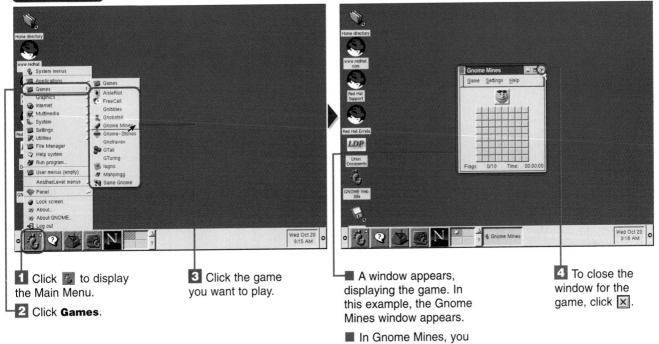

1 Click to display the Main Menu.

2 Click **Games**.

3 Click the game you want to play.

■ A window appears, displaying the game. In this example, the Gnome Mines window appears.

■ In Gnome Mines, you try to locate all of the mines without actually uncovering them.

4 To close the window for the game, click ⊠.

USING GNOTEPAD+

You can use gnotepad+ to create simple text documents.

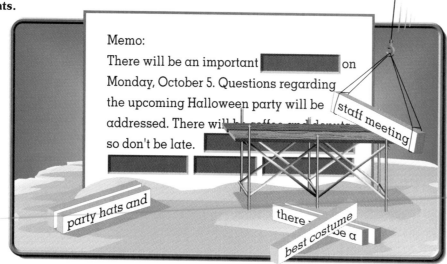

Memo:
There will be an important ▮▮▮▮▮ on Monday, October 5. Questions regarding the upcoming Halloween party will be addressed. There will be coffee and donuts so don't be late.

staff meeting

party hats and

there will be a

best costume

You can also use gnotepad+ to create Web pages. When you format text in gnotepad+, the program adds HTML tags to your document. Web browsers use the HTML tags to determine how your document should appear on the Web.

START GNOTEPAD+

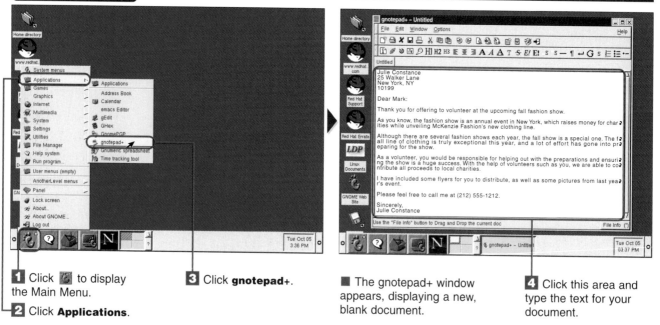

1 Click 🐾 to display the Main Menu.

2 Click **Applications**.

3 Click **gnotepad+**.

■ The gnotepad+ window appears, displaying a new, blank document.

4 Click this area and type the text for your document.

You can move or copy text to a new location in your document.

When you move text, you place the text in a new location.

When you copy text, you place an exact copy of the text in a new location.

MOVE OR COPY TEXT

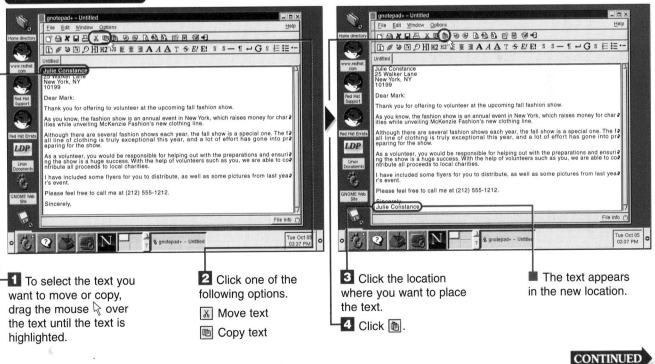

1 To select the text you want to move or copy, drag the mouse over the text until the text is highlighted.

2 Click one of the following options.

☒ Move text

▣ Copy text

3 Click the location where you want to place the text.

4 Click ▣.

■ The text appears in the new location.

CONTINUED

USING GNOTEPAD+

You should save your document to store it for future use. This allows you to later review and edit the document.

You should regularly save changes you make to a document to avoid losing your work.

SAVE A DOCUMENT

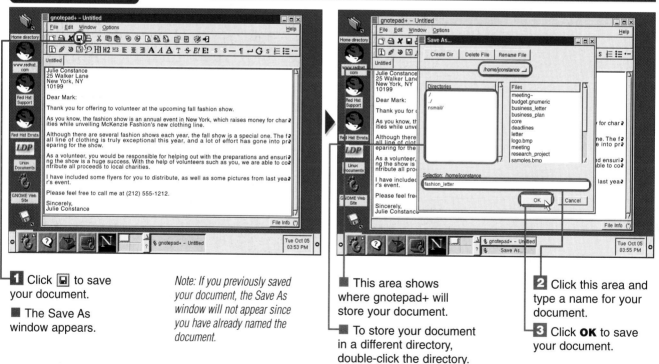

1 Click 🖫 to save your document.

■ The Save As window appears.

Note: If you previously saved your document, the Save As window will not appear since you have already named the document.

■ This area shows where gnotepad+ will store your document.

■ To store your document in a different directory, double-click the directory.

2 Click this area and type a name for your document.

3 Click **OK** to save your document.

You can open a saved
document and display the
document on your screen.
This allows you to review
and make changes to the
document.

OPEN A DOCUMENT

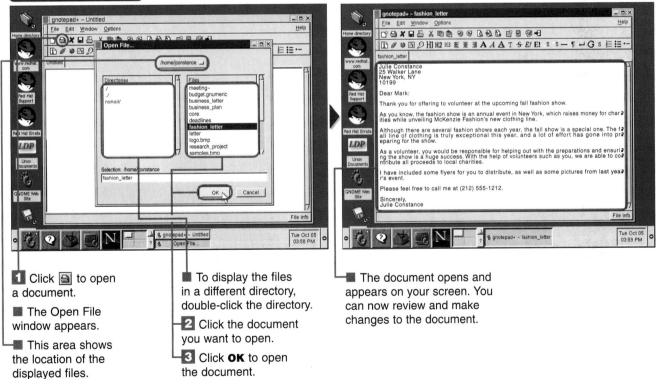

1 Click 📖 to open
a document.

■ The Open File
window appears.

■ This area shows
the location of the
displayed files.

■ To display the files
in a different directory,
double-click the directory.

2 Click the document
you want to open.

3 Click **OK** to open
the document.

■ The document opens and
appears on your screen. You
can now review and make
changes to the document.

USING XPAINT

You can use XPaint to draw pictures on your computer.

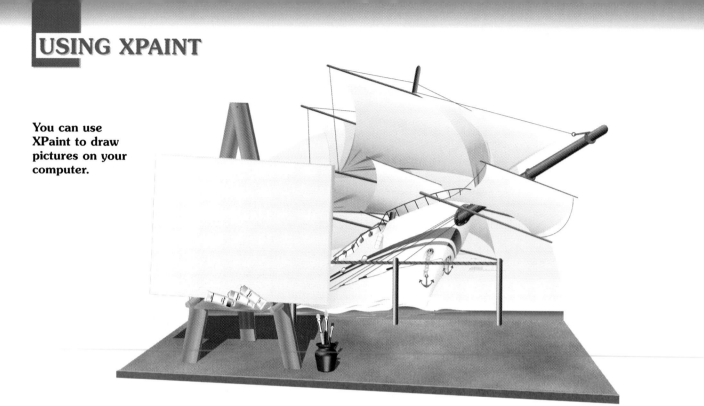

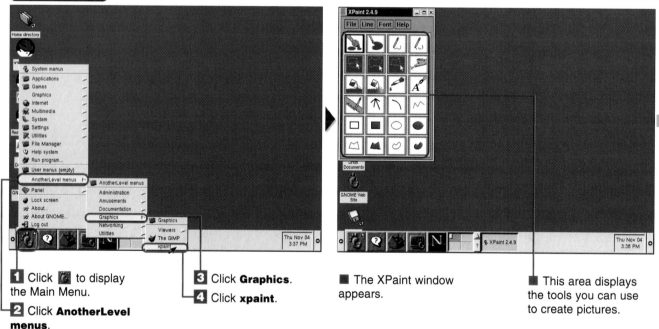

1 Click ![icon] to display the Main Menu.

2 Click **AnotherLevel menus**.

3 Click **Graphics**.

4 Click **xpaint**.

■ The XPaint window appears.

■ This area displays the tools you can use to create pictures.

Do NOT

How can I determine what each tool does?

You can display the name of a tool to help you determine what the tool does. Position the mouse over the tool and then press and hold down the right mouse button. A menu appears, displaying the name of the tool in bold type at the top of the menu.

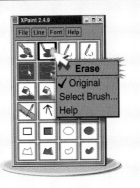

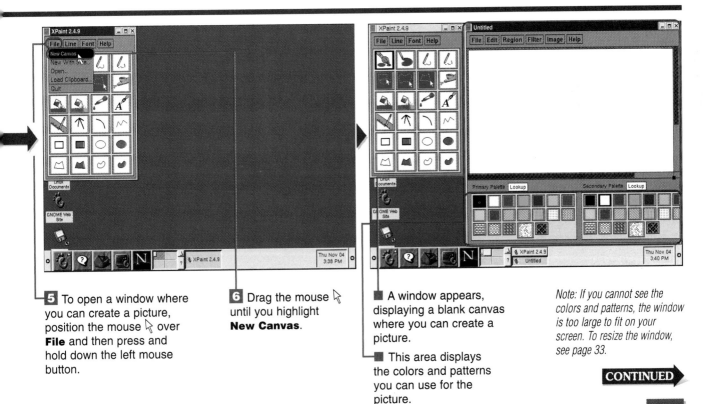

5 To open a window where you can create a picture, position the mouse over **File** and then press and hold down the left mouse button.

6 Drag the mouse until you highlight **New Canvas**.

■ A window appears, displaying a blank canvas where you can create a picture.

■ This area displays the colors and patterns you can use for the picture.

Note: If you cannot see the colors and patterns, the window is too large to fit on your screen. To resize the window, see page 33.

CONTINUED

USING XPAINT

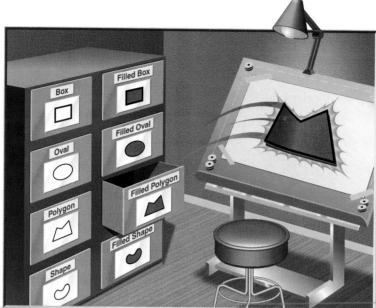

You can draw shapes such as squares, circles and polygons in various colors.

DRAW SHAPES

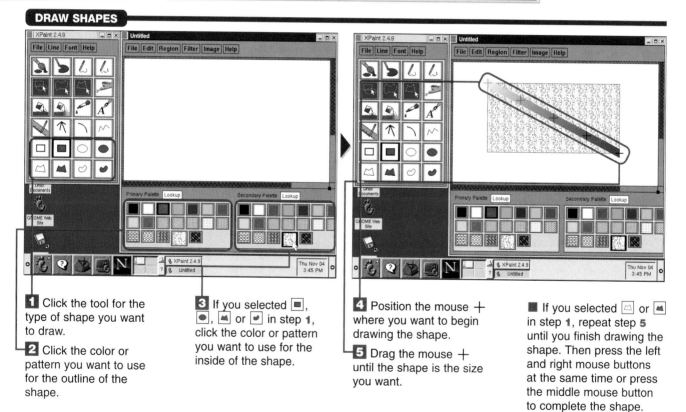

1 Click the tool for the type of shape you want to draw.

2 Click the color or pattern you want to use for the outline of the shape.

3 If you selected ▣, ●, ◪ or ✔ in step **1**, click the color or pattern you want to use for the inside of the shape.

4 Position the mouse + where you want to begin drawing the shape.

5 Drag the mouse + until the shape is the size you want.

■ If you selected ⬠ or ◪ in step **1**, repeat step **5** until you finish drawing the shape. Then press the left and right mouse buttons at the same time or press the middle mouse button to complete the shape.

You can draw
lines in various
colors using a
pencil, brush
or spray can.

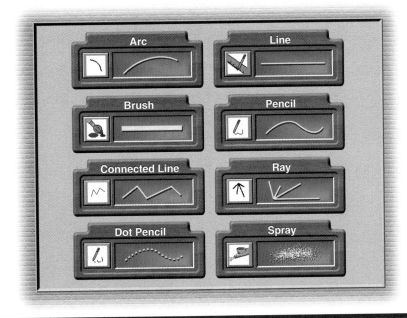

DRAW LINES

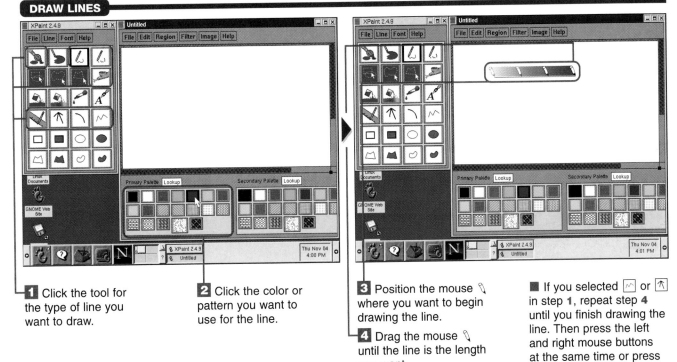

1 Click the tool for
the type of line you
want to draw.

2 Click the color or
pattern you want to
use for the line.

3 Position the mouse
where you want to begin
drawing the line.

4 Drag the mouse
until the line is the length
you want.

■ If you selected ⌐ or ⌐
in step **1**, repeat step **4**
until you finish drawing the
line. Then press the left
and right mouse buttons
at the same time or press
the middle mouse button
to complete the line.

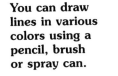

CONTINUED

You can add text
to your picture,
such as a title or
explanation.

ADD TEXT

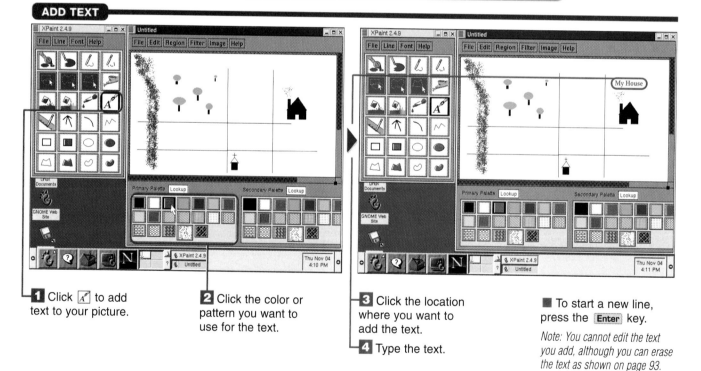

1 Click _A_ to add
text to your picture.

2 Click the color or
pattern you want to
use for the text.

3 Click the location
where you want to
add the text.

4 Type the text.

■ To start a new line,
press the **Enter** key.

Note: You cannot edit the text
you add, although you can erase
the text as shown on page 93.

You can use the
Erase tool to
remove part of
your picture.

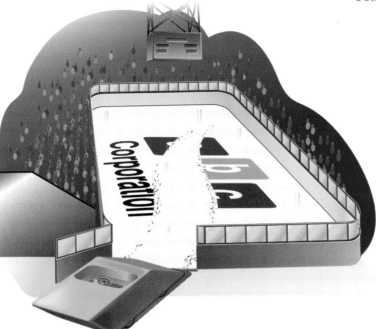

The Erase tool can only
erase changes you have
made since you last
opened your picture.

ERASE PART OF A PICTURE

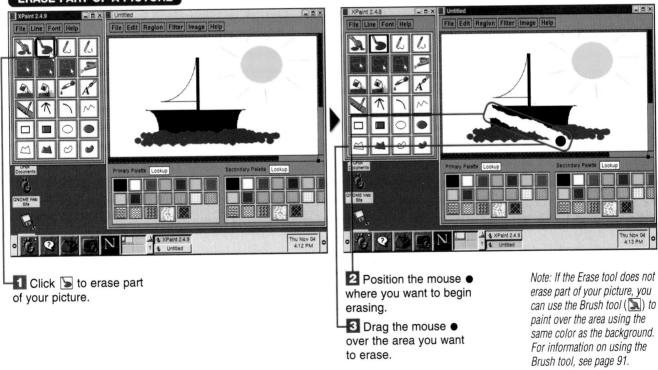

1 Click 🖉 to erase part
of your picture.

2 Position the mouse ●
where you want to begin
erasing.

3 Drag the mouse ●
over the area you want
to erase.

*Note: If the Erase tool does not
erase part of your picture, you
can use the Brush tool (🖌) to
paint over the area using the
same color as the background.
For information on using the
Brush tool, see page 91.*

CONTINUED ▶

USING XPAINT

You should save your picture to store it for future use. This allows you to later review and make changes to the picture.

You should regularly save changes you make to a picture to avoid losing your work.

SAVE A PICTURE

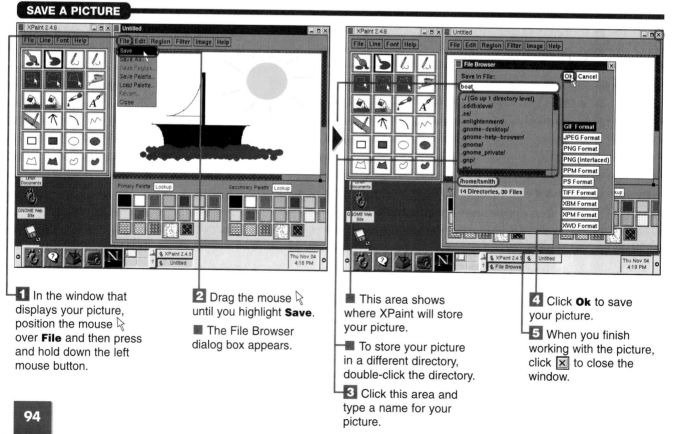

1 In the window that displays your picture, position the mouse over **File** and then press and hold down the left mouse button.

2 Drag the mouse until you highlight **Save**.

■ The File Browser dialog box appears.

■ This area shows where XPaint will store your picture.

■ To store your picture in a different directory, double-click the directory.

3 Click this area and type a name for your picture.

4 Click **Ok** to save your picture.

5 When you finish working with the picture, click ⊠ to close the window.

You can open a
saved picture to
display the picture
on your screen. This
allows you to review
and make changes
to the picture.

OPEN A PICTURE

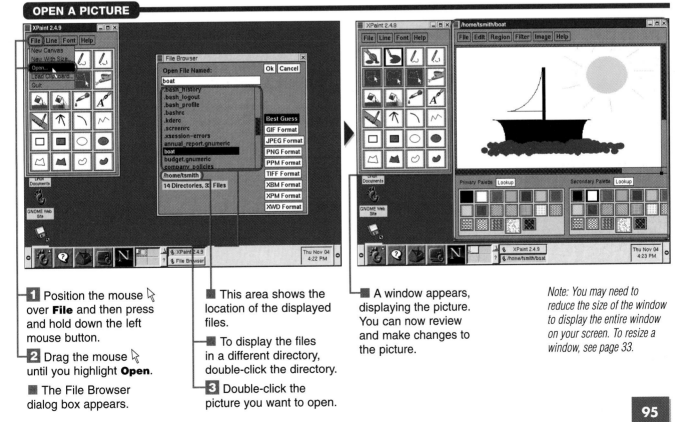

1 Position the mouse over **File** and then press and hold down the left mouse button.

2 Drag the mouse until you highlight **Open**.

■ The File Browser dialog box appears.

■ This area shows the location of the displayed files.

■ To display the files in a different directory, double-click the directory.

3 Double-click the picture you want to open.

■ A window appears, displaying the picture. You can now review and make changes to the picture.

Note: You may need to reduce the size of the window to display the entire window on your screen. To resize a window, see page 33.

USING CALENDAR

You can use Calendar to help you keep track of your appointments.

Doctor's Appt. 3

Lunch Meeting 5

Check Inventory 9

Order Supplies 11

May 2000

START CALENDAR

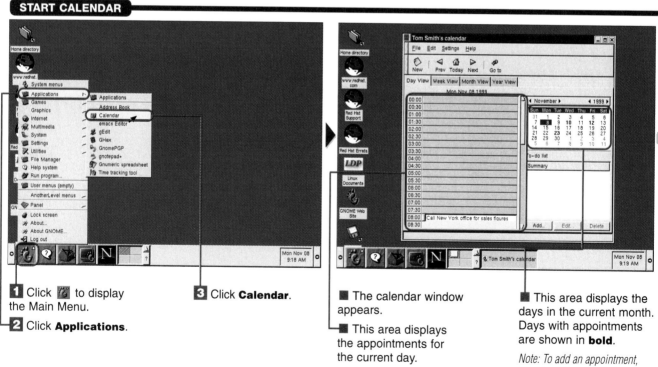

1 Click 🐾 to display the Main Menu.

2 Click **Applications**.

3 Click **Calendar**.

■ The calendar window appears.

■ This area displays the appointments for the current day.

■ This area displays the days in the current month. Days with appointments are shown in **bold**.

Note: To add an appointment, see page 98.

Why is Calendar displaying the wrong date for today?

Calendar uses the date and time set in your computer to determine today's date. Your computer's clock may be set incorrectly. To change the date and time set in your computer, see page 132.

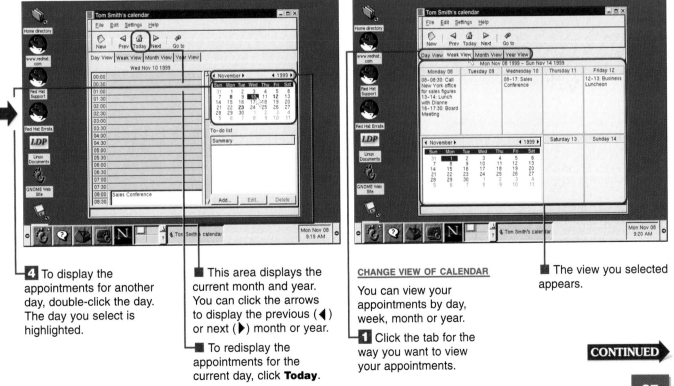

4 To display the appointments for another day, double-click the day. The day you select is highlighted.

■ This area displays the current month and year. You can click the arrows to display the previous (◀) or next (▶) month or year.

■ To redisplay the appointments for the current day, click **Today**.

CHANGE VIEW OF CALENDAR

You can view your appointments by day, week, month or year.

1 Click the tab for the way you want to view your appointments.

■ The view you selected appears.

CONTINUED ▶

USING CALENDAR

You can add an appointment to Calendar to remind you of an activity such as a business meeting, lunch date or doctor's appointment.

ADD AN APPOINTMENT

1 Click **New** to add an appointment.

■ The Create new appointment dialog box appears.

2 Click this area and type a description for the appointment.

■ These areas display the date and time the appointment will start and end.

3 To change the date or time, double-click the part of the date or time you want to change and then type the correct information.

Note: Make sure you enter the time using the 24-hour format. For example, enter 14:00 for 2 p.m.

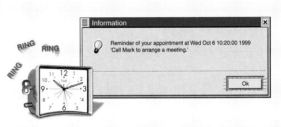

How will Calendar remind me of an appointment?

You can have Calendar display a reminder message to notify you of an upcoming appointment. By default, Calendar will remind you of an appointment 15 minutes before the appointment. The Calendar program must be open for the reminder message to appear. To close the reminder message, click **Ok**.

4 Click this option if you want Calendar to remind you of the appointment (☐ changes to ☑).

■ This area displays the amount of time before the appointment that Calendar will remind you.

5 To specify another time, double-click this area and type the new time.

6 Click **OK** to confirm the information you entered.

■ The appointment appears in the calendar window.

DELETE AN APPOINTMENT

1 Right-click the appointment you want to delete. A menu appears.

2 Click **Delete this appointment**.

USING GNOMECARD

You can use the GnomeCard address book to keep detailed information about friends, family members, colleagues and clients.

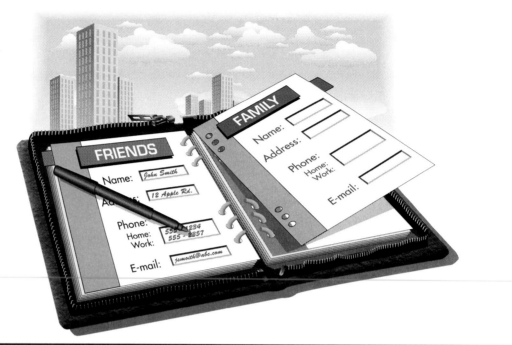

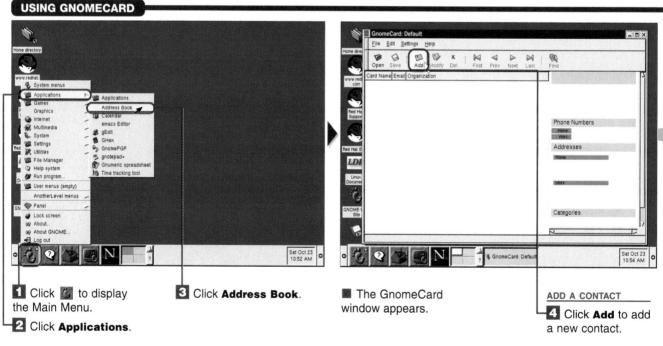

1 Click to display the Main Menu.

2 Click **Applications**.

3 Click **Address Book**.

■ The GnomeCard window appears.

ADD A CONTACT

4 Click **Add** to add a new contact.

What information can I use to file a contact?

When filing a contact, you can use information such as the contact's first name, last name, full name or nickname. For example, you can file a contact as Smith, John. You should use the same filing method for all of your contacts to help you organize the contacts in the GnomeCard window.

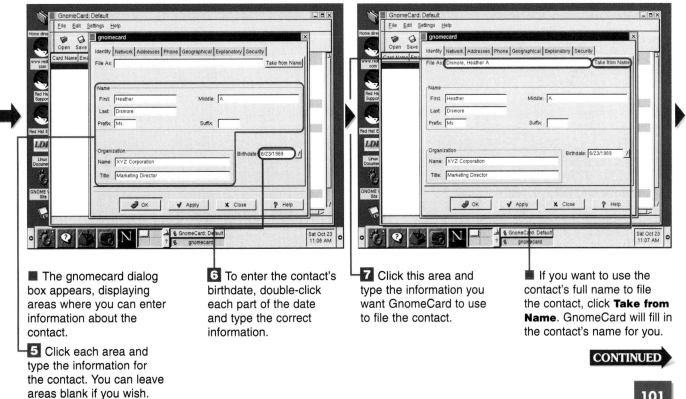

■ The gnomecard dialog box appears, displaying areas where you can enter information about the contact.

5 Click each area and type the information for the contact. You can leave areas blank if you wish.

6 To enter the contact's birthdate, double-click each part of the date and type the correct information.

7 Click this area and type the information you want GnomeCard to use to file the contact.

■ If you want to use the contact's full name to file the contact, click **Take from Name**. GnomeCard will fill in the contact's name for you.

CONTINUED

USING GNOMECARD

You can use GnomeCard to keep track of the e-mail and mailing addresses of your contacts.

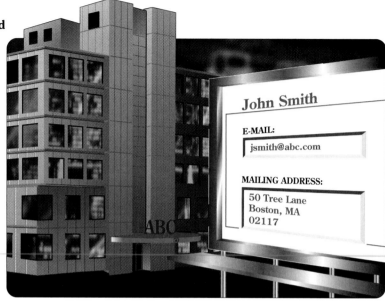

John Smith

E-MAIL:

jsmith@abc.com

MAILING ADDRESS:

50 Tree Lane
Boston, MA
02117

When entering information for a contact, you do not need to enter all of the information.

USING GNOMECARD (CONTINUED)

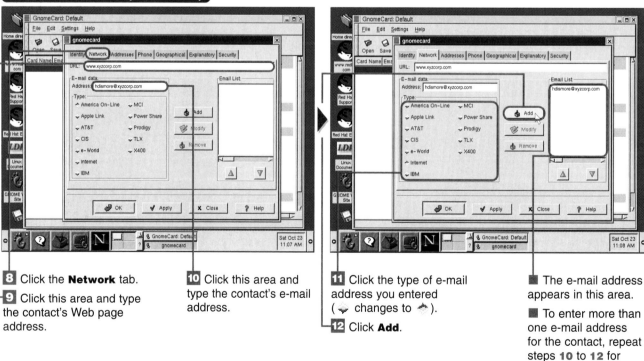

8 Click the **Network** tab.

9 Click this area and type the contact's Web page address.

10 Click this area and type the contact's e-mail address.

11 Click the type of e-mail address you entered (⌄ changes to ⌃).

12 Click **Add**.

■ The e-mail address appears in this area.

■ To enter more than one e-mail address for the contact, repeat steps **10** to **12** for each address.

Can I add comments about a contact?

You can add comments about a contact, such as their favorite restaurant and the names of their family members.

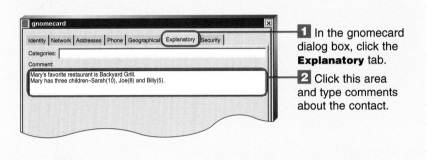

1 In the gnomecard dialog box, click the **Explanatory** tab.

2 Click this area and type comments about the contact.

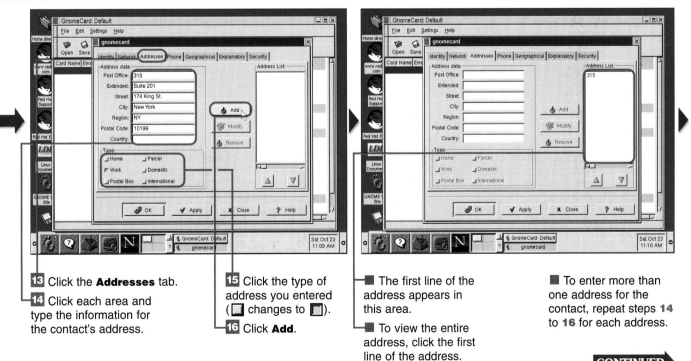

13 Click the **Addresses** tab.

14 Click each area and type the information for the contact's address.

15 Click the type of address you entered (☐ changes to ☑).

16 Click **Add**.

■ The first line of the address appears in this area.

■ To view the entire address, click the first line of the address.

■ To enter more than one address for the contact, repeat steps **14** to **16** for each address.

CONTINUED

USING GNOMECARD

You can use GnomeCard to keep track of the phone numbers of your contacts.

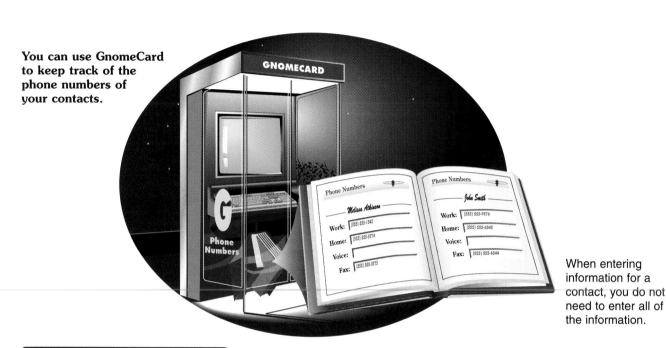

When entering information for a contact, you do not need to enter all of the information.

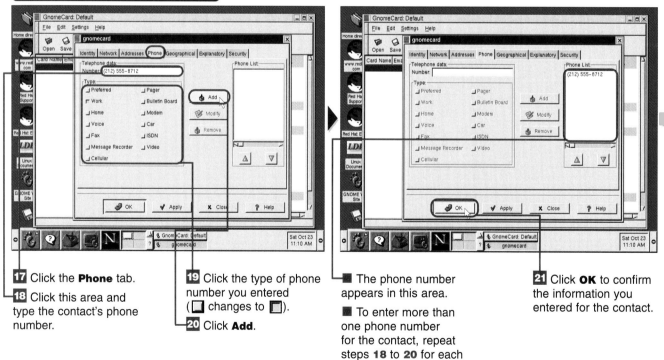

17 Click the **Phone** tab.

18 Click this area and type the contact's phone number.

19 Click the type of phone number you entered (☐ changes to ☑).

20 Click **Add**.

■ The phone number appears in this area.

■ To enter more than one phone number for the contact, repeat steps **18** to **20** for each phone number.

21 Click **OK** to confirm the information you entered for the contact.

How do I change the information for a contact?

You can update the information for a contact at any time. Double-click the contact in the GnomeCard window to redisplay the gnomecard dialog box. You can then make changes to the contact's information. When you finish changing the information, perform steps **21** and **22** below to save the changes.

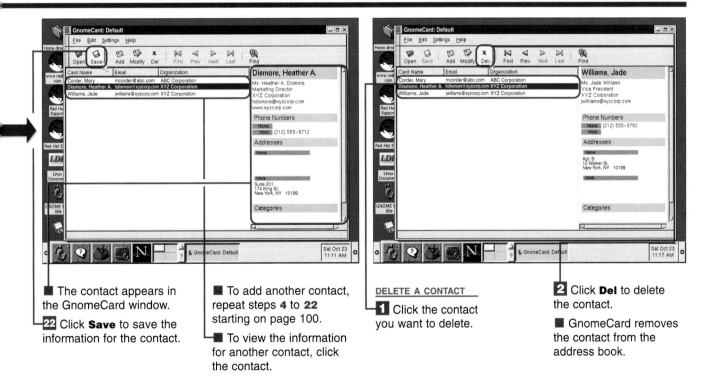

■ The contact appears in the GnomeCard window.

22 Click **Save** to save the information for the contact.

■ To add another contact, repeat steps **4** to **22** starting on page 100.

■ To view the information for another contact, click the contact.

DELETE A CONTACT

1 Click the contact you want to delete.

2 Click **Del** to delete the contact.

■ GnomeCard removes the contact from the address book.

You can use the Gnumeric spreadsheet program to organize and analyze data. Gnumeric can help you manage your business or personal finances.

1 Click  to display the Main Menu.

2 Click **Applications**.

3 Click **Gnumeric spreadsheet**.

■ The Gnumeric window appears, displaying a blank worksheet.

ENTER DATA

1 Click the cell where you want to enter data. The cell becomes the active cell and displays a thick border.

2 Type the data you want to enter and then press the Enter key.

■ The data you type appears in the active cell and in the data entry area.

What terms should I know when working with Gnumeric?

Column
A vertical line of cells. A letter identifies each column.

Cell Reference
Defines the location of each cell. A cell reference consists of a column letter followed by a row number (example: A1).

Cell
A box in a worksheet.

Row
A horizontal line of cells. A number identifies each row.

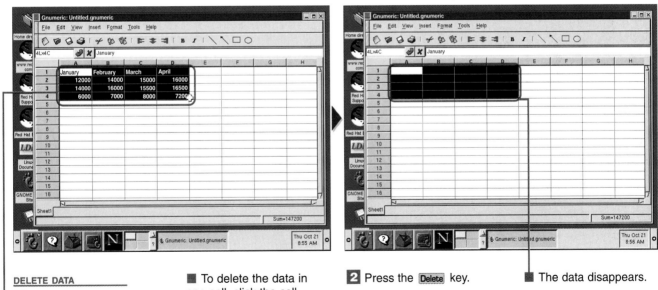

DELETE DATA

1 To select the cells containing the data you want to delete, drag the mouse ⊕ over the cells until the cells are highlighted.

■ To delete the data in one cell, click the cell.

2 Press the Delete key.

■ The data disappears.

CONTINUED

USING GNUMERIC

You can change the width of a column to display hidden data and improve the appearance of your worksheet.

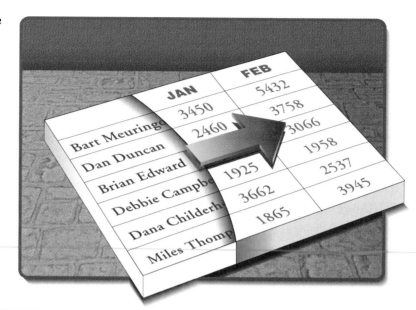

If data appears cut off or number signs (#) appear in a cell, the column is not wide enough to display the contents of the cell.

CHANGE COLUMN WIDTH

1 To change the width of a column, position the mouse ⇩ over the right edge of the column heading (⇩ changes to ⟷).

2 Drag the column edge until the line displays the column width you want.

■ The column displays the new width.

You can enter formulas to perform calculations on the data in your worksheet.

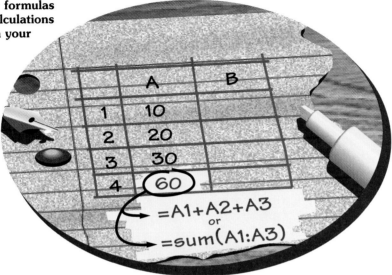

When entering formulas, use cell references (example: =A1+A2+A3) instead of actual data (example: =10+20+30) whenever possible. When you use cell references and you change a number used in a formula, Gnumeric will automatically redo the calculations for you.

ENTER A FORMULA

1 Click the cell where you want to enter a formula.

2 Type an equal sign (=) to begin the formula.

3 Type the formula and then press the Enter key.

Note: To add a list of numbers, type =sum(A:B) replacing A with the cell reference of the first cell and B with the cell reference of the last cell. For example, type =sum(B4:B7).

■ The result of the calculation appears in the cell.

4 To view the formula you entered, click the cell containing the formula.

■ The formula for the cell appears in this area.

CONTINUED

USING GNUMERIC

You should save your worksheet to store it for future use. This allows you to later review and edit the worksheet.

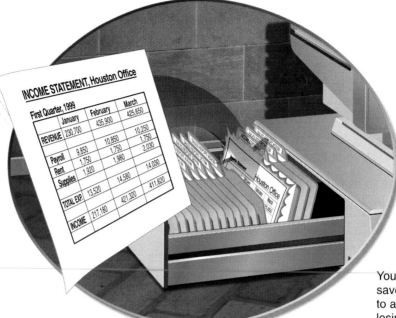

You should regularly save changes you make to a worksheet to avoid losing your work.

SAVE A WORKSHEET

1 Click 🖫 to save your worksheet.

■ The Save workbook as window appears.

Note: If you previously saved your worksheet, the Save workbook as window will not appear since you have already named the worksheet.

■ This area shows where Gnumeric will store your worksheet.

■ To store your worksheet in a different directory, double-click the directory.

2 Click this area and type a name for your worksheet.

3 Click **OK** to save your worksheet.

*Note: Gnumeric will add the **.gnumeric** file extension to the name of your worksheet (example: income.gnumeric).*

You can open a saved
worksheet and display
it on your screen. This
allows you to review
and make changes to
the worksheet.

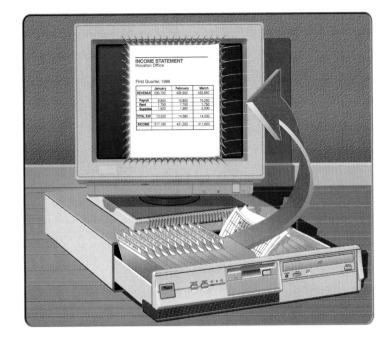

OPEN A WORKSHEET

1 Click 🖻 to open
a worksheet.

■ The Load file
dialog box appears.

■ This area shows
the location of the
displayed files.

■ To display the files
in a different directory,
double-click the directory.

2 Click the worksheet
you want to open.

3 Click **OK** to open
the worksheet.

■ A new window appears,
displaying the worksheet.
You can now review and
make changes to the
worksheet.

4 When you finish
working with the
worksheet, click ⊠
to close the window.

CHAPTER 5

Customize Linux

You can customize Linux to suit your needs. In this chapter you will learn how to add wallpaper to your desktop, set up screen savers, adjust your mouse settings and more.

USING MULTIPLE DESKTOPS

You can work with more than one desktop on your computer.

Using multiple desktops is like having more than one monitor. You can use a different desktop for each task you need to perform.

USING MULTIPLE DESKTOPS

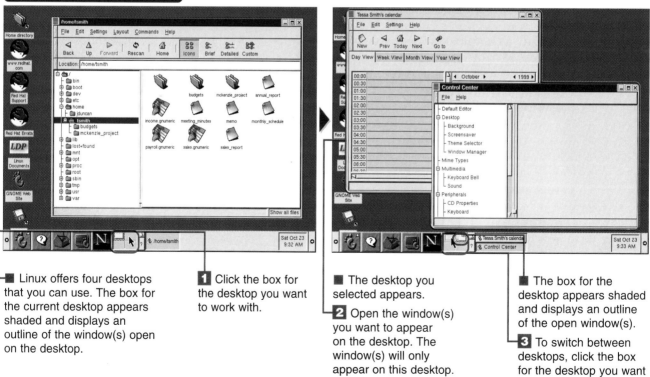

■ Linux offers four desktops that you can use. The box for the current desktop appears shaded and displays an outline of the window(s) open on the desktop.

1 Click the box for the desktop you want to work with.

■ The desktop you selected appears.

2 Open the window(s) you want to appear on the desktop. The window(s) will only appear on this desktop.

■ The box for the desktop appears shaded and displays an outline of the open window(s).

3 To switch between desktops, click the box for the desktop you want to display.

MAKE A WINDOW APPEAR ON EVERY DESKTOP

If you frequently use a window, you can have the window appear on every desktop.

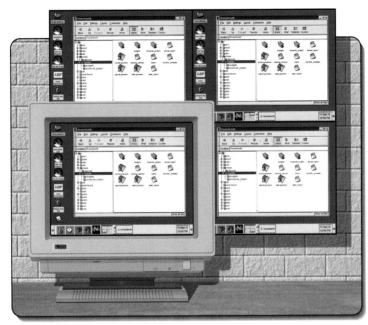

For information on using multiple desktops, see page 114.

MAKE A WINDOW APPEAR ON EVERY DESKTOP

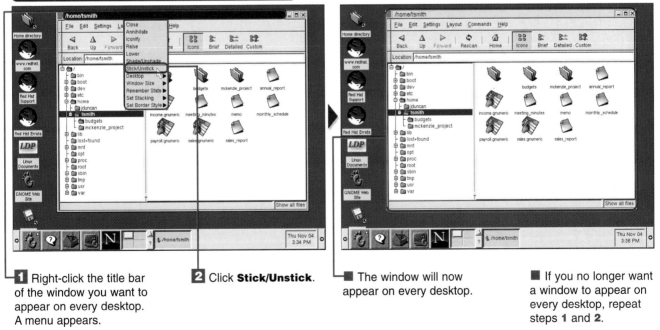

1 Right-click the title bar of the window you want to appear on every desktop. A menu appears.

2 Click **Stick/Unstick**.

■ The window will now appear on every desktop.

■ If you no longer want a window to appear on every desktop, repeat steps **1** and **2**.

DISPLAY A LIST OF OPEN WINDOWS

You can display a list of all the windows you have open on your desktops. This can help you quickly locate a window you want to work with.

For information on using multiple desktops, see page 114.

DISPLAY A LIST OF OPEN WINDOWS

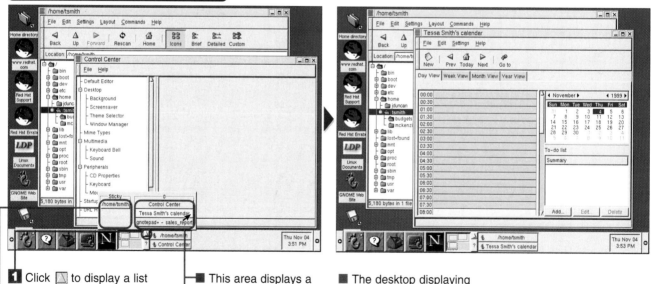

1 Click to display a list of all the windows you have open on your desktops.

■ This area displays a button for each window you chose to appear on every desktop. To make a window appear on every desktop, see page 115.

■ This area displays a button for each window you have open on your desktops.

2 Click the button for the window you want to display.

■ The desktop displaying the window appears.

You can hide the
GNOME Panel to
give you more room
on the desktop for
performing tasks.

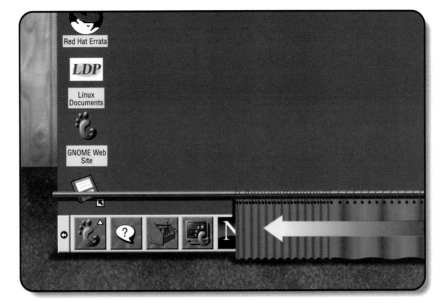

HIDE THE GNOME PANEL

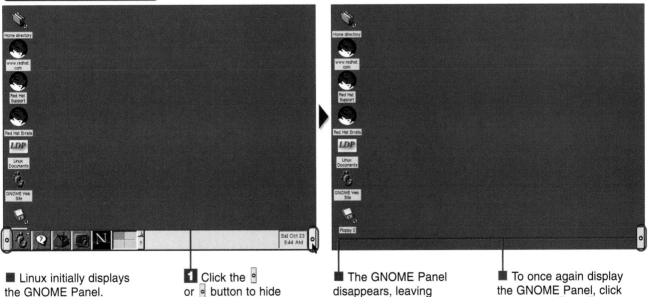

■ Linux initially displays
the GNOME Panel.

1 Click the button
or button to hide
the GNOME Panel.

■ The GNOME Panel
disappears, leaving
a button at the bottom
left or right corner
of the screen.

*Note: The location of the
button depends on the button
you selected in step 1.*

■ To once again display
the GNOME Panel, click
the button (or).

HIDE THE GNOME PANEL AUTOMATICALLY

You can have the GNOME Panel automatically disappear when you are not using the panel. This will give you more room on the desktop for performing tasks.

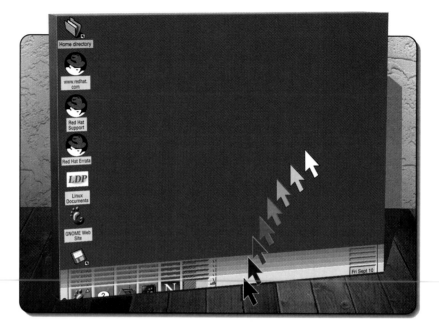

HIDE THE GNOME PANEL AUTOMATICALLY

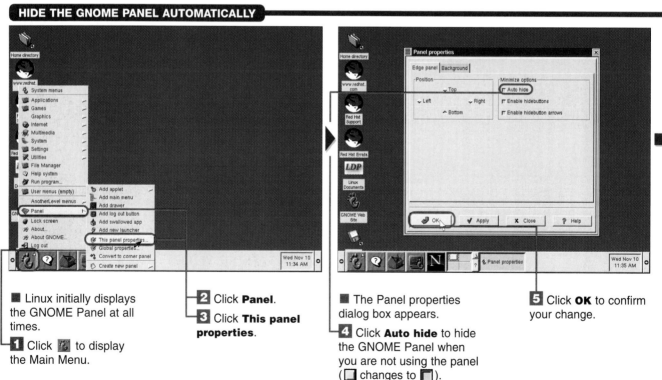

■ Linux initially displays the GNOME Panel at all times.

1 Click to display the Main Menu.

2 Click **Panel**.

3 Click **This panel properties**.

■ The Panel properties dialog box appears.

4 Click **Auto hide** to hide the GNOME Panel when you are not using the panel (☐ changes to ▓).

5 Click **OK** to confirm your change.

What information does the GNOME Panel display?

■ The Main Menu button gives you quick access to programs.

■ These application launchers allow you to get help, change settings, display the Terminal window and start Netscape Communicator.

■ The GNOME Pager allows you to switch between desktops and displays a button for each open window.

■ The clock displays the current date and time.

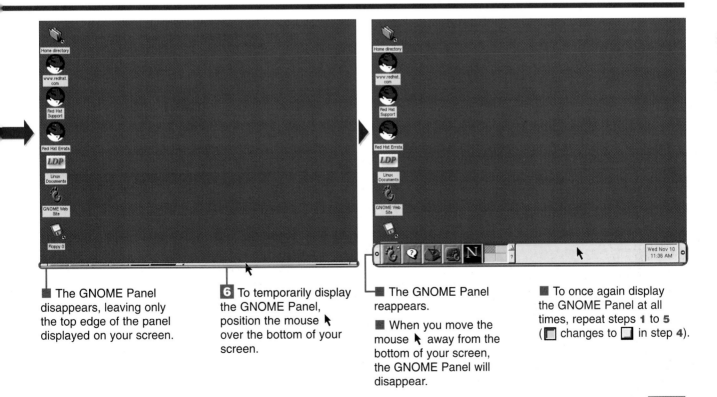

■ The GNOME Panel disappears, leaving only the top edge of the panel displayed on your screen.

6 To temporarily display the GNOME Panel, position the mouse ▶ over the bottom of your screen.

■ The GNOME Panel reappears.

■ When you move the mouse ▶ away from the bottom of your screen, the GNOME Panel will disappear.

■ To once again display the GNOME Panel at all times, repeat steps **1** to **5** (☐ changes to ☐ in step **4**).

CHANGE THE DESKTOP COLOR

You can change the color of your desktop to customize the appearance of your screen.

You can choose a solid or gradient color for your desktop.

CHANGE THE DESKTOP COLOR

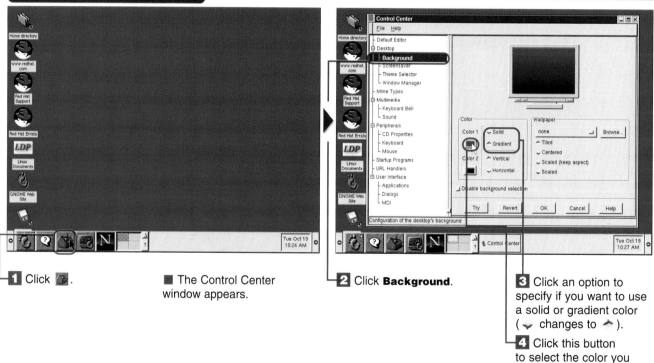

1 Click .

■ The Control Center window appears.

2 Click **Background**.

3 Click an option to specify if you want to use a solid or gradient color (changes to).

4 Click this button to select the color you want to use.

When using a gradient color, can I change the direction of the gradient?

Yes. When using a gradient color, you can have the colors blend together vertically or horizontally. In the Control Center window, click **Vertical** or **Horizontal** to change the direction of the gradient (➛ changes to ↝).

Vertical

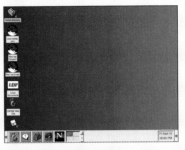

Horizontal

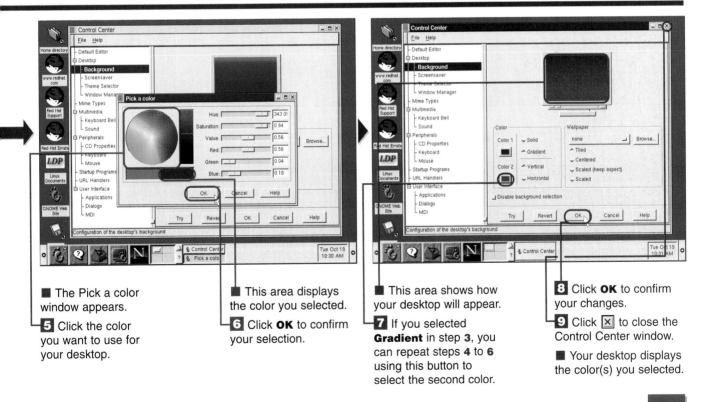

■ The Pick a color window appears.

5 Click the color you want to use for your desktop.

■ This area displays the color you selected.

6 Click **OK** to confirm your selection.

■ This area shows how your desktop will appear.

7 If you selected **Gradient** in step **3**, you can repeat steps **4** to **6** using this button to select the second color.

8 Click **OK** to confirm your changes.

9 Click ✕ to close the Control Center window.

■ Your desktop displays the color(s) you selected.

ADD WALLPAPER

You can add
wallpaper to
your desktop
to decorate
your screen.

ADD WALLPAPER

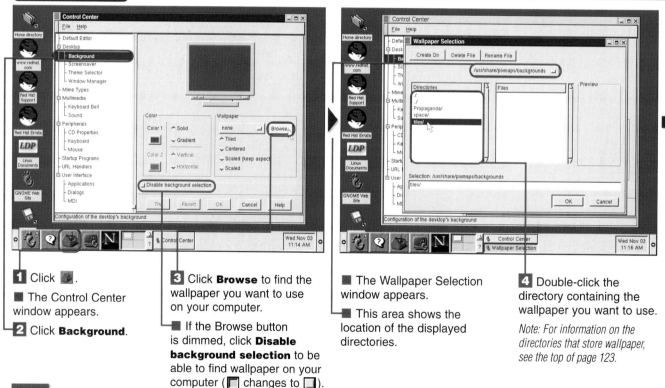

1 Click .

■ The Control Center
window appears.

2 Click **Background**.

3 Click **Browse** to find the
wallpaper you want to use
on your computer.

■ If the Browse button
is dimmed, click **Disable
background selection** to be
able to find wallpaper on your
computer (☐ changes to ■).

■ The Wallpaper Selection
window appears.

■ This area shows the
location of the displayed
directories.

4 Double-click the
directory containing the
wallpaper you want to use.

Note: For information on the
directories that store wallpaper,
see the top of page 123.

Where can I find wallpaper on my computer?

Linux stores wallpaper in three main directories on your computer.

Propaganda

Contains interesting patterns stored in six directories, named Vol1 to Vol6.

Space

Contains pictures of outer space, such as pictures of Earth, Mars and Saturn.

Tiles

Contains pictures of common objects, such as bricks, clouds and wood.

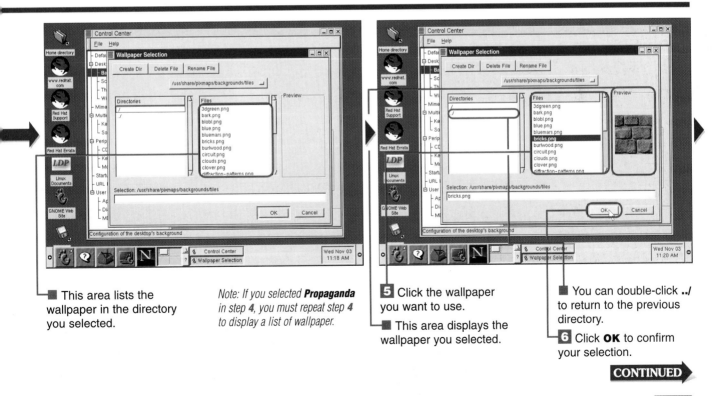

■ This area lists the wallpaper in the directory you selected.

*Note: If you selected **Propaganda** in step 4, you must repeat step 4 to display a list of wallpaper.*

5 Click the wallpaper you want to use.

■ This area displays the wallpaper you selected.

■ You can double-click **../** to return to the previous directory.

6 Click **OK** to confirm your selection.

CONTINUED

ADD WALLPAPER

You can preview
how the wallpaper
you want to use
will appear on
your screen.

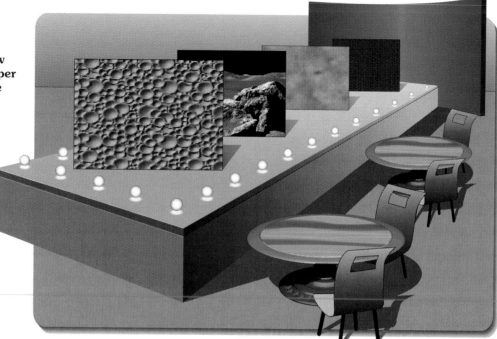

ADD WALLPAPER (CONTINUED)

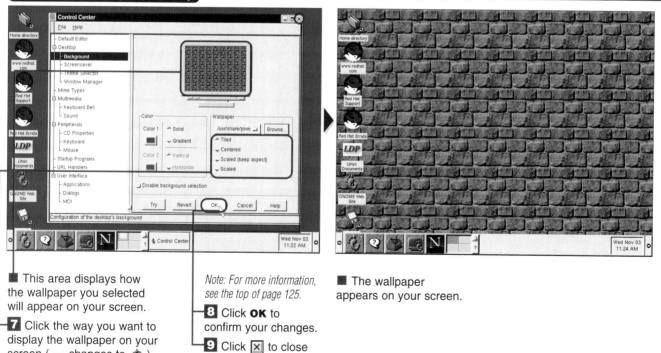

■ This area displays how
the wallpaper you selected
will appear on your screen.

7 Click the way you want to
display the wallpaper on your
screen (↧ changes to ↥).

*Note: For more information,
see the top of page 125.*

8 Click **OK** to
confirm your changes.

9 Click ⊠ to close
the Control Center
window.

■ The wallpaper
appears on your screen.

How can I display wallpaper on my screen?

Tiled

Repeats the wallpaper until it fills your screen.

Centered

Places the wallpaper in the middle of your screen.

Scaled (keep aspect)

Stretches the wallpaper to fill most of your screen without distorting the wallpaper image.

Scaled

Stretches the wallpaper to fill your screen.

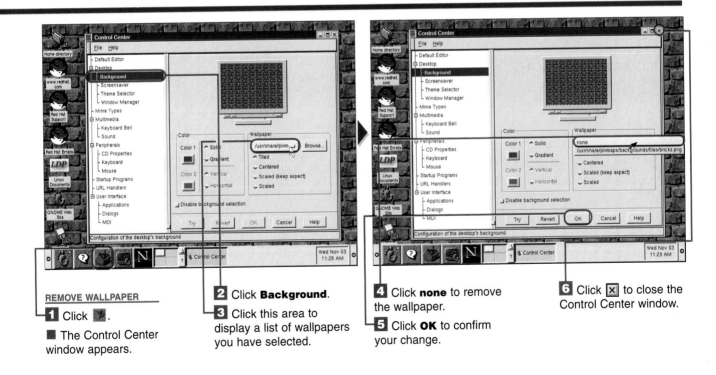

REMOVE WALLPAPER

1 Click .

■ The Control Center window appears.

2 Click **Background**.

3 Click this area to display a list of wallpapers you have selected.

4 Click **none** to remove the wallpaper.

5 Click **OK** to confirm your change.

6 Click ⊠ to close the Control Center window.

SELECT A THEME

You can select a theme to customize the appearance of your screen.

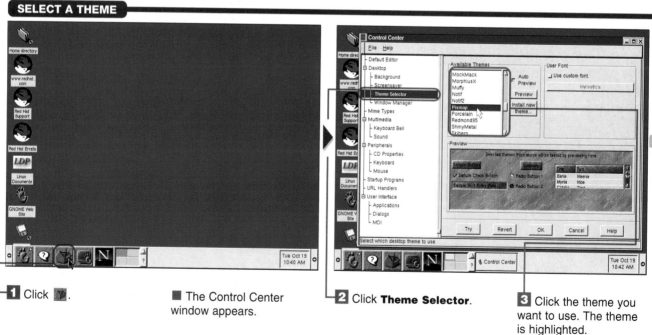

1 Click .

■ The Control Center window appears.

2 Click **Theme Selector**.

3 Click the theme you want to use. The theme is highlighted.

What items on my screen will change when I select a theme?

A theme will change the appearance of many different items on your screen, including check buttons, radio buttons and scroll bars.

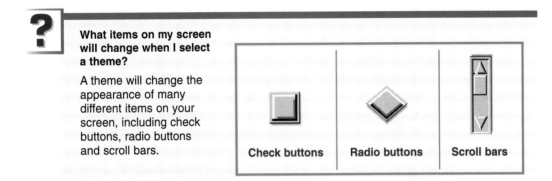

Check buttons   **Radio buttons**   **Scroll bars**

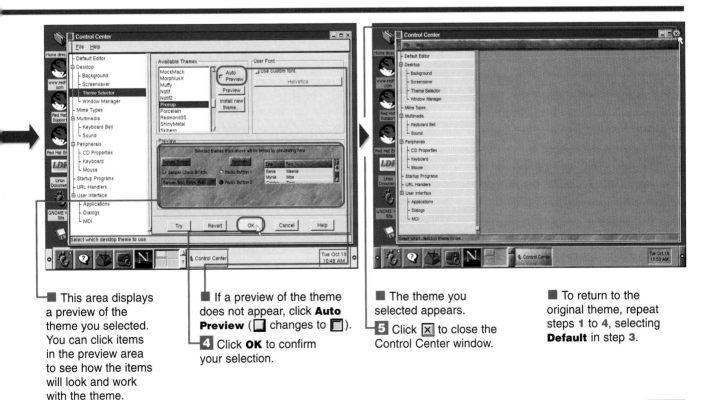

■ This area displays a preview of the theme you selected. You can click items in the preview area to see how the items will look and work with the theme.

■ If a preview of the theme does not appear, click **Auto Preview** (☐ changes to ☑).

4 Click **OK** to confirm your selection.

■ The theme you selected appears.

5 Click ☒ to close the Control Center window.

■ To return to the original theme, repeat steps **1** to **4**, selecting **Default** in step **3**.

SET UP A SCREEN SAVER

A screen saver is a moving picture or pattern that appears on the screen when you do not use your computer for a period of time.

You can only use a screen saver if you are logged on to your computer as a regular user. If you are logged on as **root**, you cannot use a screen saver.

SET UP A SCREEN SAVER

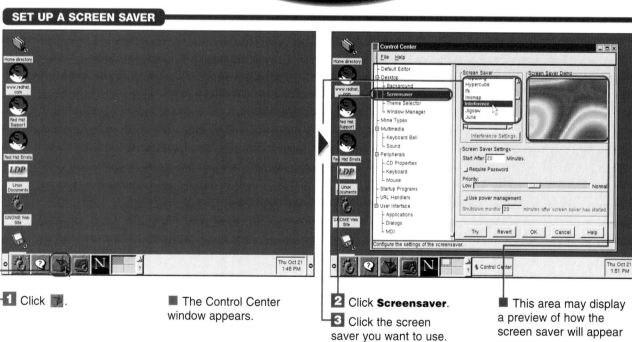

1 Click .

■ The Control Center window appears.

2 Click **Screensaver**.

3 Click the screen saver you want to use.

■ This area may display a preview of how the screen saver will appear on your screen.

How do I stop using a screen saver?

If you no longer want to use a screen saver, you can turn the screen saver off. Perform steps **1** to **3** below, selecting **No Screensaver** in step **3**. Then perform steps **6** and **7**.

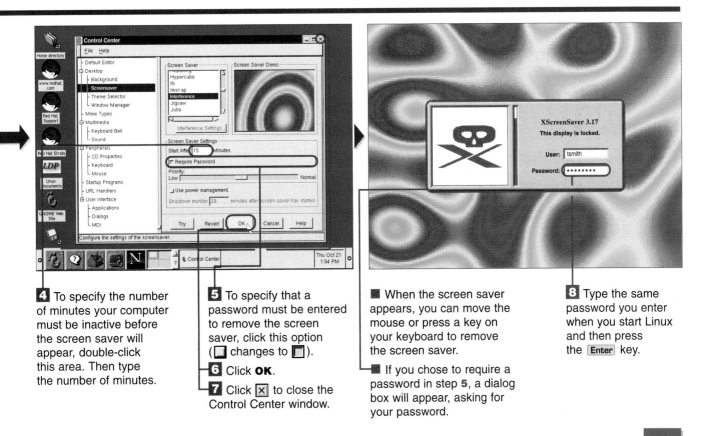

4 To specify the number of minutes your computer must be inactive before the screen saver will appear, double-click this area. Then type the number of minutes.

5 To specify that a password must be entered to remove the screen saver, click this option (☐ changes to ☐).

6 Click **OK**.

7 Click ☒ to close the Control Center window.

■ When the screen saver appears, you can move the mouse or press a key on your keyboard to remove the screen saver.

■ If you chose to require a password in step **5**, a dialog box will appear, asking for your password.

8 Type the same password you enter when you start Linux and then press the Enter key.

CHANGE THE MOUSE SETTINGS

You can change the way your mouse works to make the mouse easier to use.

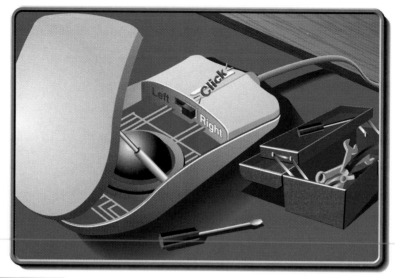

You can switch the functions of the left and right mouse buttons. You can also change how fast the mouse pointer moves on your screen.

CHANGE THE MOUSE SETTINGS

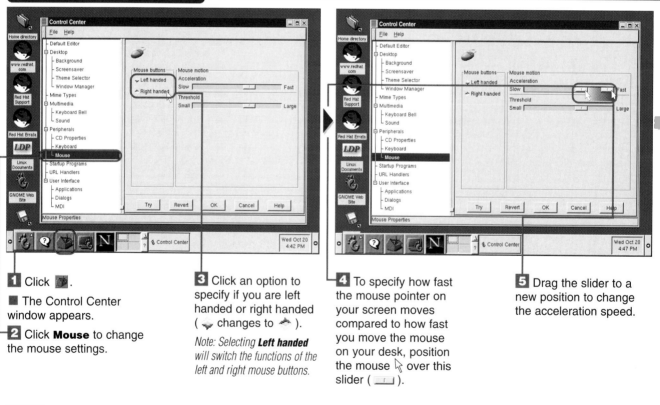

1 Click .

■ The Control Center window appears.

2 Click **Mouse** to change the mouse settings.

3 Click an option to specify if you are left handed or right handed (⌄ changes to ⌃).

*Note: Selecting **Left handed** will switch the functions of the left and right mouse buttons.*

4 To specify how fast the mouse pointer on your screen moves compared to how fast you move the mouse on your desk, position the mouse ⌖ over this slider (▭).

5 Drag the slider to a new position to change the acceleration speed.

**My mouse pointer does not move
smoothly on my screen. What can I do?**

You may need to clean your mouse.
Turn the mouse over and remove
and clean the roller ball. Then use
a cotton swab to remove the dirt
from the rollers inside the mouse.

You should use a mouse pad to
reduce the amount of dirt that enters
the mouse. Hard plastic mouse pads
attract less dirt and provide a smoother
surface than fabric mouse pads.

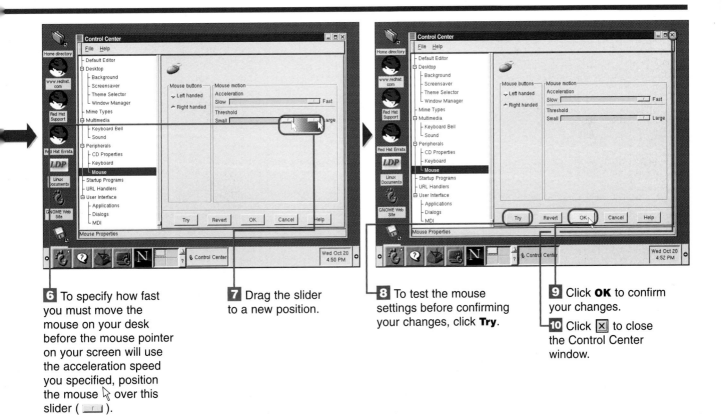

6 To specify how fast
you must move the
mouse on your desk
before the mouse pointer
on your screen will use
the acceleration speed
you specified, position
the mouse ⃕ over this
slider (▭).

7 Drag the slider
to a new position.

8 To test the mouse
settings before confirming
your changes, click **Try**.

9 Click **OK** to confirm
your changes.

10 Click ⊠ to close
the Control Center
window.

CHANGE THE DATE AND TIME

You can change the date and time displayed on your screen. Linux uses the date and time to determine when you create and update your files.

You can only change the date and time if you are logged on to your computer as **root**. If you are logged on as a regular user, you cannot change the date and time.

CHANGE THE DATE AND TIME

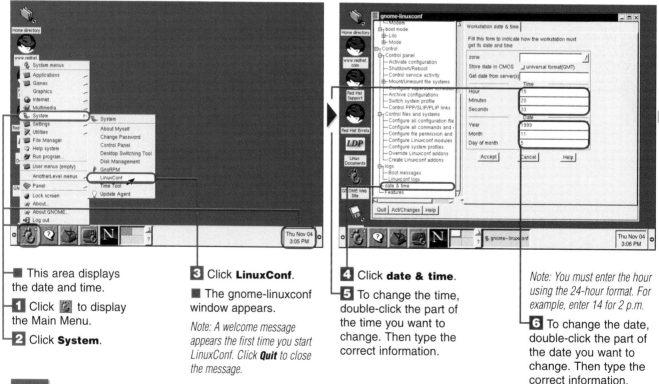

■ This area displays the date and time.

1 Click 🕐 to display the Main Menu.

2 Click **System**.

3 Click **LinuxConf**.

■ The gnome-linuxconf window appears.

Note: A welcome message appears the first time you start LinuxConf. Click Quit to close the message.

4 Click **date & time**.

5 To change the time, double-click the part of the time you want to change. Then type the correct information.

Note: You must enter the hour using the 24-hour format. For example, enter 14 for 2 p.m.

6 To change the date, double-click the part of the date you want to change. Then type the correct information.

Will Linux keep track of the date and time even when I turn off my computer?

Your computer has a built-in clock that keeps track of the date and time even when you turn off the computer.

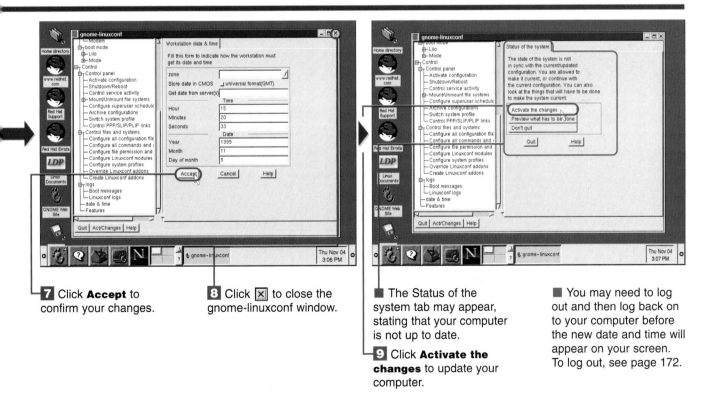

7 Click **Accept** to confirm your changes.

8 Click ✕ to close the gnome-linuxconf window.

■ The Status of the system tab may appear, stating that your computer is not up to date.

9 Click **Activate the changes** to update your computer.

■ You may need to log out and then log back on to your computer before the new date and time will appear on your screen. To log out, see page 172.

PLAY SOUNDS FOR EVENTS

You can have Linux play sounds for certain events on your computer. For example, you can hear glass break each time an error message appears.

You need a sound card and speakers to play sounds for events. You must set up your sound card as shown on page 204 before you can play sounds for events.

PLAY SOUNDS FOR EVENTS

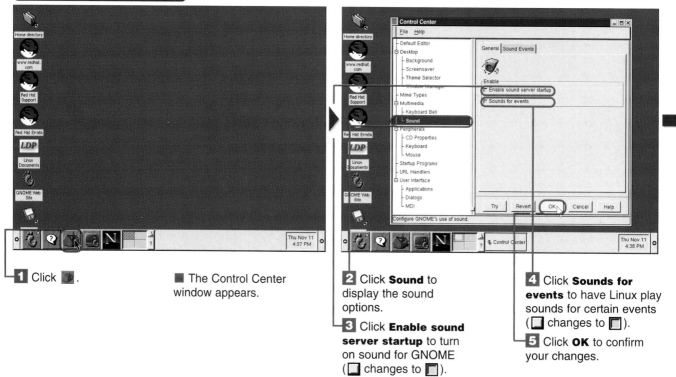

1 Click 🔧.

■ The Control Center window appears.

2 Click **Sound** to display the sound options.

3 Click **Enable sound server startup** to turn on sound for GNOME (☐ changes to ■).

4 Click **Sounds for events** to have Linux play sounds for certain events (☐ changes to ■).

5 Click **OK** to confirm your changes.

How do I stop Linux from playing sounds for events?

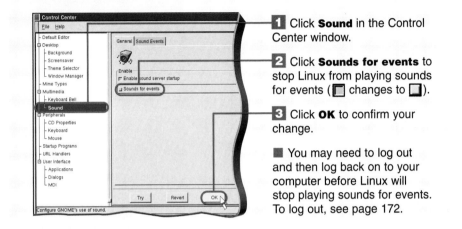

1 Click **Sound** in the Control Center window.

2 Click **Sounds for events** to stop Linux from playing sounds for events (☐ changes to ☐).

3 Click **OK** to confirm your change.

■ You may need to log out and then log back on to your computer before Linux will stop playing sounds for events. To log out, see page 172.

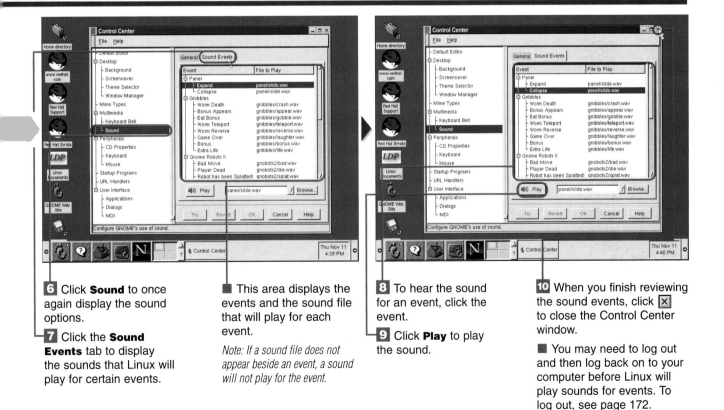

6 Click **Sound** to once again display the sound options.

7 Click the **Sound Events** tab to display the sounds that Linux will play for certain events.

■ This area displays the events and the sound file that will play for each event.

Note: If a sound file does not appear beside an event, a sound will not play for the event.

8 To hear the sound for an event, click the event.

9 Click **Play** to play the sound.

10 When you finish reviewing the sound events, click ☒ to close the Control Center window.

■ You may need to log out and then log back on to your computer before Linux will play sounds for events. To log out, see page 172.

ADJUST THE VOLUME

You can adjust the
volume of sound
for your computer.

Your computer must
be able to play sound
before you can adjust
the volume. To set up
a sound card so your
computer can play
sound, see page 204.

ADJUST THE VOLUME

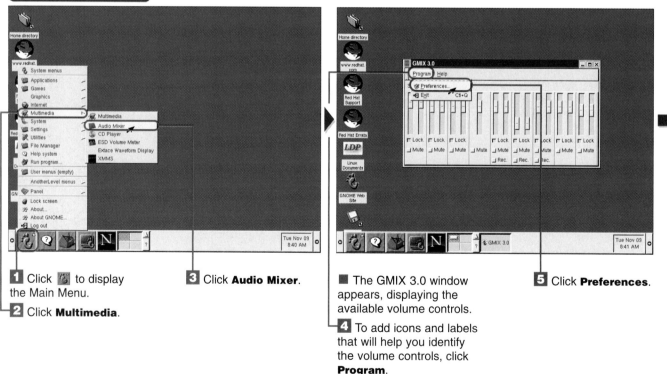

1 Click to display
the Main Menu.

2 Click **Multimedia**.

3 Click **Audio Mixer**.

■ The GMIX 3.0 window
appears, displaying the
available volume controls.

4 To add icons and labels
that will help you identify
the volume controls, click
Program.

5 Click **Preferences**.

What volume controls can I change?

Here are some volume controls that you may want to adjust. The available volume controls depend on your sound card.

CD
Volume for music CDs.

Line
Volume for a device connected to the computer, such as a cassette player or VCR.

Mic
Volume for a microphone.

Pcm
Volume for WAV files.

Spkr
Volume for speakers.

Synth
Volume for MIDI files.

Vol
Main volume control.

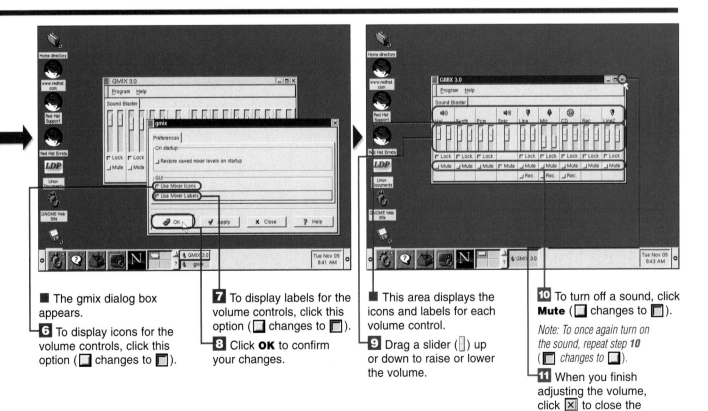

■ The gmix dialog box appears.

6 To display icons for the volume controls, click this option (☐ changes to ☑).

7 To display labels for the volume controls, click this option (☐ changes to ☑).

8 Click **OK** to confirm your changes.

■ This area displays the icons and labels for each volume control.

9 Drag a slider (⬛) up or down to raise or lower the volume.

10 To turn off a sound, click **Mute** (☐ changes to ☑).

Note: To once again turn on the sound, repeat step **10** (☑ changes to ☐).

11 When you finish adjusting the volume, click ☒ to close the window.

GIVE NEW WINDOWS THE KEYBOARD FOCUS

You can have Linux give each new window that appears on your screen the keyboard focus. Each time a new window appears, the window will become the active window.

Giving new windows the keyboard focus allows you to work in a new window without having to first click in the window.

GIVE NEW WINDOWS THE KEYBOARD FOCUS

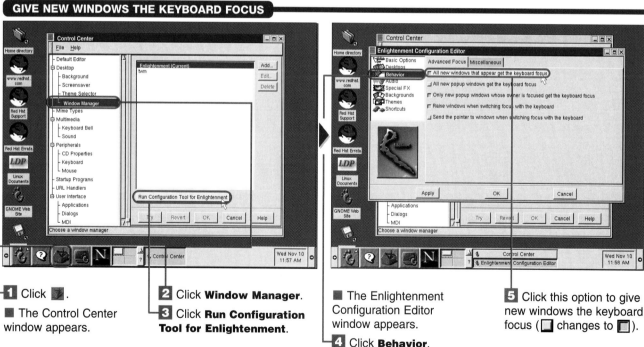

1 Click ▓.

■ The Control Center window appears.

2 Click **Window Manager**.

3 Click **Run Configuration Tool for Enlightenment**.

■ The Enlightenment Configuration Editor window appears.

4 Click **Behavior**.

5 Click this option to give new windows the keyboard focus (☐ changes to ▓).

Is there a faster way to display the Enlightenment Configuration Editor window?

You can perform the following steps to quickly display the Enlightenment Configuration Editor window.

1 Position the mouse ⌖ over a blank area on your desktop.

2 Click the left and right mouse buttons at the same time.

Note: If your mouse has a middle mouse button, click the middle mouse button.

■ A menu appears.

3 Click **Enlightenment Configuration**.

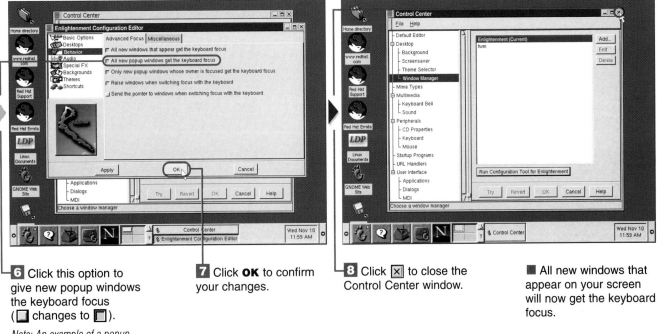

6 Click this option to give new popup windows the keyboard focus (☐ changes to ☑).

Note: An example of a popup window is an error message.

7 Click **OK** to confirm your changes.

8 Click ☒ to close the Control Center window.

■ All new windows that appear on your screen will now get the keyboard focus.

START A PROGRAM AUTOMATICALLY

If you use the same program every day, you can have the program start automatically each time you log on to your computer.

≫ Click

START A PROGRAM AUTOMATICALLY

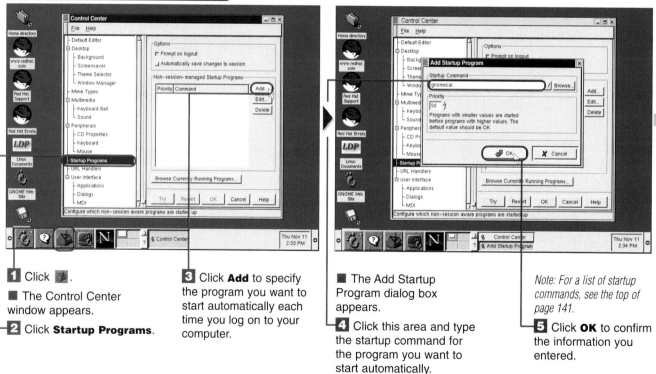

1 Click 🖳.

■ The Control Center window appears.

2 Click **Startup Programs**.

3 Click **Add** to specify the program you want to start automatically each time you log on to your computer.

■ The Add Startup Program dialog box appears.

4 Click this area and type the startup command for the program you want to start automatically.

Note: For a list of startup commands, see the top of page 141.

5 Click **OK** to confirm the information you entered.

What startup command do I type for the program I want to start automatically?

Here are some startup commands for commonly used programs.

Program	Startup Command
Calendar	gnomecal
Control Center	gnomecc
Control Panel	control-panel
Gnome Calculator	gcalc
GnomeCard	gnomecard
gnotepad+	gnp
Gnumeric	gnumeric
Netscape Communicator	/usr/bin/netscape-communicator
RH PPP Dialer	rp3
System Information	guname
Terminal window	gnome-terminal
User Mount Tool	usermount

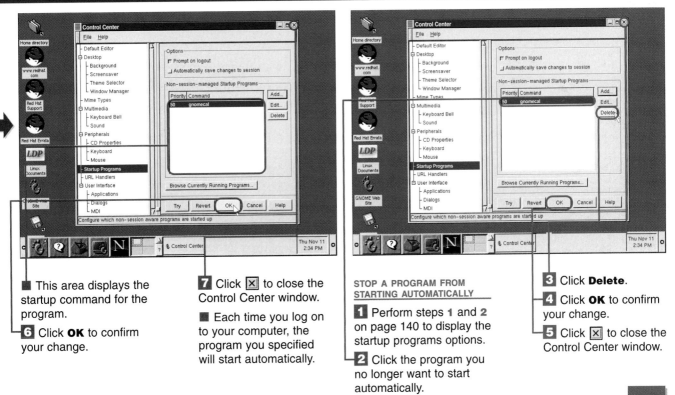

■ This area displays the startup command for the program.

6 Click **OK** to confirm your change.

7 Click ⊠ to close the Control Center window.

■ Each time you log on to your computer, the program you specified will start automatically.

STOP A PROGRAM FROM STARTING AUTOMATICALLY

1 Perform steps **1** and **2** on page 140 to display the startup programs options.

2 Click the program you no longer want to start automatically.

3 Click **Delete**.

4 Click **OK** to confirm your change.

5 Click ⊠ to close the Control Center window.

CHANGE DISPLAY SETTINGS USING XCONFIGURATOR

You can change
the settings for
your monitor and
video card by using
Xconfigurator. This
can improve the
way information
appears on your
screen.

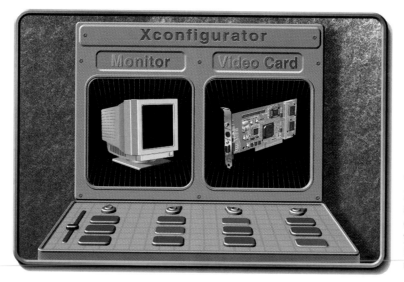

You can only use
Xconfigurator if you
are logged on to your
computer as **root**. If
you are logged on as a
regular user, you cannot
use Xconfigurator.

CHANGE DISPLAY SETTINGS USING XCONFIGURATOR

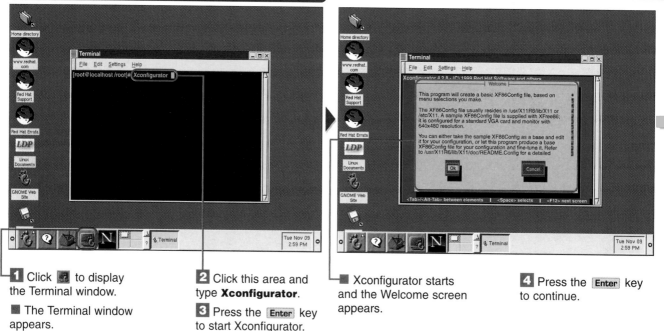

1 Click 🖳 to display
the Terminal window.

■ The Terminal window
appears.

2 Click this area and
type **Xconfigurator**.

3 Press the Enter key
to start Xconfigurator.

■ Xconfigurator starts
and the Welcome screen
appears.

4 Press the Enter key
to continue.

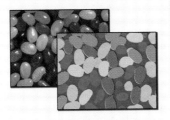 

What display settings can I change using Xconfigurator?

You can specify a new color depth to change the number of colors your screen can display.

You can specify a new resolution to change the amount of information that can fit on your screen.

You can choose to display a graphical login screen each time you log on to your computer.

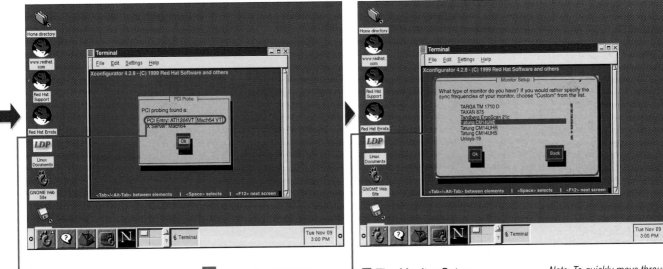

■ The Probe screen appears.

■ This area displays information about your video card.

5 Press the Enter key to continue.

■ The Monitor Setup screen appears.

6 Press the ↓ or ↑ key until you highlight the type of monitor you use. If your monitor does not appear in the list, select the **Generic** monitor option that best matches your monitor.

Note: To quickly move through the list, press the key for the first letter of your monitor type.

7 Press the Enter key to continue.

CHANGE DISPLAY SETTINGS USING XCONFIGURATOR

You can select
a color depth to
specify the number
of colors your
screen can display.
Higher color depths
result in higher
quality images.

Your video card
determines the maximum
number of colors your
screen can display.

8 bit (256 colors)

16 bit (65,536 colors)

24 bit (16.7 million colors)

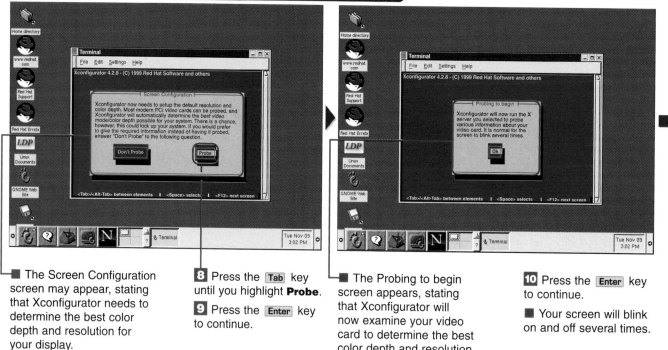

■ The Screen Configuration
screen may appear, stating
that Xconfigurator needs to
determine the best color
depth and resolution for
your display.

*Note: If this screen does not appear,
skip to step 10.*

8 Press the `Tab` key
until you highlight **Probe**.

9 Press the `Enter` key
to continue.

■ The Probing to begin
screen appears, stating
that Xconfigurator will
now examine your video
card to determine the best
color depth and resolution
for your display.

10 Press the `Enter` key
to continue.

■ Your screen will blink
on and off several times.

How will changing the resolution affect the appearance of my screen?

The resolution you select will determine the amount of information that can fit on your screen. Lower resolutions display larger images so you can see the information on your screen more clearly. Higher resolutions display smaller images so you can display more information on your screen at once.

Here are the most commonly used resolutions.

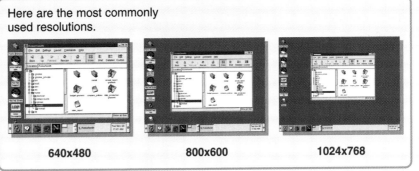

640x480 **800x600** **1024x768**

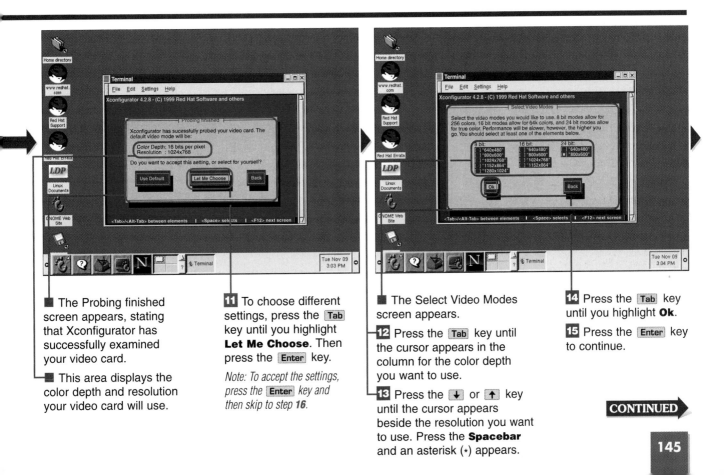

■ The Probing finished screen appears, stating that Xconfigurator has successfully examined your video card.

■ This area displays the color depth and resolution your video card will use.

11 To choose different settings, press the `Tab` key until you highlight **Let Me Choose**. Then press the `Enter` key.

Note: To accept the settings, press the `Enter` key and then skip to step 16.

■ The Select Video Modes screen appears.

12 Press the `Tab` key until the cursor appears in the column for the color depth you want to use.

13 Press the `↓` or `↑` key until the cursor appears beside the resolution you want to use. Press the **Spacebar** and an asterisk (*) appears.

14 Press the `Tab` key until you highlight **Ok**.

15 Press the `Enter` key to continue.

CONTINUED ▶

CHANGE DISPLAY SETTINGS USING XCONFIGURATOR

Xconfigurator will test the color depth and resolution you specified to make sure your video card and monitor can work with the settings.

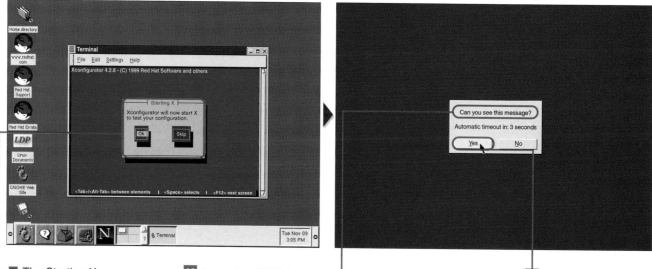

■ The Starting X screen appears, stating that Xconfigurator will now test the color depth and resolution you specified.

16 Press the Enter key to test the settings.

■ A message appears to verify that your video card and monitor can work with the settings you specified.

17 Click **Yes** if you can see the message.

Will using a graphical login screen make Linux easier to use?

Yes. When you use a graphical login screen, Linux will automatically start the GNOME desktop environment for you. If you do not use a graphical login screen, a text-based login screen will appear and you will have to manually start GNOME as shown at the top of page 29.

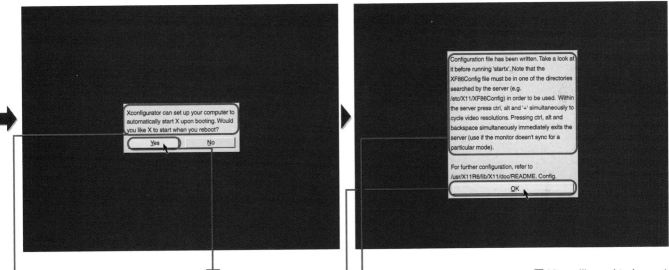

Xconfigurator can set up your computer to automatically start X upon booting. Would you like X to start when you reboot?

Yes   No

Configuration file has been written. Take a look at it before running 'startx'. Note that the XF86Config file must be in one of the directories searched by the server (e.g. /etc/X11/XF86Config) in order to be used. Within the server press ctrl, alt and '+' simultaneously to cycle video resolutions. Pressing ctrl, alt and backspace simultaneously immediately exits the server (use if the monitor doesn't sync for a particular mode).

For further configuration, refer to /usr/X11R6/lib/X11/doc/README. Config.

OK

■ A message appears, stating that Xconfigurator can set up your computer to automatically display a graphical login screen each time you log on to your computer.

18 Click **Yes** to have Linux display a graphical login screen.

■ A message appears, stating that Xconfigurator created a file to store the display settings you specified.

19 Click **OK** to close the message and exit Xconfigurator.

■ You will need to log out before the new display settings will take effect. To log out, see page 172.

147

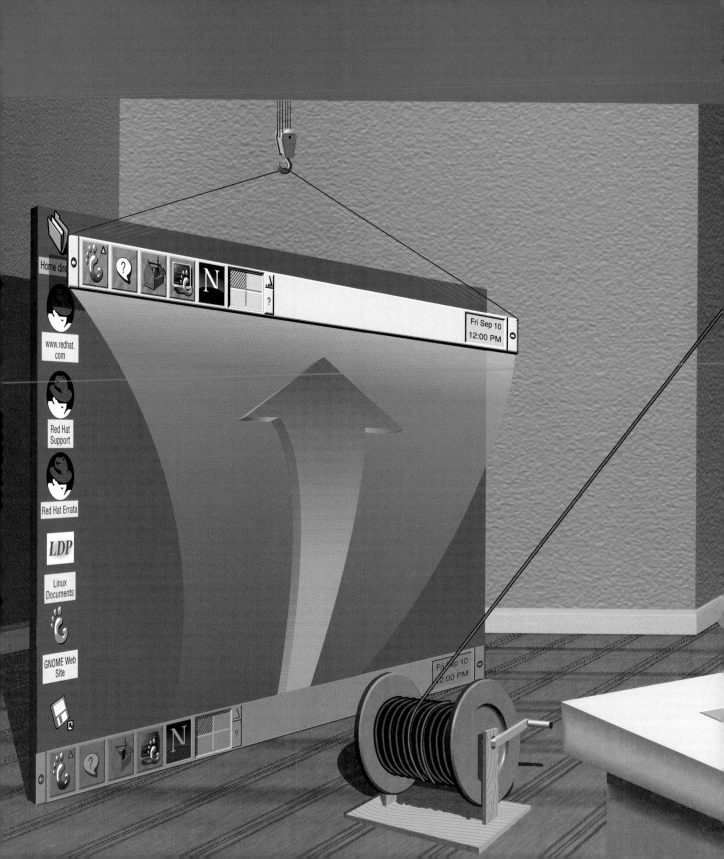

CHAPTER 6

Customize the GNOME Panel

In this chapter you will learn how to personalize the GNOME Panel to make working with your favorite programs easier.

ADD AN APPLICATION LAUNCHER

You can add an application
launcher to the GNOME Panel.
An application launcher lets
you quickly start a program
you frequently use.

ADD AN APPLICATION LAUNCHER

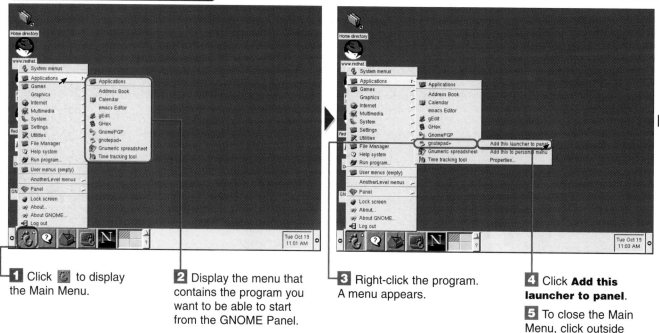

1 Click to display
the Main Menu.

2 Display the menu that
contains the program you
want to be able to start
from the GNOME Panel.

3 Right-click the program.
A menu appears.

4 Click **Add this
launcher to panel**.

5 To close the Main
Menu, click outside
the menu area.

What application launchers automatically appear on the GNOME Panel?

Starts the **GNOME Help Browser** so you can find help information about Linux.

Opens the Control Center window so you can view and change settings such as the color of the desktop.

Opens the Terminal window, where you can type Linux commands.

Starts **Netscape Communicator**, which allows you to browse the Web, exchange e-mail messages and join newsgroups.

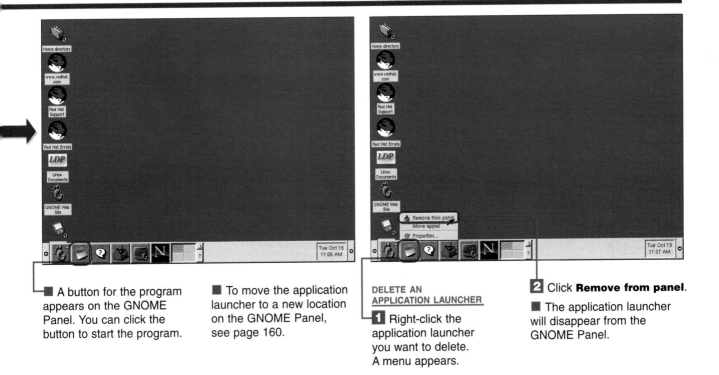

■ A button for the program appears on the GNOME Panel. You can click the button to start the program.

■ To move the application launcher to a new location on the GNOME Panel, see page 160.

DELETE AN APPLICATION LAUNCHER

1 Right-click the application launcher you want to delete. A menu appears.

2 Click **Remove from panel**.

■ The application launcher will disappear from the GNOME Panel.

CREATE A DRAWER FROM THE MAIN MENU

You can create a drawer on the GNOME Panel that contains programs from the Main Menu. This will give you quick access to programs you often use.

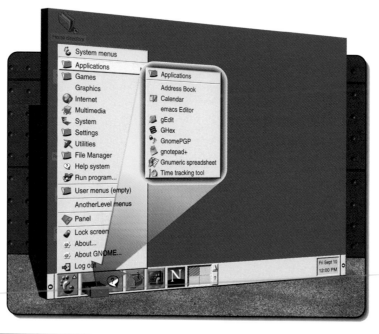

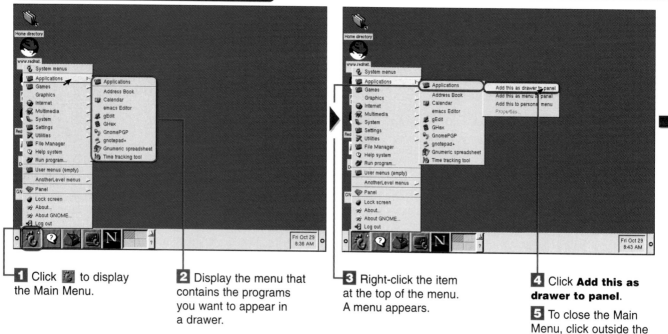

1 Click to display the Main Menu.

2 Display the menu that contains the programs you want to appear in a drawer.

3 Right-click the item at the top of the menu. A menu appears.

4 Click **Add this as drawer to panel**.

5 To close the Main Menu, click outside the menu area.

I find it difficult to remember which icon will start the program I want. What can I do?

If you find it difficult to remember which programs the icons in a drawer start, you can create a menu on the GNOME Panel instead of a drawer. A menu is similar to a drawer, but lists programs by name instead of by icon. To create a menu on the GNOME Panel, perform steps **1** to **4** on page 152, except select **Add this as menu to panel** in step **4**.

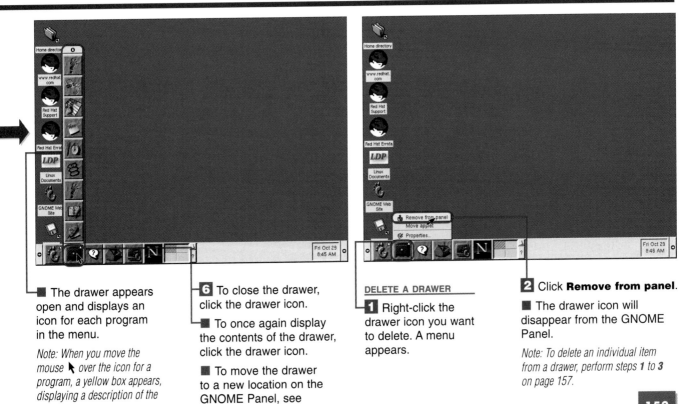

■ The drawer appears open and displays an icon for each program in the menu.

Note: When you move the mouse ▶ over the icon for a program, a yellow box appears, displaying a description of the program.

6 To close the drawer, click the drawer icon.

■ To once again display the contents of the drawer, click the drawer icon.

■ To move the drawer to a new location on the GNOME Panel, see page 160.

DELETE A DRAWER

1 Right-click the drawer icon you want to delete. A menu appears.

2 Click **Remove from panel**.

■ The drawer icon will disappear from the GNOME Panel.

Note: To delete an individual item from a drawer, perform steps 1 to 3 on page 157.

CREATE AN EMPTY DRAWER

You can create an empty drawer on the GNOME Panel that will give you quick access to programs you often use.

CREATE AN EMPTY DRAWER

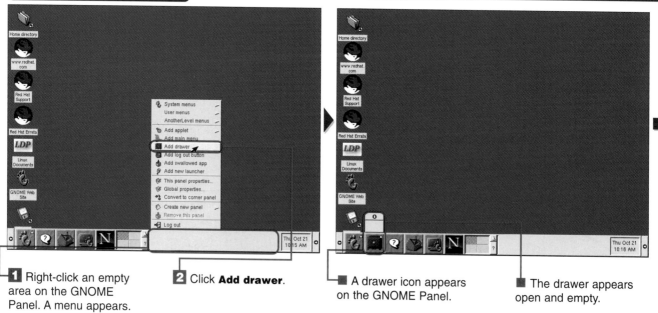

1 Right-click an empty area on the GNOME Panel. A menu appears.

2 Click **Add drawer**.

■ A drawer icon appears on the GNOME Panel.

■ The drawer appears open and empty.

When would I create an empty drawer?

Creating an empty drawer is useful when you want to keep together all the programs you need to perform a task. For example, you can create a drawer for programs you use to write letters or work with images.

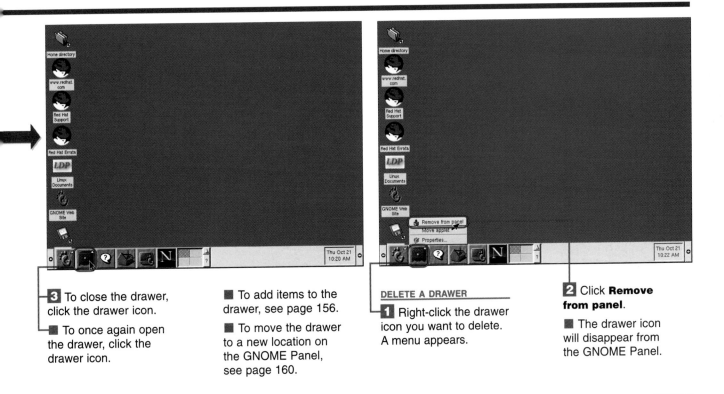

3 To close the drawer, click the drawer icon.

■ To once again open the drawer, click the drawer icon.

■ To add items to the drawer, see page 156.

■ To move the drawer to a new location on the GNOME Panel, see page 160.

DELETE A DRAWER

1 Right-click the drawer icon you want to delete. A menu appears.

2 Click **Remove from panel**.

■ The drawer icon will disappear from the GNOME Panel.

ADD ITEMS TO A DRAWER

After creating a drawer, you can add programs you want to quickly access to the drawer.

To create a drawer, see page 152 or 154.

ADD ITEMS TO A DRAWER

1 Click the icon for the drawer you want to add items to.

■ The contents of the drawer appear.

2 Click 🐾 to display the Main Menu.

3 Display the menu that contains a program you want to add to the drawer.

4 Position the mouse ➤ over the program.

Note: If the Main Menu covers the open drawer, you must move the drawer before you can add the program. To move a drawer, see page 160.

5 Drag the program to the right of the menu and then to the open drawer.

Does deleting a program from a drawer permanently delete the program?

When you delete a program from a drawer, you do not permanently delete the program from your computer. You can still access the program using the Main Menu.

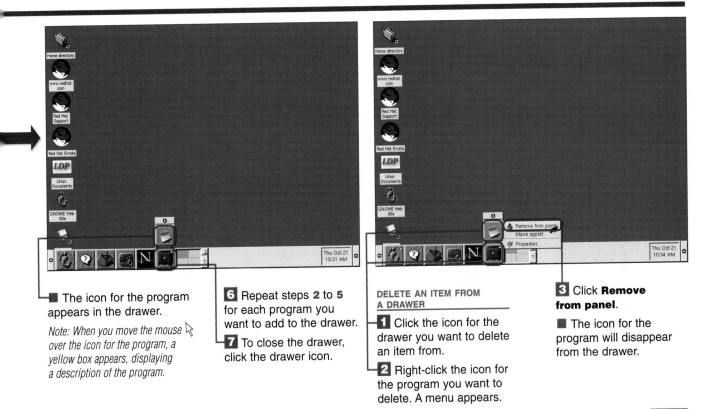

■ The icon for the program appears in the drawer.

Note: When you move the mouse over the icon for the program, a yellow box appears, displaying a description of the program.

6 Repeat steps **2** to **5** for each program you want to add to the drawer.

7 To close the drawer, click the drawer icon.

DELETE AN ITEM FROM A DRAWER

1 Click the icon for the drawer you want to delete an item from.

2 Right-click the icon for the program you want to delete. A menu appears.

3 Click **Remove from panel**.

■ The icon for the program will disappear from the drawer.

CHANGE DRAWER ICON

You can change the icon
for a drawer you added
to the GNOME Panel.

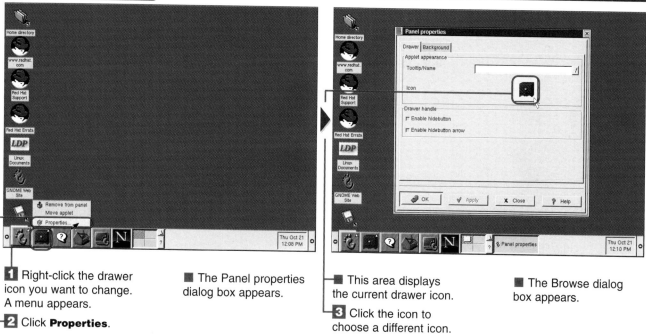

CHANGE DRAWER ICON

■ **1** Right-click the drawer
icon you want to change.
A menu appears.

■ **2** Click **Properties**.

■ The Panel properties
dialog box appears.

■ This area displays
the current drawer icon.

■ **3** Click the icon to
choose a different icon.

■ The Browse dialog
box appears.

Can I change the icon for other items on the GNOME Panel?

You can use the method shown below to change the icon for items such as the Help feature (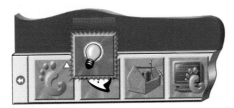) and Control Center ( ). You can also use the method shown below to change the icon for items in a drawer.

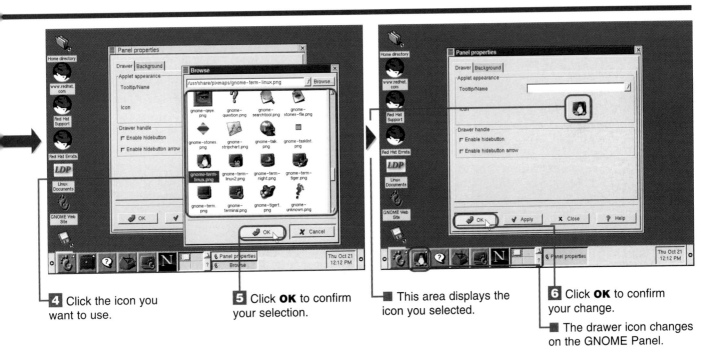

■4 Click the icon you want to use.

■5 Click **OK** to confirm your selection.

■ This area displays the icon you selected.

■6 Click **OK** to confirm your change.

■ The drawer icon changes on the GNOME Panel.

MOVE AN APPLET

You can move an applet to a new location on the GNOME Panel.

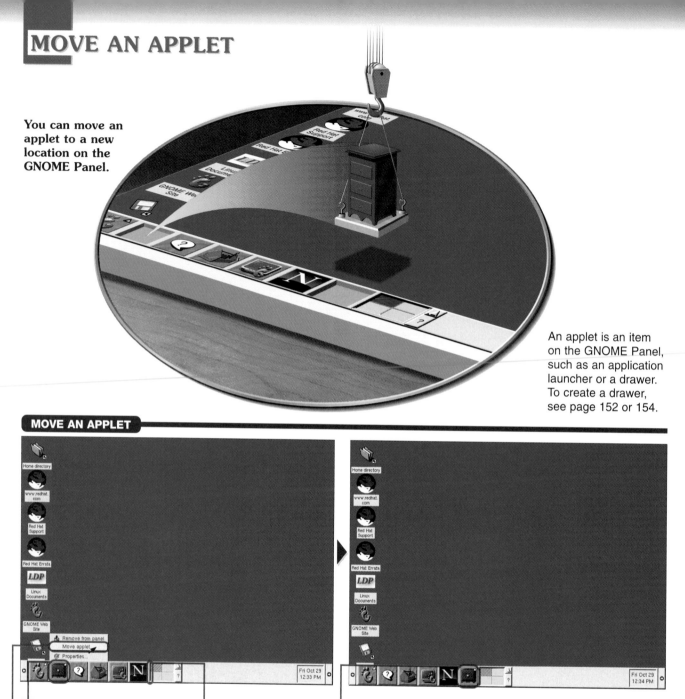

An applet is an item on the GNOME Panel, such as an application launcher or a drawer. To create a drawer, see page 152 or 154.

1 Right-click the applet you want to move. A menu appears.

2 Click **Move applet**.

3 Click the location on the GNOME Panel where you want to place the applet.

■ The applet appears in the new location.

You can move the
**GNOME Panel to a
more convenient
location on your
screen.**

You can move the
GNOME Panel to
the top, bottom,
left or right edge
of your screen.

MOVE THE GNOME PANEL

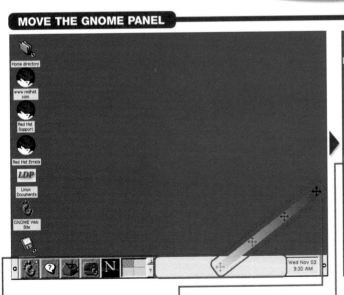

1 Position the mouse ▸
over a blank area on the
GNOME Panel.

2 Press and hold down the
left and right mouse buttons
at the same time as you drag
the GNOME Panel to a new
location on your screen.

*Note: If your mouse has a middle
mouse button, press and hold
down the middle mouse button
as you drag the GNOME Panel.*

■ The GNOME Panel
moves to the new location.

CHAPTER 7

Work With Accounts

In this chapter you will learn how to create accounts for people who use your computer, change your password and more.

CREATE A NEW USER ACCOUNT

If you share your computer with family members or colleagues, you can create a user account for each person so they can have their own personalized settings.

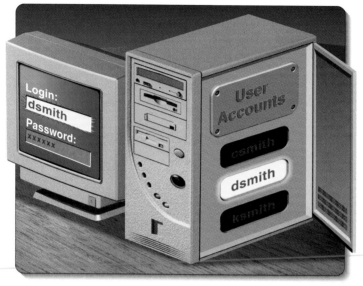

You may have created user accounts when you installed Linux.

You can only create a new user account if you are logged on to your computer as **root**. If you are logged on as a regular user, you cannot create a new user account.

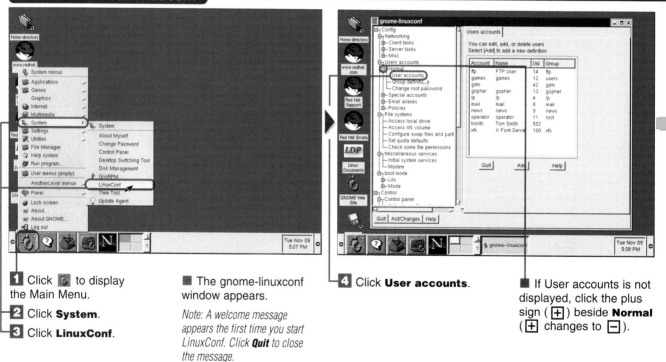

1 Click ![icon] to display the Main Menu.

2 Click **System**.

3 Click **LinuxConf**.

■ The gnome-linuxconf window appears.

*Note: A welcome message appears the first time you start LinuxConf. Click **Quit** to close the message.*

4 Click **User accounts**.

■ If User accounts is not displayed, click the plus sign (⊞) beside **Normal** (⊞ changes to ⊟).

Do I need to create a user account if I am the only person using my computer?

If you did not create a user account for yourself when you installed Linux, you should create a user account for performing daily tasks. The root account should only be used to perform administrative and maintenance tasks, since you can damage the computer when using the root account. The root account was automatically created when you installed Linux.

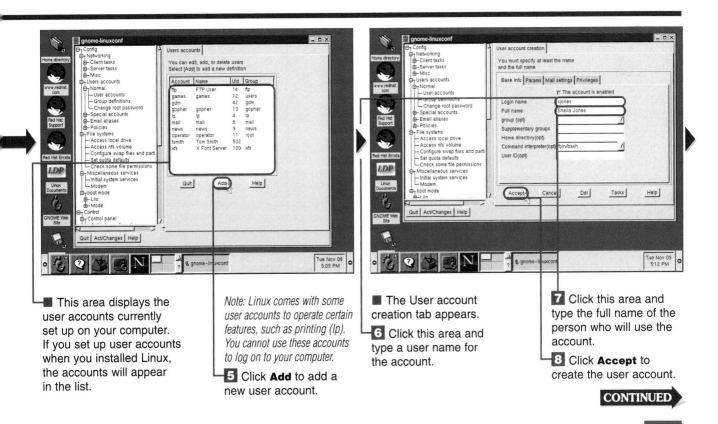

■ This area displays the user accounts currently set up on your computer. If you set up user accounts when you installed Linux, the accounts will appear in the list.

Note: Linux comes with some user accounts to operate certain features, such as printing (lp). You cannot use these accounts to log on to your computer.

5 Click **Add** to add a new user account.

■ The User account creation tab appears.

6 Click this area and type a user name for the account.

7 Click this area and type the full name of the person who will use the account.

8 Click **Accept** to create the user account.

CONTINUED

CREATE A NEW USER ACCOUNT

When you create a
new user account,
you will need to
enter a password
for the account.

CREATE A NEW USER ACCOUNT (CONTINUED)

■ The Changing
password tab appears.

9 Type a password for
the new user account.
A symbol (ˣ) appears for
each character you type
to prevent others from
seeing the password.

*Note: For information on
choosing a password,
see the top of page 167.*

10 Click **Accept**.

11 Retype the password
to confirm the password.

12 Click **Accept**.

What password should I use?

You should follow these guidelines when choosing a password.

A password should contain between 6 and 8 characters.

A password should contain a mixture of letters and numbers.

A password should not be a word in the dictionary.

A password should not contain repeated characters, such as aaabbb.

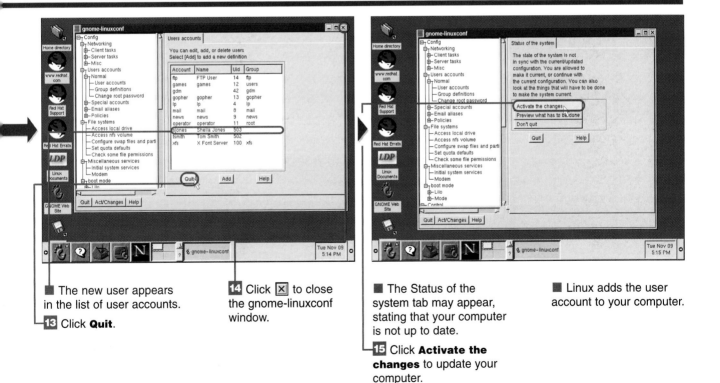

■ The new user appears in the list of user accounts.

13 Click **Quit**.

14 Click ⊠ to close the gnome-linuxconf window.

■ The Status of the system tab may appear, stating that your computer is not up to date.

15 Click **Activate the changes** to update your computer.

■ Linux adds the user account to your computer.

DELETE A USER ACCOUNT

You can delete the user account for a family member or colleague who will no longer be using your computer.

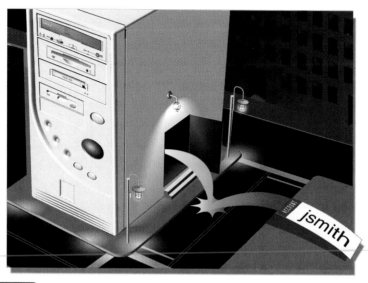

You can only delete a user account if you are logged on to your computer as **root**. If you are logged on as a regular user, you cannot delete a user account.

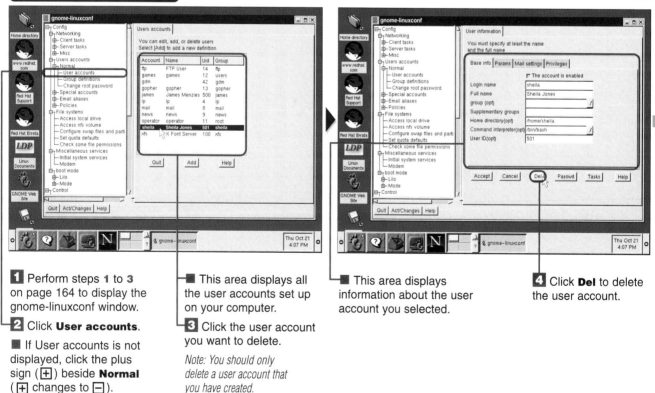

1 Perform steps **1** to **3** on page 164 to display the gnome-linuxconf window.

2 Click **User accounts**.

■ If User accounts is not displayed, click the plus sign (⊞) beside **Normal** (⊞ changes to ⊟).

■ This area displays all the user accounts set up on your computer.

3 Click the user account you want to delete.

Note: You should only delete a user account that you have created.

■ This area displays information about the user account you selected.

4 Click **Del** to delete the user account.

When I delete a user account, what can I do with the account's data?

Archive the account's data

Compresses the data for the account into a single file that Linux stores in a directory named oldaccounts within the home directory.

Delete the account's data

Removes the data for the account.

Leave the account's data in place

Leaves the data for the account in a directory with the user's name within the home directory.

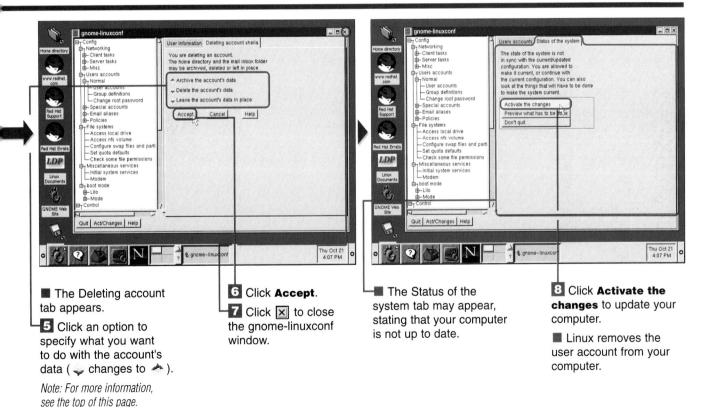

■ The Deleting account tab appears.

5 Click an option to specify what you want to do with the account's data (changes to).

Note: For more information, see the top of this page.

6 Click **Accept**.

7 Click ⊠ to close the gnome-linuxconf window.

■ The Status of the system tab may appear, stating that your computer is not up to date.

8 Click **Activate the changes** to update your computer.

■ Linux removes the user account from your computer.

CHANGE YOUR PASSWORD

You should regularly change your password to prevent others from accessing your information.

CHANGE YOUR PASSWORD

1 Click ▓ to display the Main Menu.

2 Click **System**.

3 Click **Change Password**.

■ The Input window appears, asking you to enter your password.

Note: If you are changing the password for the root account, skip to step 6.

4 Click this area and type your current password.

Note: A symbol (x) appears for each character you type to prevent others from seeing the password.

5 Click **OK** to continue.

How can I protect my password?

▶ Change your password once a month.

▶ Change your password immediately if you suspect someone knows your password.

▶ Never write down your password.

▶ Never share your password with other people.

▶ Use a different password for each account set up on your computer.

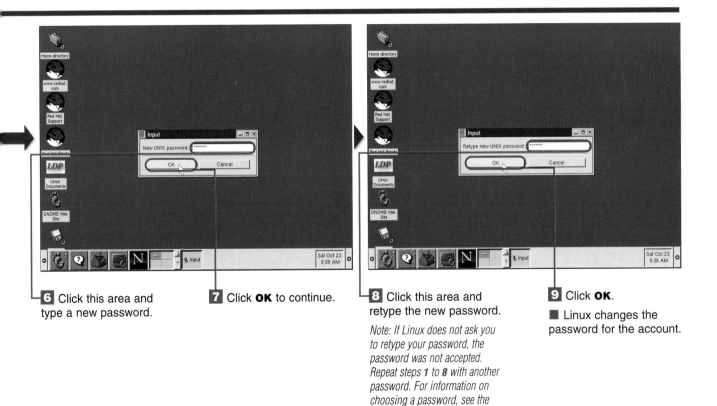

6 Click this area and type a new password.

7 Click **OK** to continue.

8 Click this area and retype the new password.

Note: If Linux does not ask you to retype your password, the password was not accepted. Repeat steps 1 to 8 with another password. For information on choosing a password, see the top of page 167.

9 Click **OK**.

■ Linux changes the password for the account.

LOG ON AS ANOTHER USER

If you share your computer with others, you can log out so another person can log on and use the computer.

When you installed Linux, you created one or more user accounts. To create a user account after you install Linux, see page 164.

LOG ON AS ANOTHER USER

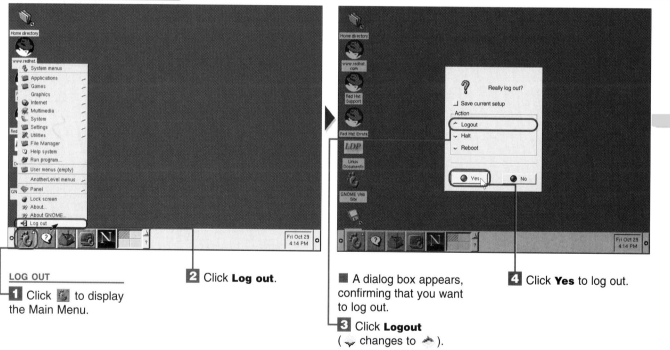

LOG OUT

1 Click ![icon] to display the Main Menu.

2 Click **Log out**.

■ A dialog box appears, confirming that you want to log out.

3 Click **Logout** (⇥ changes to ⇤).

4 Click **Yes** to log out.

Will I ever need to log on as another user if I am the only person using my computer?

If you are the only person using your computer, you can log on as another user to switch between the root account and your user account. When performing daily tasks, you should work in a user account. You should only use the root account when performing administrative tasks, such as setting up hardware.

LOG ON

■ A dialog box appears, asking for the user name of the person who wants to log on to the computer.

5 Type the user name and then press the `Enter` key.

6 Type the password and then press the `Enter` key.

Note: A symbol (ˣ) appears for each character you type to prevent others from seeing the password.

■ The person is logged on to the computer and can begin using Linux.

Note: For information on the windows that appear when Linux starts, see page 29.

CHAPTER 8

Work With Floppy and CD-ROM Drives

This chapter will teach you how to use Linux to work with information stored on floppy disks and CD-ROM discs.

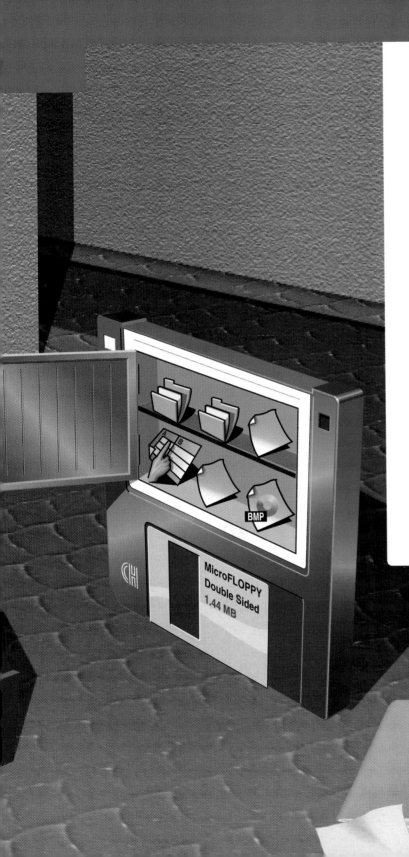

DISPLAY CONTENTS OF A LINUX FLOPPY DISK

You can display the contents of a Linux floppy disk. This lets you review and make changes to the files stored on the disk.

MicroFLOPPY
Double Sided
1.44 MB

To display the contents of an MS-DOS floppy disk, see pages 182 to 185.

DISPLAY CONTENTS OF A LINUX FLOPPY DISK

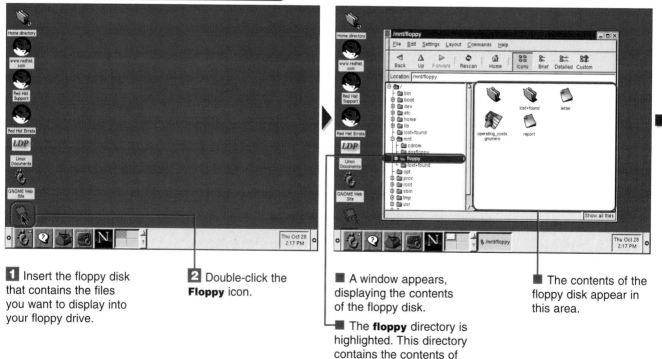

1 Insert the floppy disk that contains the files you want to display into your floppy drive.

2 Double-click the **Floppy** icon.

■ A window appears, displaying the contents of the floppy disk.

■ The **floppy** directory is highlighted. This directory contains the contents of the floppy disk.

■ The contents of the floppy disk appear in this area.

Why can't I save the changes I made to a file on a floppy disk?

You may not have permission to make changes to the file. To change the file, perform one of the following tasks.

▶ Log on to your computer using the root account as shown on page 172. The root account can always make changes to the files on a floppy disk.

▶ Change the permissions for the file as shown on page 74. You must be logged on to your computer using the root account to change the permissions for the file.

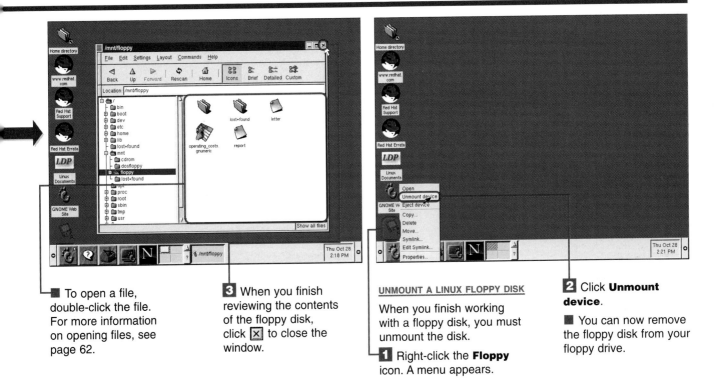

■ To open a file, double-click the file. For more information on opening files, see page 62.

3 When you finish reviewing the contents of the floppy disk, click ⊠ to close the window.

UNMOUNT A LINUX FLOPPY DISK

When you finish working with a floppy disk, you must unmount the disk.

1 Right-click the **Floppy** icon. A menu appears.

2 Click **Unmount device**.

■ You can now remove the floppy disk from your floppy drive.

SET UP LINUX TO USE MS-DOS FLOPPY DISKS

If you want to use floppy disks that contain files created in MS-DOS or Windows, you must set up Linux to use MS-DOS floppy disks.

You can only set up Linux to use MS-DOS floppy disks if you are logged on to your computer as **root**. If you are logged on as a regular user, you cannot set up Linux to use MS-DOS floppy disks.

SET UP LINUX TO USE MS-DOS FLOPPY DISKS

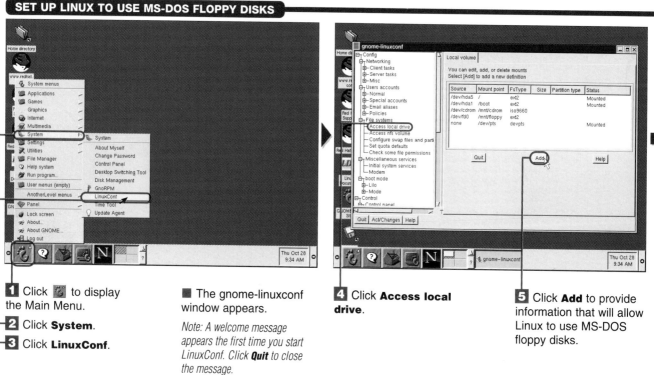

1 Click 🐾 to display the Main Menu.

2 Click **System**.

3 Click **LinuxConf**.

■ The gnome-linuxconf window appears.

*Note: A welcome message appears the first time you start LinuxConf. Click **Quit** to close the message.*

4 Click **Access local drive**.

5 Click **Add** to provide information that will allow Linux to use MS-DOS floppy disks.

178

Why would I want to use MS-DOS floppy disks?

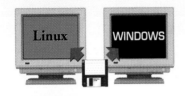

Share Information

Using MS-DOS floppy disks is useful if you want to exchange information with colleagues or family members who use MS-DOS or Windows.

Dual-Boot Setup

If you have set up your computer to run both Linux and Windows, known as a dual-boot setup, you can use MS-DOS floppy disks to exchange information between Linux and Windows.

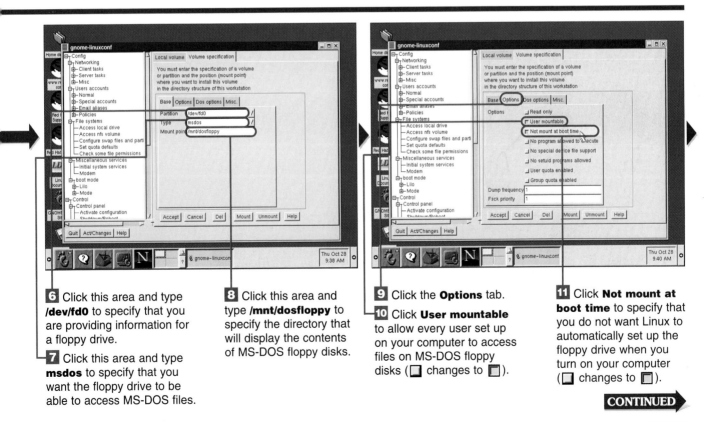

6 Click this area and type **/dev/fd0** to specify that you are providing information for a floppy drive.

7 Click this area and type **msdos** to specify that you want the floppy drive to be able to access MS-DOS files.

8 Click this area and type **/mnt/dosfloppy** to specify the directory that will display the contents of MS-DOS floppy disks.

9 Click the **Options** tab.

10 Click **User mountable** to allow every user set up on your computer to access files on MS-DOS floppy disks (☐ changes to ☑).

11 Click **Not mount at boot time** to specify that you do not want Linux to automatically set up the floppy drive when you turn on your computer (☐ changes to ☑).

CONTINUED

SET UP LINUX TO USE MS-DOS FLOPPY DISKS

When you set up Linux to use MS-DOS floppy disks, Linux creates a directory on your computer that will display the contents of the disks.

SET UP LINUX TO USE MS-DOS FLOPPY DISKS (CONTINUED)

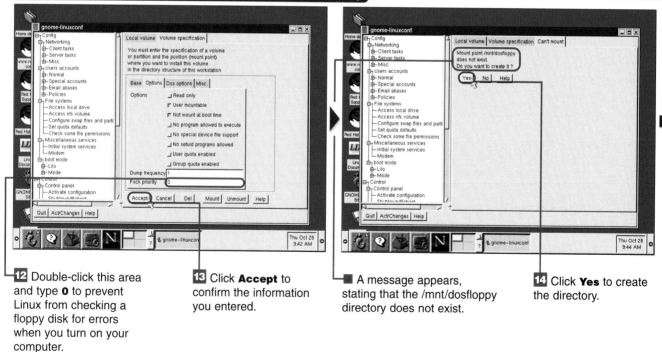

12 Double-click this area and type **0** to prevent Linux from checking a floppy disk for errors when you turn on your computer.

13 Click **Accept** to confirm the information you entered.

■ A message appears, stating that the /mnt/dosfloppy directory does not exist.

14 Click **Yes** to create the directory.

Where can I get MS-DOS floppy disks?

You can purchase floppy disks that are formatted as MS-DOS floppy disks at computer stores. You can also format floppy disks as MS-DOS floppy disks on your own computer. Any floppy disk can be formatted as an MS-DOS floppy disk. To format a floppy disk, see page 188.

■ This area displays the information for the MS-DOS floppy drive.

15 Click **Quit**.

16 Click ⊠ to close the gnome-linuxconf window.

■ The Status of the system tab may appear, stating that your computer is not up to date.

17 Click **Activate the changes** to update your computer.

■ You can now access information on MS-DOS floppy disks. For more information, see pages 182 to 185.

MOUNT AN MS-DOS FLOPPY DISK

You must mount an MS-DOS floppy disk before you can access the information on the disk.

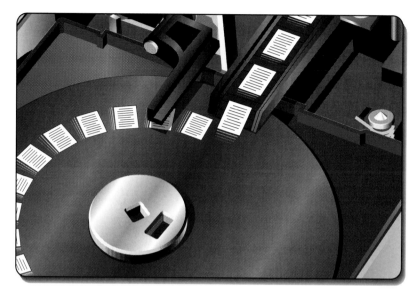

Before you can mount an MS-DOS floppy disk, you must set up Linux to use MS-DOS floppy disks as shown on page 178.

MOUNT AN MS-DOS FLOPPY DISK

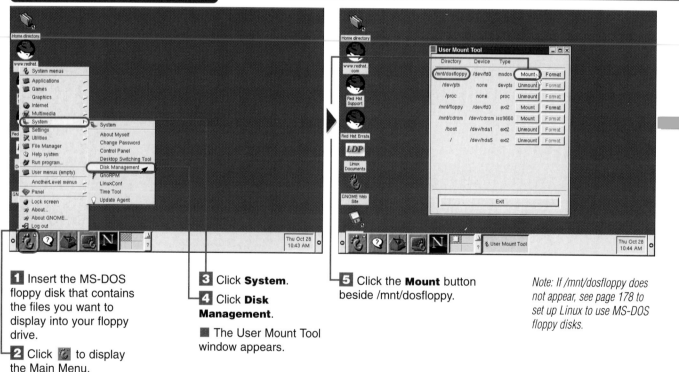

1 Insert the MS-DOS floppy disk that contains the files you want to display into your floppy drive.

2 Click to display the Main Menu.

3 Click **System**.

4 Click **Disk Management**.

■ The User Mount Tool window appears.

5 Click the **Mount** button beside /mnt/dosfloppy.

Note: If /mnt/dosfloppy does not appear, see page 178 to set up Linux to use MS-DOS floppy disks.

Do I need to mount an MS-DOS floppy disk every time I use the disk?

Each time you insert an MS-DOS floppy disk into your floppy drive, you must mount the disk. Mounting the disk allows you to access the information stored on the disk. Before you remove the disk from your floppy drive, you must unmount the disk to indicate that you no longer want to access the information on the disk.

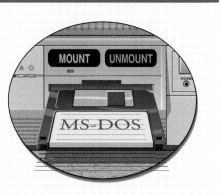

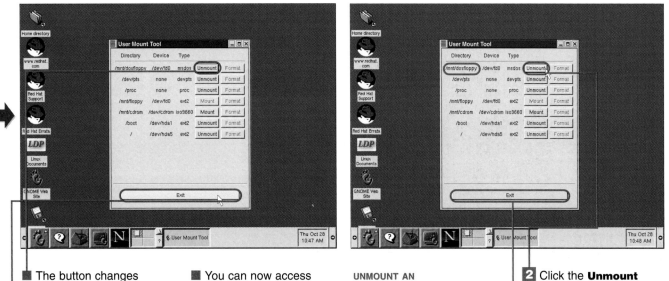

■ The button changes from Mount to Unmount.

6 Click **Exit** to close the window.

■ You can now access the information on the MS-DOS floppy disk. To display the contents of an MS-DOS floppy disk, see page 184.

**UNMOUNT AN
MS-DOS FLOPPY DISK**

When you finish working with an MS-DOS floppy disk, you must unmount the disk.

1 Perform steps **2** to **4** on page 182 to display the User Mount Tool window.

2 Click the **Unmount** button beside /mnt/dosfloppy.

Note: The button will change from Unmount to Mount.

3 Click **Exit** to close the window.

4 Remove the floppy disk from your floppy drive.

DISPLAY CONTENTS OF AN MS-DOS FLOPPY DISK

You can display the contents of an MS-DOS floppy disk to review and make changes to the files stored on the disk.

DISPLAY CONTENTS OF AN MS-DOS FLOPPY DISK

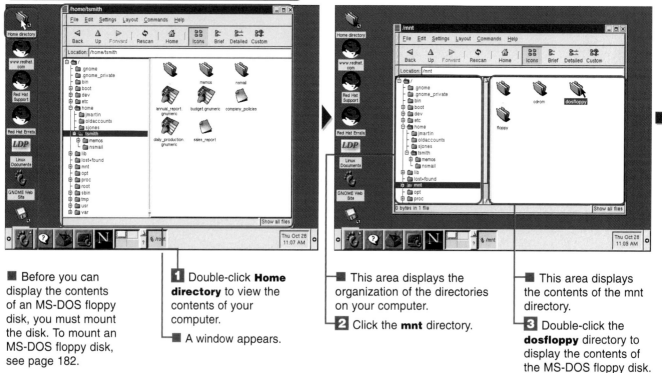

■ Before you can display the contents of an MS-DOS floppy disk, you must mount the disk. To mount an MS-DOS floppy disk, see page 182.

1 Double-click **Home directory** to view the contents of your computer.

■ A window appears.

■ This area displays the organization of the directories on your computer.

2 Click the **mnt** directory.

■ This area displays the contents of the mnt directory.

3 Double-click the **dosfloppy** directory to display the contents of the MS-DOS floppy disk.

?

**Can I open any file stored on an
MS-DOS floppy disk?**

You must have the appropriate
program installed on your computer
before you can open a file stored
on an MS-DOS floppy disk. For
example, to open a Microsoft Word
file, you will need a program that
can understand the file, such as
StarOffice.

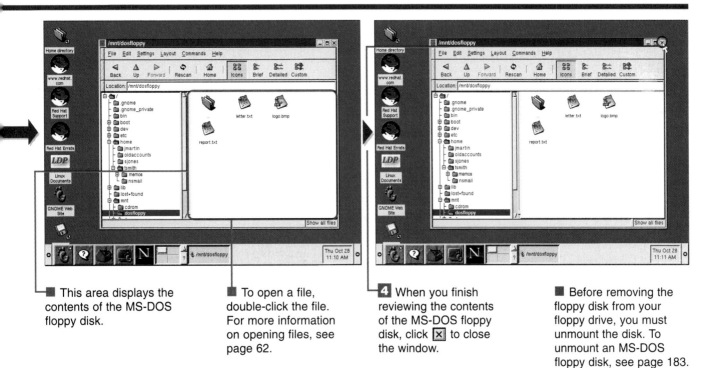

■ This area displays the
contents of the MS-DOS
floppy disk.

■ To open a file,
double-click the file.
For more information
on opening files, see
page 62.

4 When you finish
reviewing the contents
of the MS-DOS floppy
disk, click ⊠ to close
the window.

■ Before removing the
floppy disk from your
floppy drive, you must
unmount the disk. To
unmount an MS-DOS
floppy disk, see page 183.

COPY A FILE TO A FLOPPY DISK

You can copy a
file stored on your
computer to a
floppy disk. This
is useful if you
want to share the
file with a friend,
family member
or colleague.

When copying a file to
a floppy disk, you must
use a formatted floppy
disk. To format a floppy
disk, see page 188.

COPY A FILE TO A FLOPPY DISK

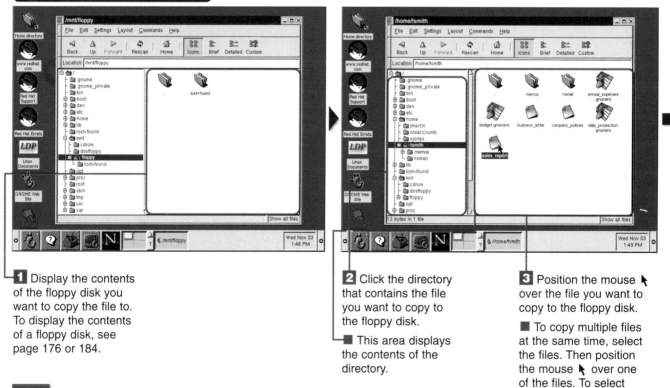

1 Display the contents
of the floppy disk you
want to copy the file to.
To display the contents
of a floppy disk, see
page 176 or 184.

2 Click the directory
that contains the file
you want to copy to
the floppy disk.

■ This area displays
the contents of the
directory.

3 Position the mouse ▶
over the file you want to
copy to the floppy disk.

■ To copy multiple files
at the same time, select
the files. Then position
the mouse ▶ over one
of the files. To select
multiple files, see page 60.

I am having trouble copying a file to a floppy disk. What can I do?

To copy the file to a floppy disk, perform one of the following tasks.

▶ Log on to your computer using the root account as shown on page 172. The root account can always copy files to a floppy disk.

▶ Format the floppy disk in the user account you will use to copy files to the floppy disk. To format a floppy disk, see page 188.

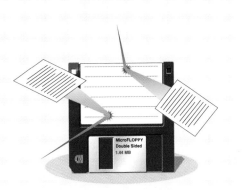

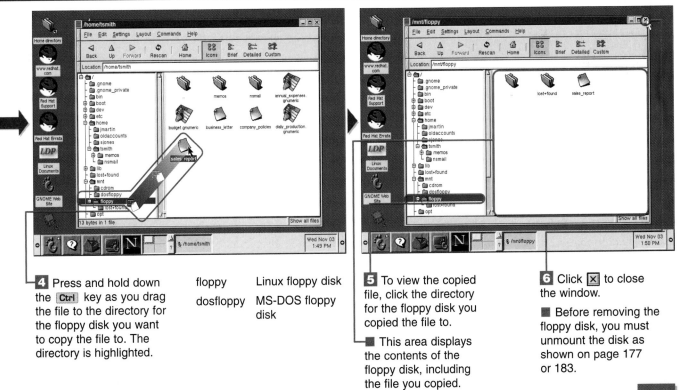

4 Press and hold down the **Ctrl** key as you drag the file to the directory for the floppy disk you want to copy the file to. The directory is highlighted.

floppy — Linux floppy disk

dosfloppy — MS-DOS floppy disk

5 To view the copied file, click the directory for the floppy disk you copied the file to.

■ This area displays the contents of the floppy disk, including the file you copied.

6 Click ⊠ to close the window.

■ Before removing the floppy disk, you must unmount the disk as shown on page 177 or 183.

FORMAT A FLOPPY DISK

You must format a
floppy disk before
you can use the disk
to store information.

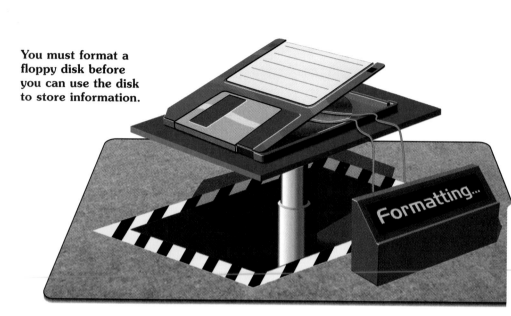

You can format a floppy disk
in the Linux or MS-DOS
format. To format a floppy
disk in the MS-DOS format,
you must first set up Linux
to use MS-DOS floppy disks
as shown on page 178.

FORMAT A FLOPPY DISK

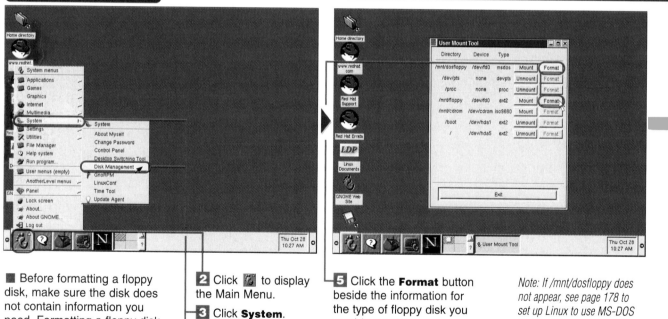

■ Before formatting a floppy
disk, make sure the disk does
not contain information you
need. Formatting a floppy disk
will permanently remove all
the information on the disk.

1 Insert the floppy disk
you want to format into
your floppy drive.

2 Click 🐾 to display
the Main Menu.

3 Click **System**.

4 Click **Disk
Management**.

■ The User Mount Tool
window appears.

5 Click the **Format** button
beside the information for
the type of floppy disk you
want to create.

/mnt/floppy   Linux
                   floppy disk

/mnt/dosfloppy   MS-DOS
                   floppy disk

*Note: If /mnt/dosfloppy does
not appear, see page 178 to
set up Linux to use MS-DOS
floppy disks.*

■ If the Format button is
dimmed, click **Unmount**.

? I get an error message when I try to format a floppy disk. What can I do?

If an error message appears when you try to format a floppy disk, repeat step **5** below. In the confirmation window that appears, click the **Do low level format** option to turn the option off (☐ changes to ☐). Then perform steps **6** and **7**.

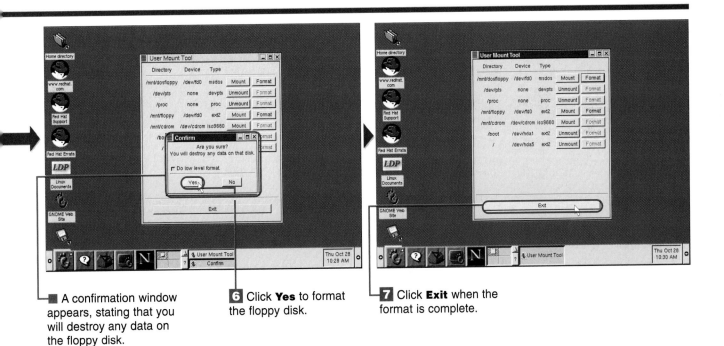

■ A confirmation window appears, stating that you will destroy any data on the floppy disk.

6 Click **Yes** to format the floppy disk.

7 Click **Exit** when the format is complete.

DISPLAY CONTENTS OF A CD-ROM DISC

You can display the contents of a CD-ROM disc to view the files stored on the disc.

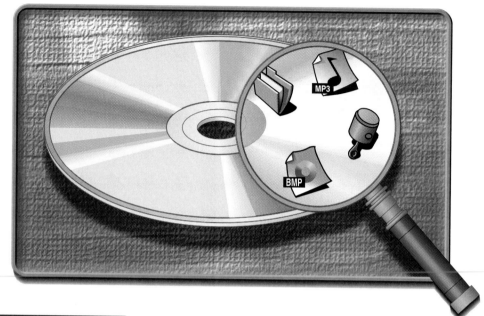

DISPLAY CONTENTS OF A CD-ROM DISC

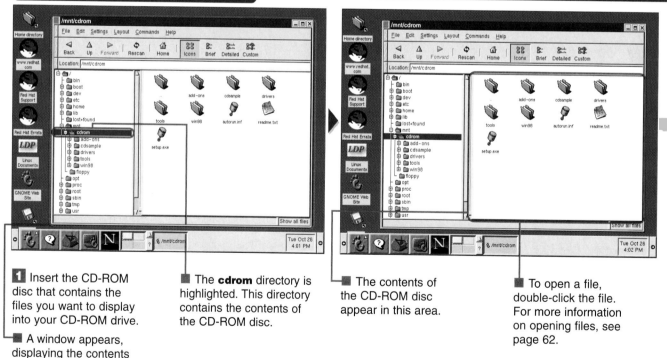

1 Insert the CD-ROM disc that contains the files you want to display into your CD-ROM drive.

■ A window appears, displaying the contents of the CD-ROM disc.

■ The **cdrom** directory is highlighted. This directory contains the contents of the CD-ROM disc.

■ The contents of the CD-ROM disc appear in this area.

■ To open a file, double-click the file. For more information on opening files, see page 62.

? What type of information can
I find on a CD-ROM disc?

Programs

CD-ROM discs can
store programs that
you can install on
your computer.

Multimedia Files

CD-ROM discs can store
pictures, sounds and
videos that you can use
in documents you create.

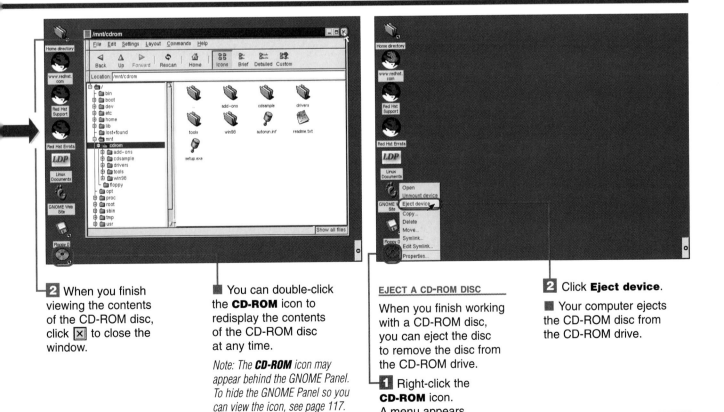

2 When you finish
viewing the contents
of the CD-ROM disc,
click ☒ to close the
window.

■ You can double-click
the **CD-ROM** icon to
redisplay the contents
of the CD-ROM disc
at any time.

*Note: The **CD-ROM** icon may
appear behind the GNOME Panel.
To hide the GNOME Panel so you
can view the icon, see page 117.*

EJECT A CD-ROM DISC

When you finish working
with a CD-ROM disc,
you can eject the disc
to remove the disc from
the CD-ROM drive.

1 Right-click the
CD-ROM icon.
A menu appears.

2 Click **Eject device**.

■ Your computer ejects
the CD-ROM disc from
the CD-ROM drive.

PLAY A MUSIC CD

You can use your computer to play music CDs while you work.

You need a CD-ROM drive, a sound card and speakers to play music CDs. You must set up your sound card as shown on page 204 before you can play music CDs.

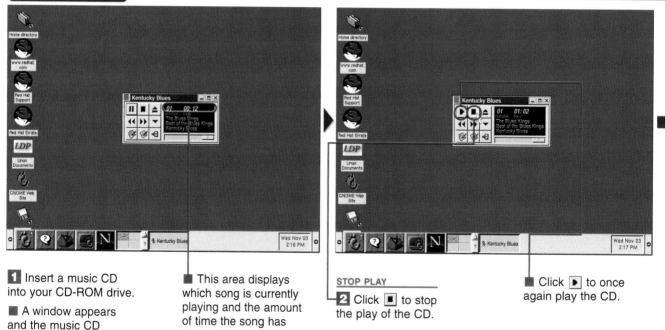

1 Insert a music CD into your CD-ROM drive.

■ A window appears and the music CD begins to play.

■ This area displays which song is currently playing and the amount of time the song has played.

STOP PLAY

2 Click ■ to stop the play of the CD.

■ Click ▶ to once again play the CD.

Can I listen to music privately?

You can listen to music privately
by turning your speakers off
and plugging a headset into
your CD-ROM drive.

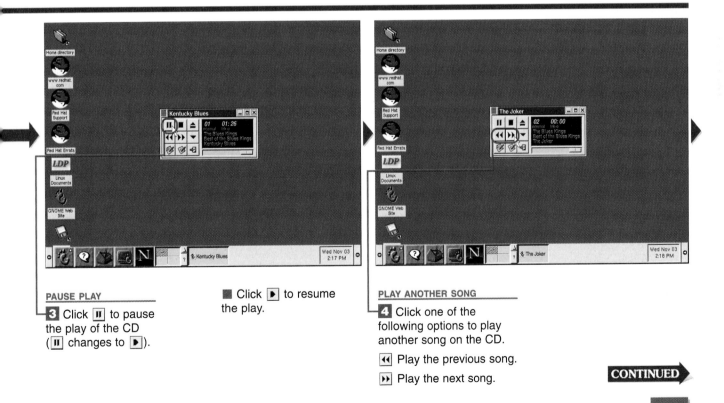

PAUSE PLAY

3 Click ⏸ to pause
the play of the CD
(⏸ changes to ▶).

■ Click ▶ to resume
the play.

PLAY ANOTHER SONG

4 Click one of the
following options to play
another song on the CD.

⏪ Play the previous song.

⏩ Play the next song.

CONTINUED▶

PLAY A MUSIC CD

You can switch
between the
songs on a CD.

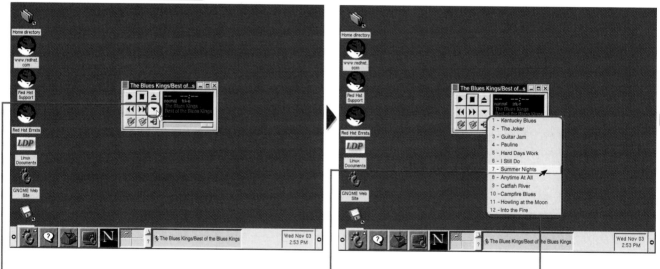

5 Click ▼ to display
a list of the songs on
the CD.

■ If you are connected
to the Internet, the title
of each song on the CD
appears.

*Note: If you are not connected
to the Internet, Linux will not
display the title of each song.*

6 Click the song you
want to play.

How does the CD Player know the title of each song on my CD?

If you are connected to the Internet, the CD Player can automatically access the largest collection of music CD information on the Web. If the CD you are playing exists in the collection, the CD Player can display the name of the album, the artist and each song on the CD. To connect to the Internet, see page 250.

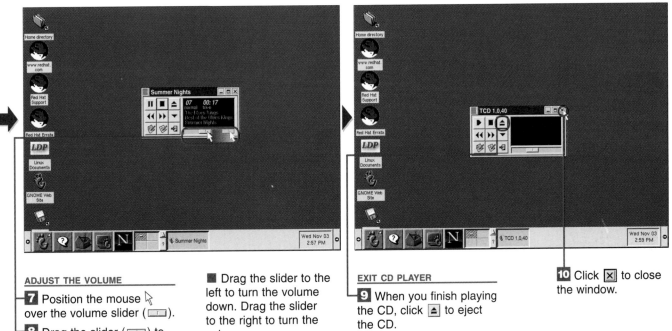

ADJUST THE VOLUME

7 Position the mouse ⌖ over the volume slider (▭).

8 Drag the slider (▭) to turn the volume up or down.

■ Drag the slider to the left to turn the volume down. Drag the slider to the right to turn the volume up.

Note: You can also use the volume control on your speakers to adjust the volume.

EXIT CD PLAYER

9 When you finish playing the CD, click ▲ to eject the CD.

10 Click ⊠ to close the window.

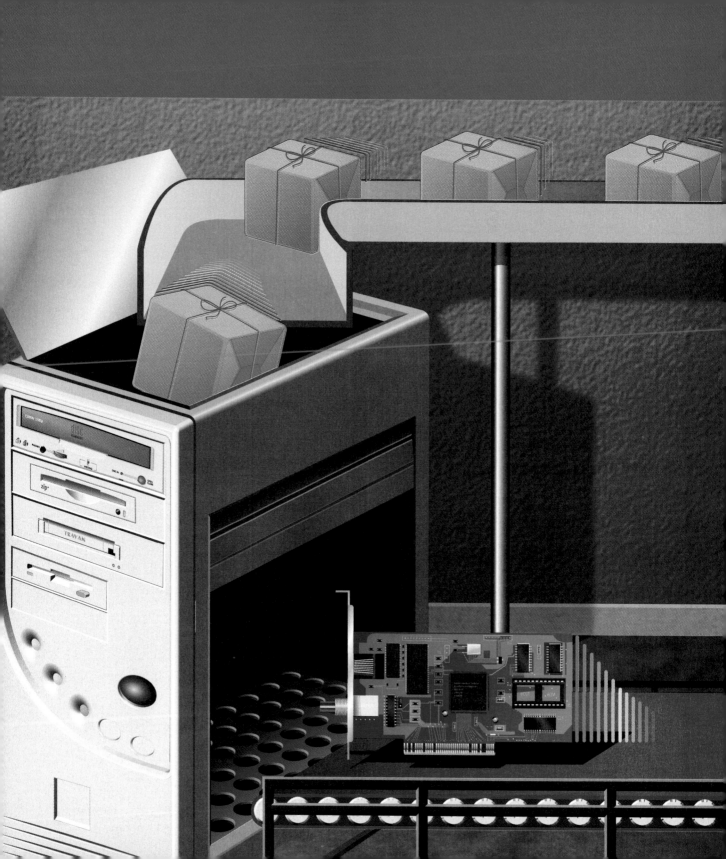

CHAPTER 9

Work With Hardware and Software

You can use Linux to set up hardware and software on your computer. This chapter shows you how to set up a printer, sound card and network card, as well as how to install software packages.

You must set up a printer on your computer before you can print files. You only need to set up a printer once.

You can only set up a printer if you are logged on to your computer as **root**. If you are logged on as a regular user, you cannot set up a printer.

SET UP A PRINTER

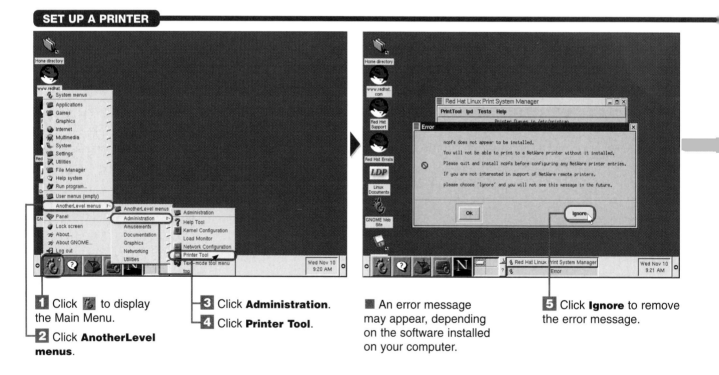

1 Click 🐾 to display the Main Menu.

2 Click **AnotherLevel menus**.

3 Click **Administration**.

4 Click **Printer Tool**.

■ An error message may appear, depending on the software installed on your computer.

5 Click **Ignore** to remove the error message.

Why do I need to set up a printer?

Setting up a printer lets you specify
the printer driver Linux should use
for your printer. A printer driver is
special software that enables Linux
to communicate with your printer.
When you set up a printer using
the steps below, Linux helps you
select the correct printer driver for
your printer.

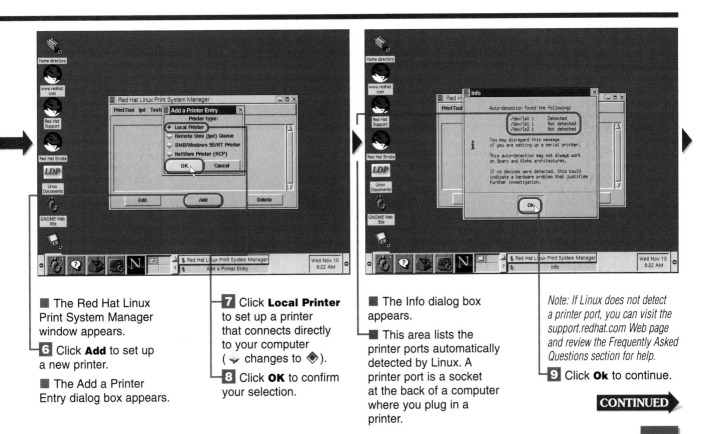

■ The Red Hat Linux
Print System Manager
window appears.

6 Click **Add** to set up
a new printer.

■ The Add a Printer
Entry dialog box appears.

7 Click **Local Printer**
to set up a printer
that connects directly
to your computer
(✦ changes to ◈).

8 Click **OK** to confirm
your selection.

■ The Info dialog box
appears.

■ This area lists the
printer ports automatically
detected by Linux. A
printer port is a socket
at the back of a computer
where you plug in a
printer.

*Note: If Linux does not detect
a printer port, you can visit the
support.redhat.com Web page
and review the Frequently Asked
Questions section for help.*

9 Click **Ok** to continue.

CONTINUED ▶

SET UP A PRINTER

When setting up a printer, you must specify the type of printer you will use.

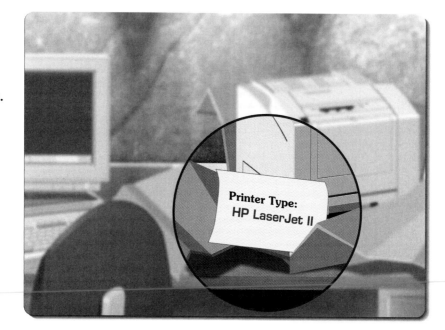

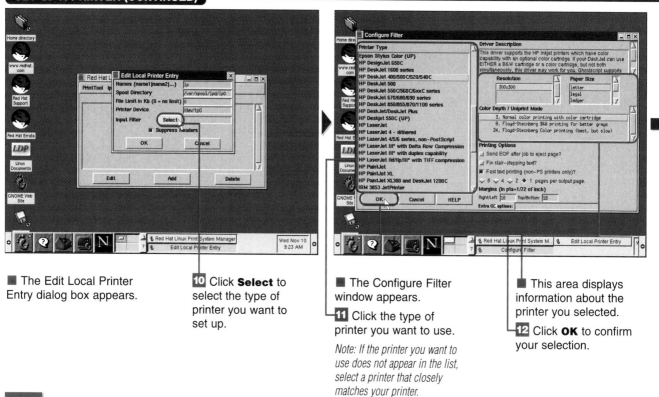

■ The Edit Local Printer Entry dialog box appears.

10 Click **Select** to select the type of printer you want to set up.

■ The Configure Filter window appears.

11 Click the type of printer you want to use.

Note: If the printer you want to use does not appear in the list, select a printer that closely matches your printer.

■ This area displays information about the printer you selected.

12 Click **OK** to confirm your selection.

**What information does
Linux display about my
printer?**

Linux displays the following
information about the
printer you select in the
Configure Filter window.
Linux automatically selects
the most commonly used
settings for the printer.

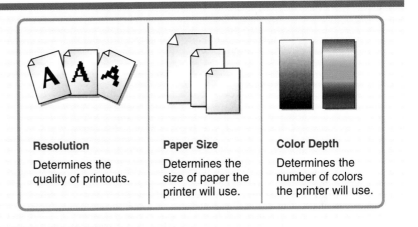

Resolution

Determines the
quality of printouts.

Paper Size

Determines the
size of paper the
printer will use.

Color Depth

Determines the
number of colors
the printer will use.

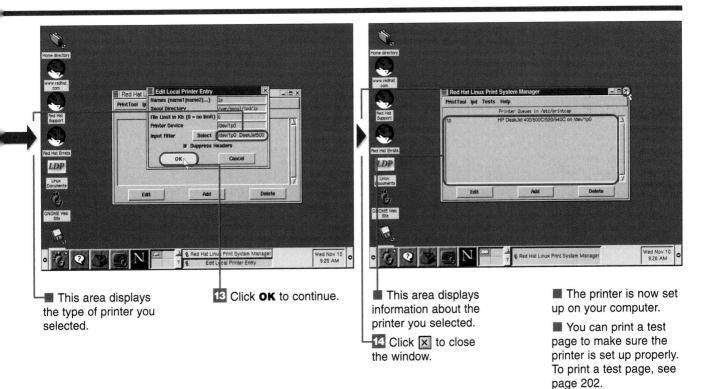

■ This area displays
the type of printer you
selected.

13 Click **OK** to continue.

■ This area displays
information about the
printer you selected.

14 Click ⊠ to close
the window.

■ The printer is now set
up on your computer.

■ You can print a test
page to make sure the
printer is set up properly.
To print a test page, see
page 202.

PRINT A TEST PAGE

You can print
a test page to
confirm that
your printer is
set up properly.

You can only print a test page if you are logged on to your computer as **root**. If you are logged on as a regular user, you cannot print a test page.

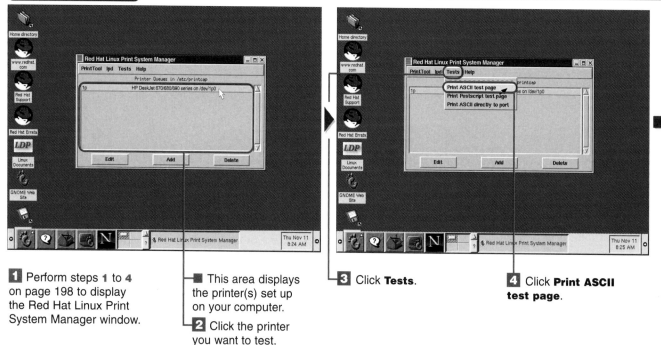

1 Perform steps **1** to **4** on page 198 to display the Red Hat Linux Print System Manager window.

■ This area displays the printer(s) set up on your computer.

2 Click the printer you want to test.

3 Click **Tests**.

4 Click **Print ASCII test page**.

My test page did not print correctly. What can I do?

If your test page did not print correctly, try changing one of these settings.

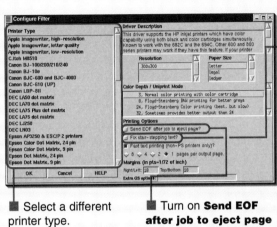

■ Turn on **Fix stair-stepping text** if the text printed off the page.

Note: If you are still having problems printing, you can visit the support.redhat.com Web page and review the Frequently Asked Questions section for help.

■ Select a different printer type.

■ Turn on **Send EOF after job to eject page** if the page did not eject from the printer.

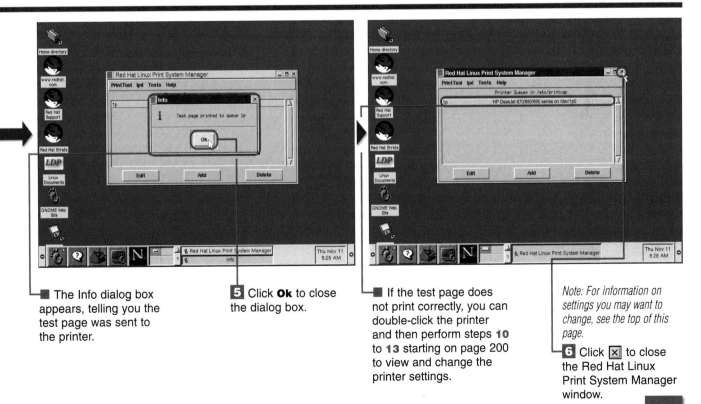

■ The Info dialog box appears, telling you the test page was sent to the printer.

5 Click **Ok** to close the dialog box.

■ If the test page does not print correctly, you can double-click the printer and then perform steps **10** to **13** starting on page 200 to view and change the printer settings.

Note: For information on settings you may want to change, see the top of this page.

6 Click ⊠ to close the Red Hat Linux Print System Manager window.

SET UP A SOUND CARD

You can set up
a sound card on
your computer.
A sound card is a
device that allows
a computer to
play and record
sound.

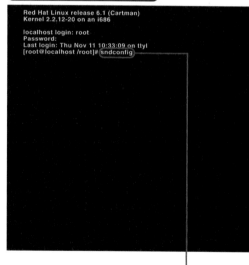

SET UP A SOUND CARD

```
Red Hat Linux release 6.1 (Cartman)
Kernel 2.2.12-20 on an i686

localhost login: root
Password:
Last login: Thu Nov 11 10:33:09 on tty1
[root@localhost /root]# sndconfig
```

Sound Configuration Utility 0.38   (C) 1999 Red Hat Software

┤ Introduction ├

sndconfig is a configuration tool for sound cards.

A probe will now be performed for any PnP cards that
will be automatically configured.

Report bugs to sound-list@redhat.com

Ok   Cancel

<Tab>/<Alt-Tab> between elements | Use <Enter> to edit a selection

1 Perform steps 1 to 3 on page 233 to display the command line using a full screen. You must log in using the root account.

2 Type **sndconfig** and then press the `Enter` key to start the program that allows you to set up a sound card.

■ The Introduction screen appears, stating that the program will determine information about your sound card.

3 Press the `Enter` key to continue.

What will setting up a sound card allow me to do?

Play Music CDs

A sound card allows you to play music CDs on your computer while you work. To play a music CD, see page 192.

Play Sounds for Events

A sound card allows you to hear sounds for certain events, such as when an error message appears. To play sounds for events, see page 134.

Play Sounds in Games

A sound card allows you to hear music and sound effects while playing games.

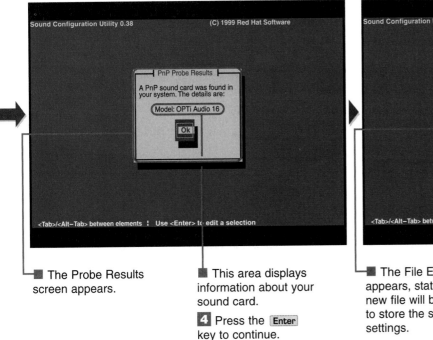

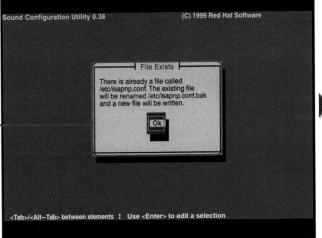

■ The Probe Results screen appears.

■ This area displays information about your sound card.

4 Press the `Enter` key to continue.

■ The File Exists screen appears, stating that a new file will be created to store the sound card settings.

5 Press the `Enter` key to continue.

CONTINUED

SET UP A SOUND CARD

When setting up your sound card, you will need to test the sound card to make sure the card is set up correctly.

Before testing your sound card, make sure your speakers are plugged into your computer and the speaker volume is turned up.

SET UP A SOUND CARD (CONTINUED)

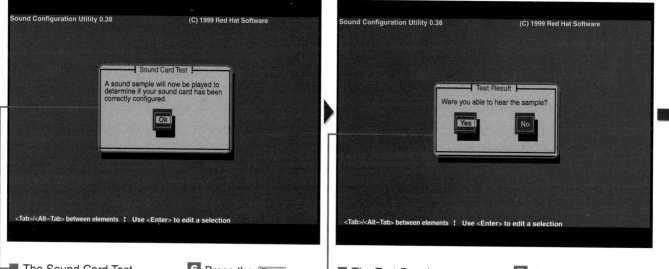

■ The Sound Card Test screen appears, stating that a sound sample will be played to determine if your sound card is set up correctly.

6 Press the `Enter` key to continue.

■ The Test Result screen appears.

7 If you heard the sound, press the `Enter` key.

? What devices can I plug into a sound card?

You can see the edge of a sound card at the back of a computer. A sound card has a port and several jacks where you can plug in devices.

Spk Out

Allows you to connect speakers or headphones to hear sound.

Game Port

Allows you to connect a joystick or other device used to play games.

Mic In

Allows you to connect a microphone to record sound.

Line In

Allows you to connect a cassette player, radio or CD player to play or record music.

Line Out

Allows you to connect an amplifier to play sound through your home stereo.

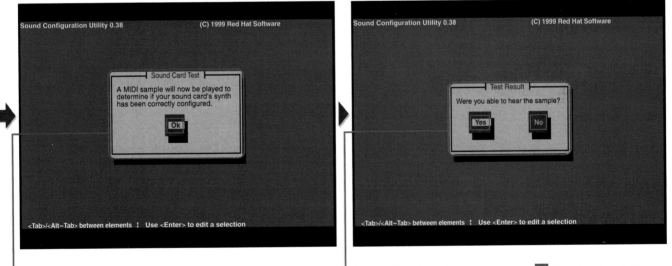

■ The Sound Card Test screen appears, stating that a MIDI sound file will be played to determine if your sound card will properly play MIDI files.

Note: MIDI files usually contain instrumental music and are more complicated sound files than the sound sample you tested in step 6.

8 Press the Enter key to continue.

■ The Test Result screen appears.

9 If you heard the sound, press the Enter key.

10 To return to your desktop, press and hold down the Ctrl and Alt keys as you press the F7 key.

■ The sound card is now set up on your computer.

SET UP A NETWORK CARD

You can set up a network card on your computer. A network card allows you to exchange information with other computers on a network.

You may have already set up your network card when you installed Linux.

You can only set up a network card if you are logged on to your computer as **root**. If you are logged on as a regular user, you cannot set up a network card.

SET UP A NETWORK CARD

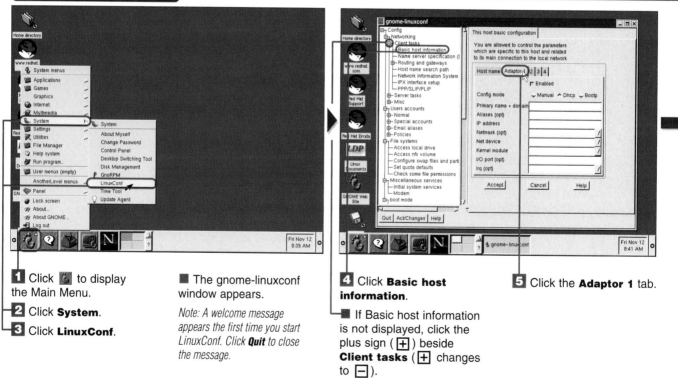

1 Click ⚙ to display the Main Menu.

2 Click **System**.

3 Click **LinuxConf**.

■ The gnome-linuxconf window appears.

*Note: A welcome message appears the first time you start LinuxConf. Click **Quit** to close the message.*

4 Click **Basic host information**.

■ If Basic host information is not displayed, click the plus sign (⊞) beside **Client tasks** (⊞ changes to ⊟).

5 Click the **Adaptor 1** tab.

What information do I need to set up my network card?

You will need some or all of the following information from your network administrator. The information you need depends on the setup of your network and whether your network has a DHCP server. A DHCP server automatically assigns an IP address to each computer on a network.

IP address

Identifies your computer on the network.

Primary name + domain

Name of your computer and name of your domain on the network.

Net device

Identifies the type of network card.

Kernel module

Identifies the software your computer uses to communicate with the network card.

Note: To determine the correct software for your network card, consult the Reference Guide that came with Linux or visit the www.redhat.com Web site.

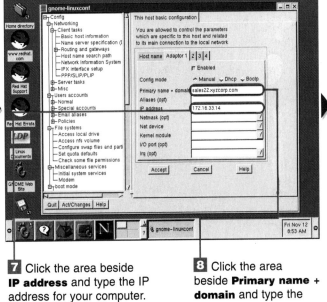

■6 If your network does not have a DHCP server, click **Manual** (changes to).

■ If your network has a DHCP server, click **Dhcp** (changes to). Then skip to step 8.

■7 Click the area beside **IP address** and type the IP address for your computer.

■8 Click the area beside **Primary name + domain** and type the name of your computer and the name of your domain on the network.

When setting up a network card, you need to specify the type of the network card and the software your computer will use to communicate with the card.

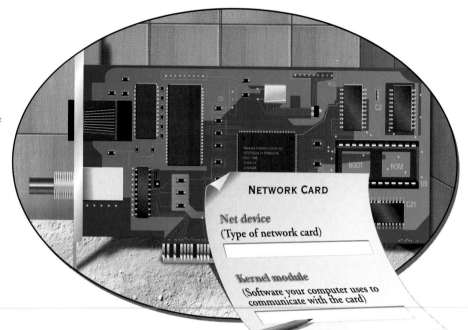

NETWORK CARD

Net device
(Type of network card)

Kernel module
(Software your computer uses to communicate with the card)

SET UP A NETWORK CARD (CONTINUED)

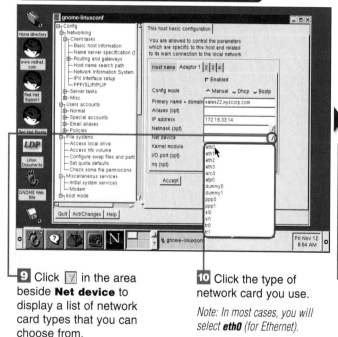

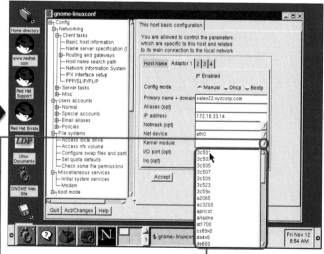

9 Click ☑ in the area beside **Net device** to display a list of network card types that you can choose from.

10 Click the type of network card you use.

*Note: In most cases, you will select **eth0** (for Ethernet).*

11 Click ☑ in the area beside **Kernel module** to specify the software your computer will use to communicate with the network card.

12 Click the software your computer will use to communicate with the network card.

Note: For more information, see the top of page 209.

**Can Linux automatically
detect my network card?**

Linux can automatically
detect some types of network
cards. If Linux detects your
network card, this screen
will appear when you turn
on your computer. Press the
Enter key and then follow
the instructions that appear
on your screen to set up the
network card.

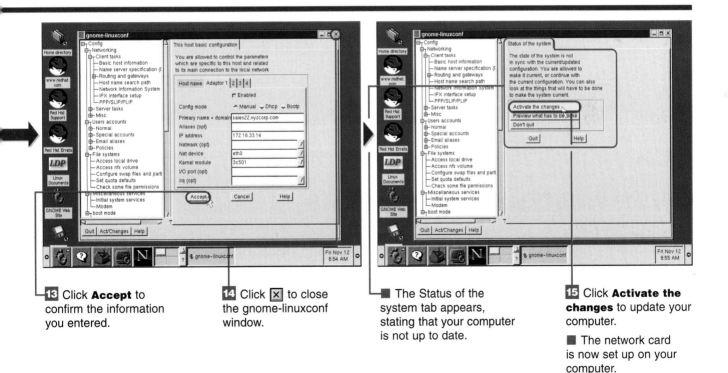

13 Click **Accept** to
confirm the information
you entered.

14 Click ✕ to close
the gnome-linuxconf
window.

■ The Status of the
system tab appears,
stating that your computer
is not up to date.

15 Click **Activate the
changes** to update your
computer.

■ The network card
is now set up on your
computer.

DISPLAY SYSTEM INFORMATION

You can display information about your computer, such as the amount of free hard disk space and the total amount of memory.

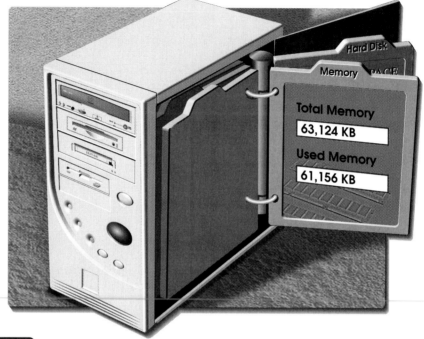

DISPLAY SYSTEM INFORMATION

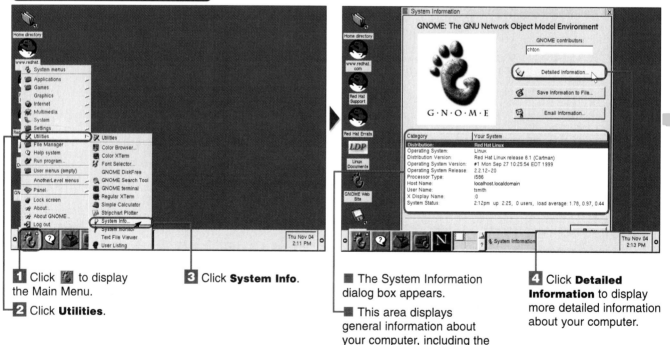

1 Click to display the Main Menu.

2 Click **Utilities**.

3 Click **System Info**.

■ The System Information dialog box appears.

■ This area displays general information about your computer, including the version of Linux you use.

4 Click **Detailed Information** to display more detailed information about your computer.

How can I increase the amount of free hard disk space and free memory on my computer?

Hard Disk Space

To increase the amount of free hard disk space, you can delete files and programs you no longer need and move files you rarely use to a storage medium such as a floppy disk.

Memory

You can increase the amount of free memory by reducing the number of programs you have open at the same time or by purchasing more memory.

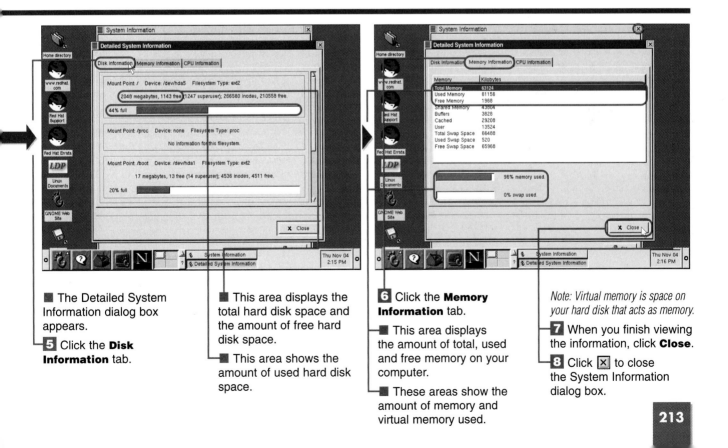

■ The Detailed System Information dialog box appears.

5 Click the **Disk Information** tab.

■ This area displays the total hard disk space and the amount of free hard disk space.

■ This area shows the amount of used hard disk space.

6 Click the **Memory Information** tab.

■ This area displays the amount of total, used and free memory on your computer.

■ These areas show the amount of memory and virtual memory used.

Note: Virtual memory is space on your hard disk that acts as memory.

7 When you finish viewing the information, click **Close**.

8 Click ⊠ to close the System Information dialog box.

INSTALL A PACKAGE

You can use Gnome RPM to install packages on your computer that will add new capabilities to Linux. Packages can contain programs and files.

You cannot use Gnome RPM to install some programs. You can check the documentation that came with a program to determine how to install the program.

INSTALL A PACKAGE

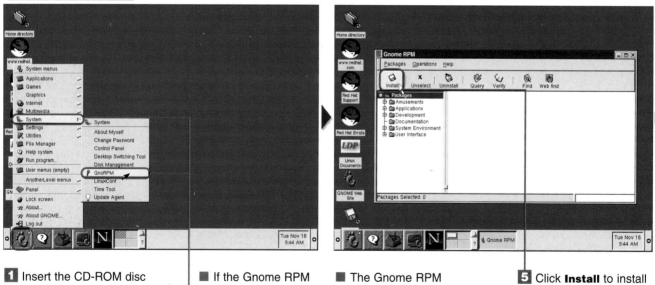

1 Insert the CD-ROM disc that contains the package you want to install into your CD-ROM drive.

Note: A window may appear, asking for the password for the root account. Type the password and then press the Enter *key.*

■ If the Gnome RPM window appears, skip to step **5**.

2 Click  to display the Main Menu.

3 Click **System**.

4 Click **GnoRPM**.

■ The Gnome RPM window appears.

5 Click **Install** to install a package.

?

Does Linux come with packages that I can install?

The Red Hat Linux box set comes with CD-ROM discs that contain hundreds of packages that you can install. Here are some packages you will find on CD-ROM disc 1.

Package	Description
apache	Allows your computer to act as a Web server.
cdparanoia	Allows you to record music on your computer from music CDs.
macutils	Provides utilities for working with Macintosh files.
pilot-link	Allows you to transfer files between Linux and a 3Com Palm Pilot organizer.
xpuzzles	Provides puzzles and toys for Linux.

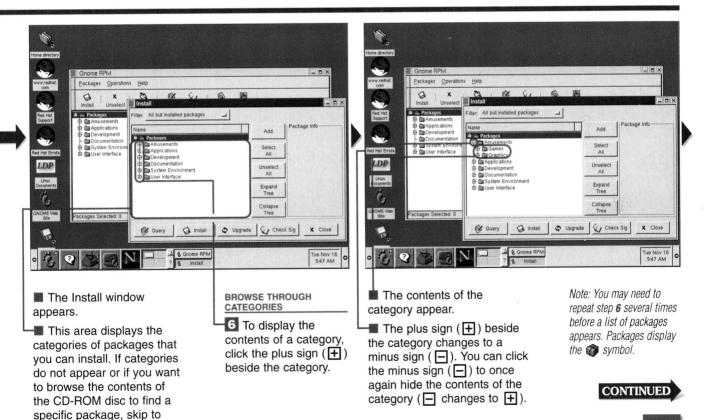

■ The Install window appears.

■ This area displays the categories of packages that you can install. If categories do not appear or if you want to browse the contents of the CD-ROM disc to find a specific package, skip to step **10**.

BROWSE THROUGH CATEGORIES

6 To display the contents of a category, click the plus sign (⊞) beside the category.

■ The contents of the category appear.

■ The plus sign (⊞) beside the category changes to a minus sign (⊟). You can click the minus sign (⊟) to once again hide the contents of the category (⊟ changes to ⊞).

*Note: You may need to repeat step **6** several times before a list of packages appears. Packages display the ● symbol.*

CONTINUED

INSTALL A PACKAGE

You can view a brief
description of a package
to help you determine
if you want to install
the package.

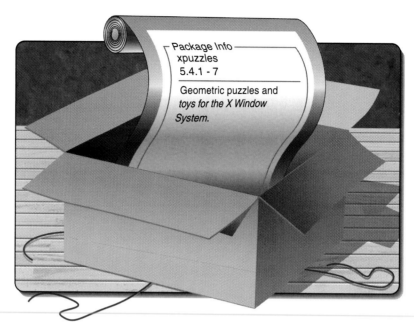

Package Info
xpuzzles
5.4.1 - 7

Geometric puzzles and
*toys for the X Window
System.*

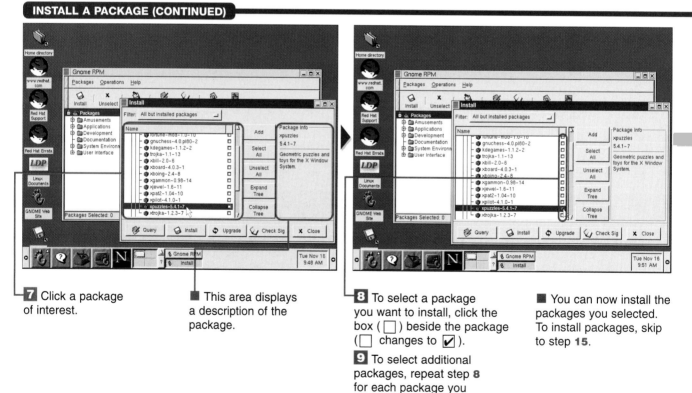

7 Click a package
of interest.

■ This area displays
a description of the
package.

8 To select a package
you want to install, click the
box (☐) beside the package
(☐ changes to ☑).

9 To select additional
packages, repeat step **8**
for each package you
want to install.

■ You can now install the
packages you selected.
To install packages, skip
to step **15**.

Where else can I get packages that I can install?

Computer Stores

Many computer stores offer CD-ROM discs containing Linux packages that you can install.

Internet

You can obtain packages on the Internet that you can install. For example, you can find packages at the www.tucows.com Web site.

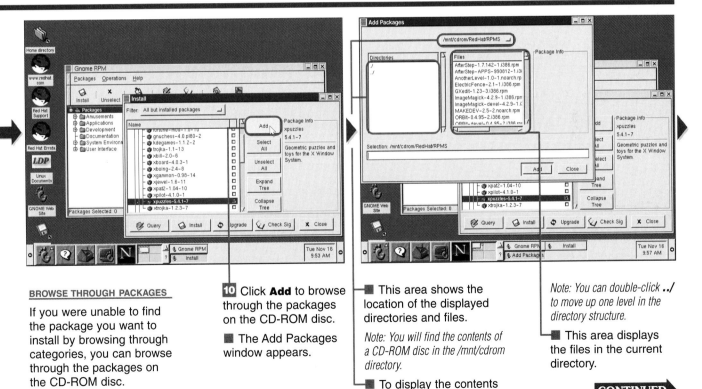

BROWSE THROUGH PACKAGES

If you were unable to find the package you want to install by browsing through categories, you can browse through the packages on the CD-ROM disc.

10 Click **Add** to browse through the packages on the CD-ROM disc.

■ The Add Packages window appears.

■ This area shows the location of the displayed directories and files.

Note: You will find the contents of a CD-ROM disc in the /mnt/cdrom directory.

■ To display the contents of a different directory, double-click the directory in this area.

Note: You can double-click ../ to move up one level in the directory structure.

■ This area displays the files in the current directory.

CONTINUED

INSTALL A PACKAGE

After you select the packages you want to install, you can install the packages on your computer.

After you install a package, you may need to run a setup program before you can use the software. For help information, read the documentation that came with the package or look for a README file.

INSTALL A PACKAGE (CONTINUED)

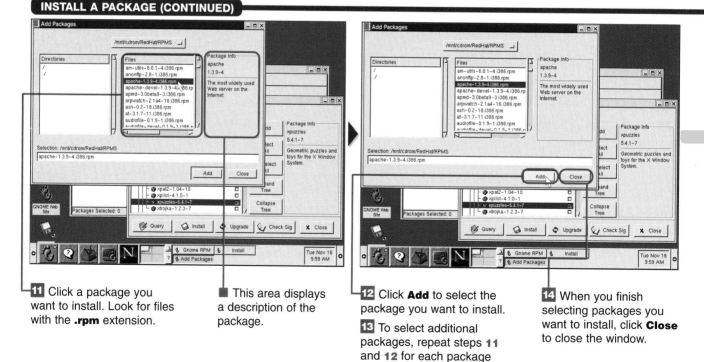

11 Click a package you want to install. Look for files with the **.rpm** extension.

■ This area displays a description of the package.

12 Click **Add** to select the package you want to install.

13 To select additional packages, repeat steps **11** and **12** for each package you want to install.

14 When you finish selecting packages you want to install, click **Close** to close the window.

Why does this dialog box appear when I try to install a package?

This dialog box appears if the package you are installing requires you to install additional packages to work properly. Some Linux programs require more than one package to operate. Select all the packages the program requires and then install all the packages at the same time.

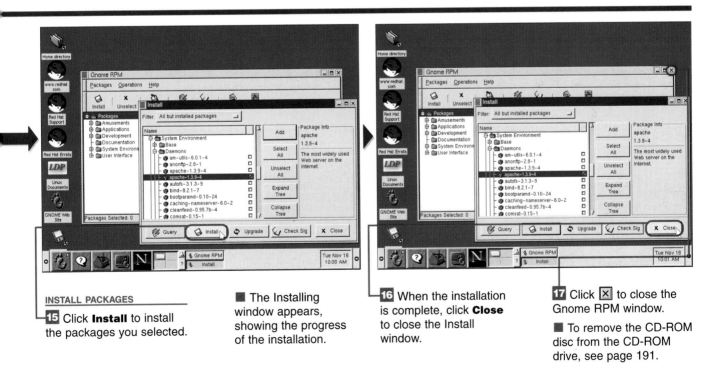

<u>INSTALL PACKAGES</u>

15 Click **Install** to install the packages you selected.

■ The Installing window appears, showing the progress of the installation.

16 When the installation is complete, click **Close** to close the Install window.

17 Click ⊠ to close the Gnome RPM window.

■ To remove the CD-ROM disc from the CD-ROM drive, see page 191.

USING UPDATE AGENT

You can use Update Agent to obtain new and updated packages on the Internet. Update Agent helps you download and install the packages on your computer.

Update Agent allows you to obtain packages that contain new programs for Linux and updates to Linux features.

USING UPDATE AGENT

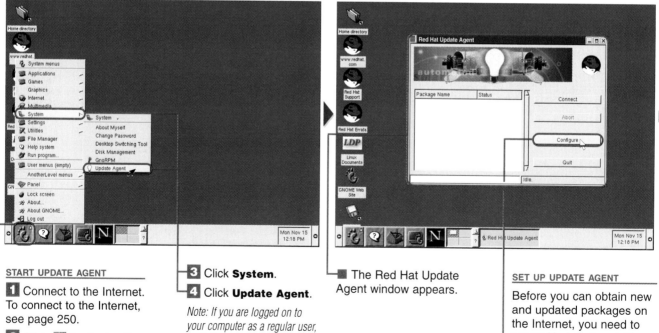

START UPDATE AGENT

1 Connect to the Internet. To connect to the Internet, see page 250.

2 Click 🐚 to display the Main Menu.

3 Click **System**.

4 Click **Update Agent**.

Note: If you are logged on to your computer as a regular user, a window appears, asking for the password for the root account. Type the password and then press the **Enter** *key.*

■ The Red Hat Update Agent window appears.

SET UP UPDATE AGENT

Before you can obtain new and updated packages on the Internet, you need to set up Update Agent. You only need to set up Update Agent once.

1 Click **Configure** to set up Update Agent.

What do I need to do before using Update Agent?

Before you can use Update Agent, you must register your copy of Red Hat Linux at the www.redhat.com/now Web page. When you register, you specify a user name and password that you will need to set up Update Agent.

■ The Configuration dialog box appears.

2 Click this area and type the user name you specified when you registered your copy of Linux.

3 Click this area and type the password you specified when you registered your copy of Linux.

Note: For more information, see the top of this page.

4 Click the **Retrieval** tab.

5 Click this option to have Linux automatically install packages after you download them from the Internet (■ changes to ■).

6 Click **OK** to confirm your changes.

CONTINUED

USING UPDATE AGENT

Update Agent compares the packages on your computer to the packages available on the Internet and then displays a list of packages that you may want to download and install.

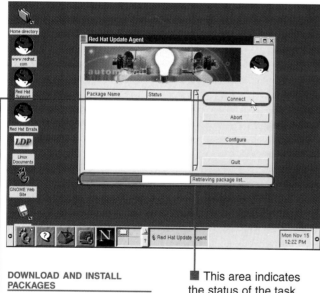

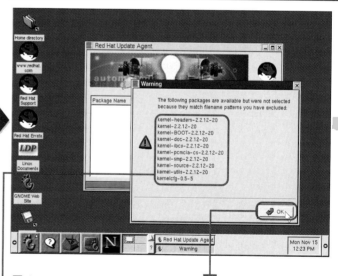

DOWNLOAD AND INSTALL PACKAGES

1 Click **Connect** to have Update Agent compare the packages on your computer to the packages available on the Internet.

■ This area indicates the status of the task Update Agent is currently performing and a brief description of the task.

■ A warning dialog box appears.

■ This area displays a list of packages that Update Agent will not update. By default, Update Agent will not update packages that begin with "kernel." The kernel is the central part of the Linux operating system.

2 Click **OK** to continue.

■ Update Agent now determines which packages you can update. This may take a few minutes.

What types of packages can I obtain using Update Agent?

Security Advisories

You can obtain packages that can improve the security of Linux. These packages can help prevent unauthorized users from accessing information on your computer.

Bug Fixes

You can obtain packages that can fix errors that prevent Linux programs from working properly.

Package Enhancements

You can obtain packages that can update Linux features and add new capabilities to Linux.

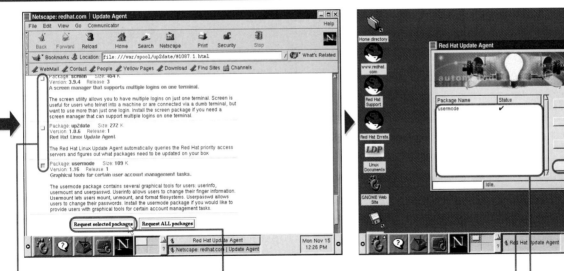

■ A Web page appears, displaying the name and a description of each package you can update.

3 Click the box (☐) beside each package you want to update (☐ changes to ▓).

4 When you finish selecting packages, click **Request selected packages** at the bottom of the Web page.

*Note: A warning dialog box may appear. Click **Continue Submission** to continue.*

■ Update Agent downloads the packages to your computer. This may take a few minutes.

*Note: A dialog box may appear, asking if you want to close a window. Click **OK** to close the dialog box.*

■ This area displays the packages you selected. When a package has successfully downloaded and installed, a check mark (✔) appears beside the package.

5 Click **Quit** to close the Red Hat Update Agent window.

CHAPTER 10

Using KDE

In this chapter you will learn about the KDE desktop environment.

KDE (K Desktop Environment) is a graphical desktop environment that you can use to work with Linux.

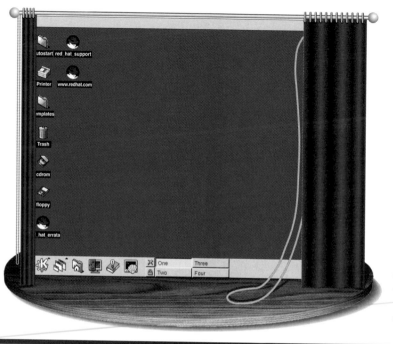

KDE is an alternative to the GNOME desktop environment that is shown throughout this book. Some people prefer using KDE since it came with earlier versions of Linux and is more like the Windows operating system.

You can find out more about KDE at the www.kde.org Web site.

START KDE

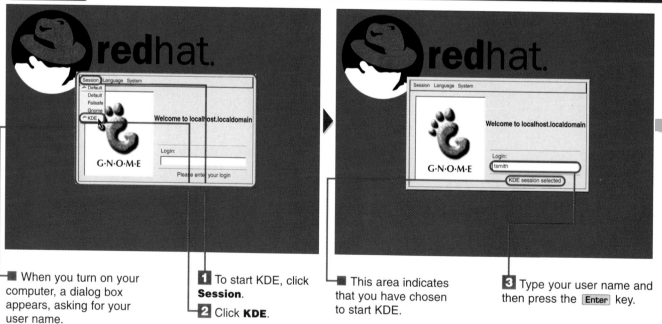

■ When you turn on your computer, a dialog box appears, asking for your user name.

Note: If you have already logged on to your computer, you can display the dialog box by logging out. To log out, see page 172.

1 To start KDE, click **Session**.

2 Click **KDE**.

Note: If KDE is not available, see the top of page 227.

■ This area indicates that you have chosen to start KDE.

3 Type your user name and then press the Enter key.

What do I need to do before I can use KDE?

Before you can use KDE, you need to install the following packages. You can find the packages on the CD-ROM disc 1 that came with Linux. To install a package, see page 214.

REQUIRED PACKAGES			
✔ kdebase	✔ kdelibs	✔ kdesupport	✔ qt1x

OPTIONAL PACKAGES	
kdeadmin	Contains utilities for the system administrator.
kdegames	Contains games.
kdegraphics	Contains graphics applications.
kdemultimedia	Contains multimedia applications.
kdenetwork	Contains applications for use on a network or on the Internet.
kdetoys	Contains amusing applications for the desktop.
kdeutils	Contains utilities, such as a calculator and text editor.
kdeorganizer	Contains a calendar and scheduling program.

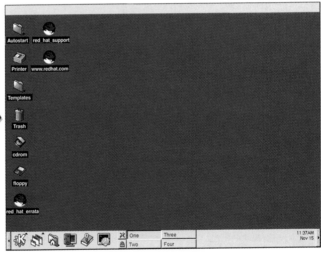

4 Type your password and then press the **Enter** key.

Note: A symbol (ˣ) appears for each character you type to prevent others from seeing the password.

■ The KDE desktop appears.

PARTS OF THE KDE SCREEN

The KDE screen displays various items. The items that appear depend on the KDE packages you installed and the account you used to log on to your computer.

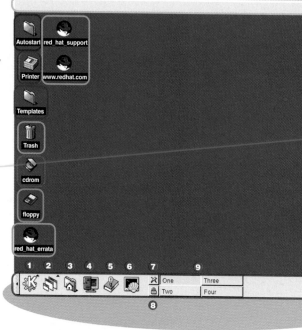

AUTOSTART

Allows you to have programs start automatically each time you start KDE.

PRINTER

Allows you to print files.

TEMPLATES

Allows you to create shortcuts to items such as programs.

TRASH

Stores files you have deleted.

TASKBAR

Displays a button for each open window.

CDROM

Allows you to display the contents of a CD-ROM disc.

FLOPPY

Allows you to display the contents of a floppy disk.

HELP WEB PAGES

Allows you to quickly display Web pages that offer help on using Linux.

KDE PANEL

❶ Application Starter

Gives you quick access to programs.

❷ Window List

Allows you to display a list of all open windows.

❸ Home Directory

Allows you to display the contents of the directory that stores your personal files.

❹ KDE Control Center

Allows you to view and change KDE settings.

❺ KDE Help

Provides help on using KDE.

❻ Terminal

Allows you to display the Konsole window where you can type Linux commands.

❼ Logout

Allows you to log out of KDE.

❽ Lock Screen

Allows you to secure your computer while you are away from your desk.

❾ Virtual Desktops

Allows you to switch between different desktops.

❿ Clock

Displays the current time and date.

When you finish
using KDE, you
can log out of
KDE.

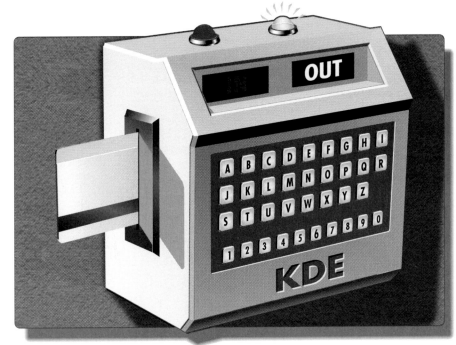

LOG OUT OF KDE

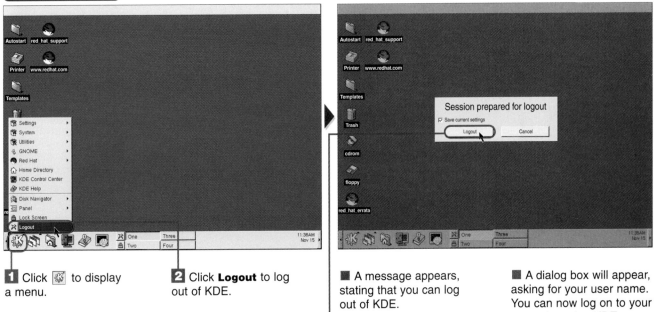

1 Click to display
a menu.

2 Click **Logout** to log
out of KDE.

■ A message appears,
stating that you can log
out of KDE.

3 Click **Logout**.

■ A dialog box will appear,
asking for your user name.
You can now log on to your
computer using KDE or
GNOME. To log on using
KDE, see page 226. To
log on using GNOME,
see page 173.

CHAPTER 11

Using the Command Line

This chapter will teach you how to use some basic commands to accomplish tasks in Linux.

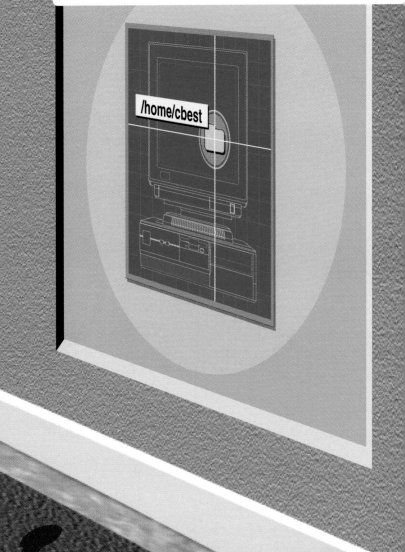

DISPLAY THE COMMAND LINE

You can display the
command line so
you can enter Linux
commands. The
command line displays
text without any
graphics.

DISPLAY THE COMMAND LINE

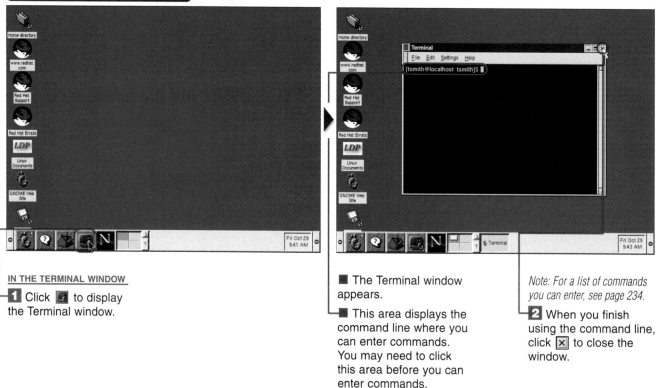

1 Click to display
the Terminal window.

■ The Terminal window
appears.

■ This area displays the
command line where you
can enter commands.
You may need to click
this area before you can
enter commands.

*Note: For a list of commands
you can enter, see page 234.*

2 When you finish
using the command line,
click ⊠ to close the
window.

232

Why would I want to use the command line?

▶ You can perform some tasks, such as stopping a file from printing, only in the command line.

▶ You can perform many tasks, such as moving files, much faster in the command line.

▶ If you are having a problem with Linux, you can use the command line to fix the problem.

▶ Some people prefer to work with a screen that shows only text.

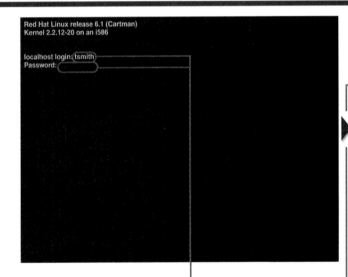

IN A FULL SCREEN

1 To display the command line using a full screen, press and hold down the `Ctrl` and `Alt` keys as you press the `F1` key.

■ Linux displays a line where you can log in.

2 Type your user name and then press the `Enter` key.

3 Type your password and then press the `Enter` key.

Note: The password does not appear on the screen to prevent others from seeing the password.

■ The command line appears.

4 When you finish using the command line, type **exit** and then press the `Enter` key to log out of the command line.

5 To return to your desktop, press and hold down the `Ctrl` and `Alt` keys as you press the `F7` key.

COMMON LINUX COMMANDS

Terminal

File   Edit   Settings   Help

[root@localhost /root]# cd /home/tduncan/mckenzie_project
[root@localhost mckenzie_project]# ▮

CD

Changes the current directory.

1 Type **cd** followed by the location and name of the directory you want to change to. Then press the [Enter] key.

Note: If you do not type the location and name of a directory, Linux changes to your home directory.

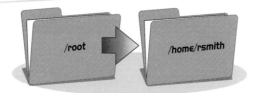

Terminal

File   Edit   Settings   Help

[root@localhost /root]# chmod a + w /root/employee_suggestions

CHMOD

Changes the read, write, and execute permissions for a file.

1 Type **chmod** followed by **u**, **g**, **o** or **a** (user, group, other users or all users) to specify who you want to change the permissions for.

2 Type **+** or **-** to allow or deny permissions for the file.

3 Type **r**, **w** or **x** (read, write or execute) to specify the type of permission you want to allow or deny.

4 Type the location and name of the file you want to change the permissions for. Then press the [Enter] key.

Terminal

File   Edit   Settings   Help

[root@localhost /root]# clear

CLEAR

Clears the screen.

1 Type **clear** and then press the [Enter] key.

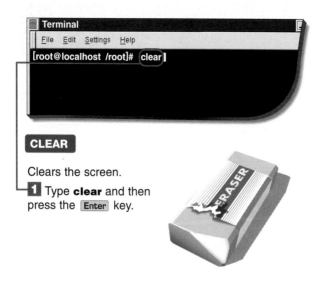

Terminal

File   Edit   Settings   Help

[root@localhost /root]# cp /root/deadlines /home/tsmith ▮

CP

Makes an exact copy of a file and places the copy in a new location.

1 Type **cp** followed by the location and name of the file you want to copy.

2 Type the location and name of the directory where you want to place the copy. Then press the [Enter] key.

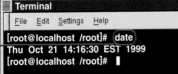

DATE

Displays the current date and time.

1 Type **date** and then press the Enter key.

EXIT

Closes the Terminal window or logs off the current user.

1 Type **exit** and then press the Enter key.

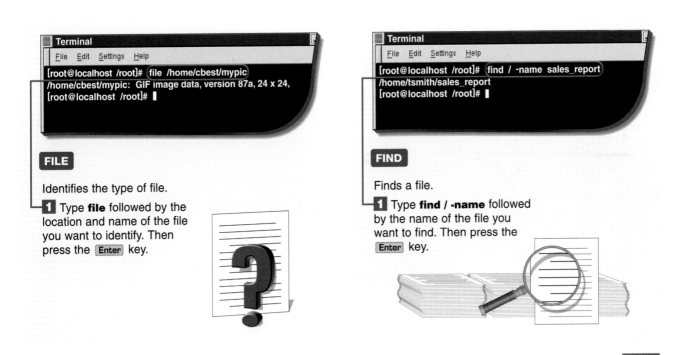

FILE

Identifies the type of file.

1 Type **file** followed by the location and name of the file you want to identify. Then press the Enter key.

FIND

Finds a file.

1 Type **find / -name** followed by the name of the file you want to find. Then press the Enter key.

COMMON LINUX COMMANDS

GUNZIP

Uncompresses a file so you can work with the file. Files are compressed to reduce the file size.

1 To uncompress a file with the .gz extension, type **gunzip** and then type the location and name of the file. Then press the [Enter] key.

■ To uncompress a file with the .zip extension, type **gunzip -S .zip** and then type the location and name of the file. Then press the [Enter] key.

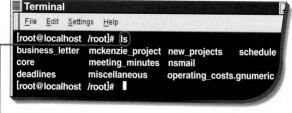

KILL

Closes a program. This is useful when a program has stopped responding.

1 Type **kill** followed by the process identification (PID) number for the program you want to close. Then press the [Enter] key.

Note: You may be able to determine the PID number for the program by using the ps command as shown on page 238.

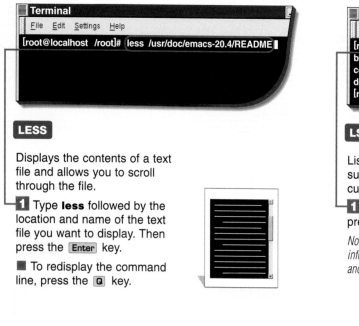

LESS

Displays the contents of a text file and allows you to scroll through the file.

1 Type **less** followed by the location and name of the text file you want to display. Then press the [Enter] key.

■ To redisplay the command line, press the [Q] key.

LS

Lists the files and subdirectories in the current directory.

1 Type **ls** and then press the [Enter] key.

*Note: If you want to display information about each file and subdirectory, type **ls -la**.*

Terminal

File   Edit   Settings   Help

[root@localhost   /root]#   man   kill

MAN

Displays help information about a command.

1 Type **man** followed by the name of the command you want information on. Then press the Enter key.

■ To redisplay the command line, press the Q key.

HELP

Terminal

File   Edit   Settings   Help

[root@localhost   /root]#   mkdir   /home/tsmith/work_folder

MKDIR

Creates a new directory.

1 Type **mkdir** followed by a location and name for the directory you want to create. Then press the Enter key.

NEW

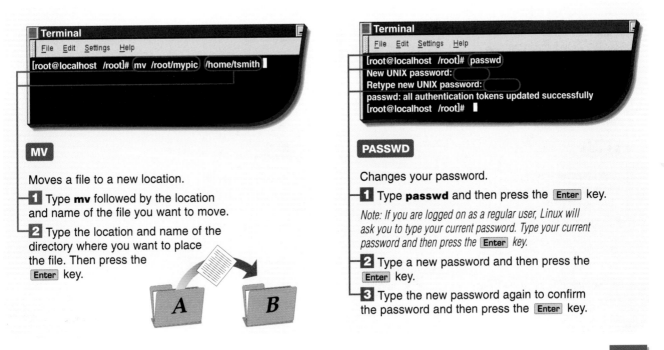

Terminal

File   Edit   Settings   Help

[root@localhost   /root]#   mv   /root/mypic   /home/tsmith

MV

Moves a file to a new location.

1 Type **mv** followed by the location and name of the file you want to move.

2 Type the location and name of the directory where you want to place the file. Then press the Enter key.

A   B

Terminal

File   Edit   Settings   Help

[root@localhost   /root]#   passwd
New UNIX password:
Retype new UNIX password:
passwd: all authentication tokens updated successfully
[root@localhost   /root]#

PASSWD

Changes your password.

1 Type **passwd** and then press the Enter key.

Note: If you are logged on as a regular user, Linux will ask you to type your current password. Type your current password and then press the Enter key.

2 Type a new password and then press the Enter key.

3 Type the new password again to confirm the password and then press the Enter key.

COMMON LINUX COMMANDS

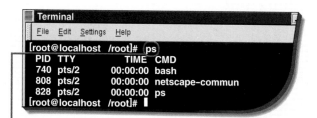

PICO

Starts a program that allows you to create and edit text files.

1 Type **pico** and then press the `Enter` key.

■ To redisplay the command line, press and hold down the `Ctrl` key as you press the `X` key.

PS

Displays a list of currently running programs that were started from the command line.

1 Type **ps** and then press the `Enter` key.

CURRENTLY RUNNING PROGRAMS

Gnome Mines
gnotepad+
Gnumeric
Netscape Communicator

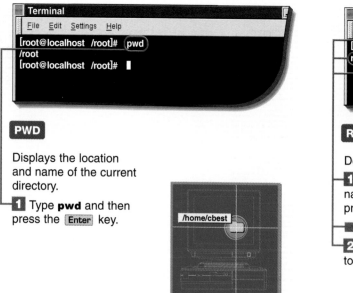

PWD

Displays the location and name of the current directory.

1 Type **pwd** and then press the `Enter` key.

/home/cbest

RM

Deletes a file.

1 Type **rm** followed by the location and name of the file you want to delete. Then press the `Enter` key.

■ A confirmation message may appear.

2 Type **Y** and then press the `Enter` key to delete the file.

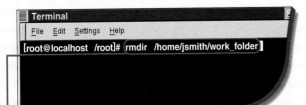

RMDIR

Deletes a directory. You must delete all the files in a directory before you can delete the directory.

1 Type **rmdir** followed by the location and name of the directory you want to delete. Then press the Enter key.

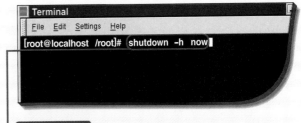

SHUTDOWN

Shuts down or restarts your computer.

1 To shut down your computer, type **shutdown –h now** and then press the Enter key.

■ To restart your computer, type **shutdown –r now** and then press the Enter key.

Note: If you are logged on as a regular user, Linux will ask you to type your password. Type your password and then press the Enter key.

TAR

Extracts files from an archive so you can work with the files. An archive is a group of files that are stored as a single file to save storage space. The tar command extracts files from archives with the .tar extension and is often used after using the gunzip command.

1 Type **tar –xf** and then type the location and name of the archive file you want to extract files from. Then press the Enter key.

WHO

Displays a list of the users who are logged on to the computer at the command line.

1 Type **who** and then press the Enter key.

Note: You can type **who am i** to determine which account you used to log on.

Users Logged On
- jsmith
- bmckenzie
- mrobinson
- rbest

CHAPTER 12

Connect to the Internet

This chapter shows you how to set up a connection to the Internet so you can access information on the World Wide Web.

SET UP A CONNECTION TO THE INTERNET

You need to set up a
connection to the Internet
before you can browse the
Web, exchange electronic
mail and join newsgroups.

SET UP A CONNECTION TO THE INTERNET

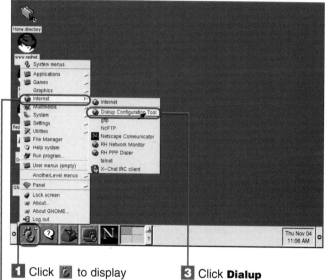

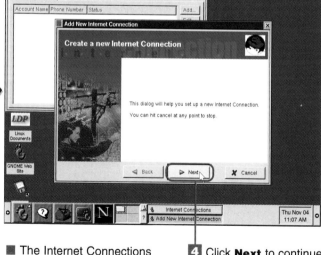

1 Click 🐾 to display
the Main Menu.

2 Click **Internet**.

3 Click **Dialup
Configuration Tool**.

*Note: If you are logged on to
your computer as a regular user,
a window appears, asking for the
password for the root account.
Type the password and then
press the* Enter *key.*

■ The Internet Connections
window and the Add New
Internet Connection dialog
box appear. The dialog
box will help you set up a
connection to the Internet.

4 Click **Next** to continue.

Why didn't Linux detect my modem?

Linux may not be able to detect some types of modems, such as Plug and Play modems and modems designed specifically to work with computers using the Windows operating system. To find out if your modem will work with Linux, check the documentation that came with the modem or visit the following Web page.

www.redhat.com/corp/support/hardware

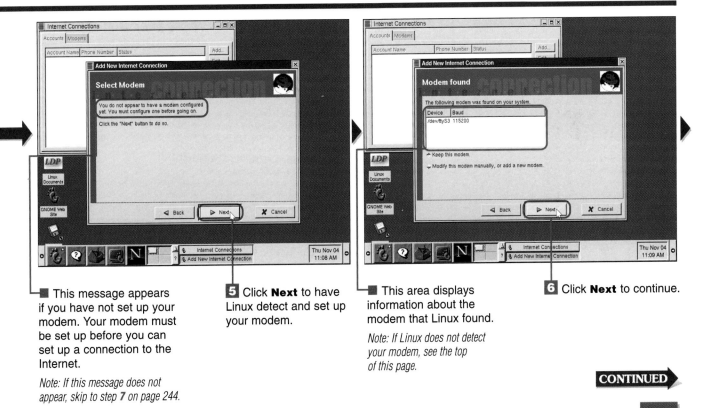

■ This message appears if you have not set up your modem. Your modem must be set up before you can set up a connection to the Internet.

Note: If this message does not appear, skip to step 7 on page 244.

5 Click **Next** to have Linux detect and set up your modem.

■ This area displays information about the modem that Linux found.

Note: If Linux does not detect your modem, see the top of this page.

6 Click **Next** to continue.

CONTINUED

When setting up a connection to the Internet, you need to enter information such as the phone number you need to dial to access your Internet Service Provider (ISP).

SET UP A CONNECTION TO THE INTERNET (CONTINUED)

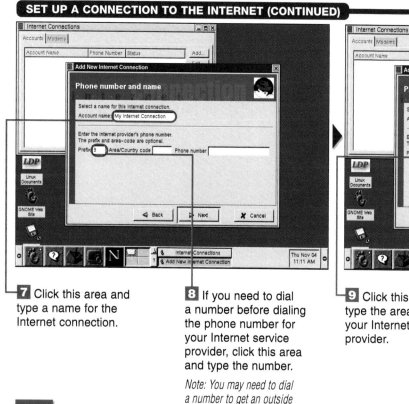

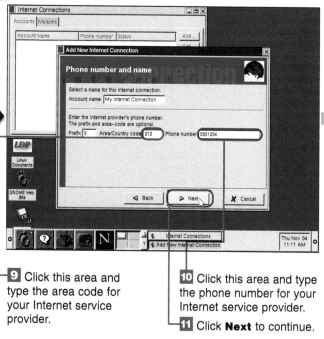

7 Click this area and type a name for the Internet connection.

8 If you need to dial a number before dialing the phone number for your Internet service provider, click this area and type the number.

Note: You may need to dial a number to get an outside line or disable call waiting.

9 Click this area and type the area code for your Internet service provider.

10 Click this area and type the phone number for your Internet service provider.

11 Click **Next** to continue.

What information do I need to set up a connection to the Internet?

You will need the following information from your Internet Service Provider (ISP) to set up a connection to the Internet.

Information	Example
Phone number for ISP	(212) 555-1234
User name	tsmith
Password	2p5mu6vo
Domain name server (DNS) number 1	192.168.30.1
Domain name server (DNS) number 2	192.168.30.2
Gateway number	192.168.48.5

Note: Your ISP may not require you to enter DNS and gateway numbers.

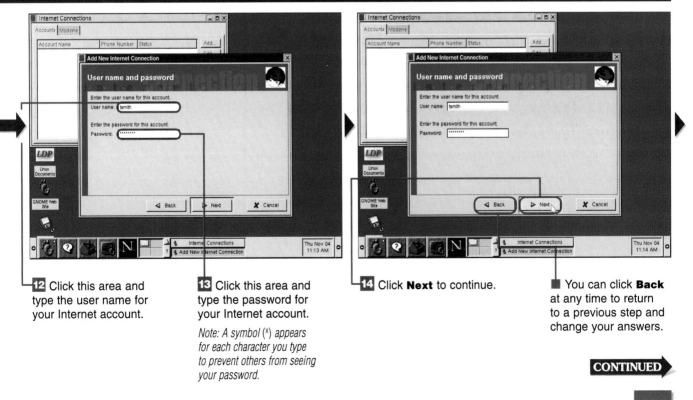

12 Click this area and type the user name for your Internet account.

13 Click this area and type the password for your Internet account.

Note: A symbol (ˣ) appears for each character you type to prevent others from seeing your password.

14 Click **Next** to continue.

■ You can click **Back** at any time to return to a previous step and change your answers.

CONTINUED

SET UP A CONNECTION TO THE INTERNET

You only need to set up a connection to the Internet once. Each user set up on your computer will be able to use the connection to access the Internet.

SET UP A CONNECTION TO THE INTERNET (CONTINUED)

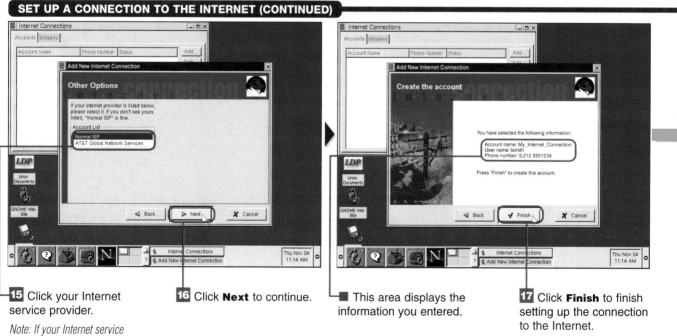

15 Click your Internet service provider.

*Note: If your Internet service provider does not appear in the list, click **Normal ISP**.*

16 Click **Next** to continue.

■ This area displays the information you entered.

17 Click **Finish** to finish setting up the connection to the Internet.

Does Linux come with the programs I need to access information on the Internet?

Linux comes with Netscape Communicator, which includes programs that allow you to access information on the Internet.

Netscape Navigator

Allows you to browse through the information on the Web. For more information, see page 254.

Netscape Messenger

Allows you to exchange electronic mail (e-mail) and join newsgroups. For more information, see pages 270 and 286.

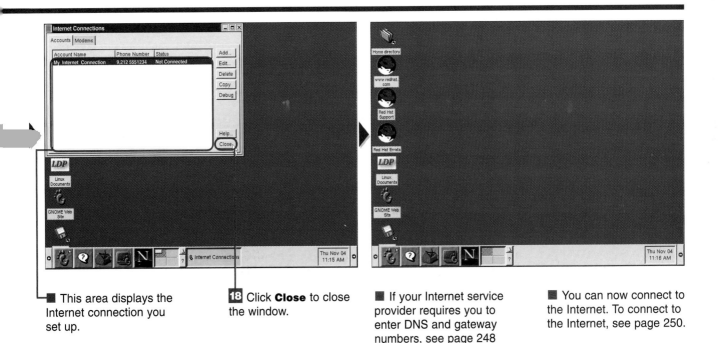

■ This area displays the Internet connection you set up.

18 Click **Close** to close the window.

■ If your Internet service provider requires you to enter DNS and gateway numbers, see page 248 to enter the numbers.

■ You can now connect to the Internet. To connect to the Internet, see page 250.

ENTER DNS AND GATEWAY NUMBERS

Your Internet service provider may require you to enter Domain Name Server (DNS) and gateway numbers before you can connect to the Internet.

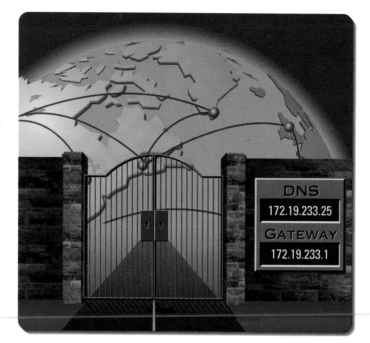

DNS
172.19.233.25

GATEWAY
172.19.233.1

You can contact your Internet service provider to determine if you need to enter DNS and gateway numbers.

You can only enter DNS and gateway numbers if you are logged on to your computer as **root**. If you are logged on as a regular user, you cannot enter the numbers.

ENTER DNS AND GATEWAY NUMBERS

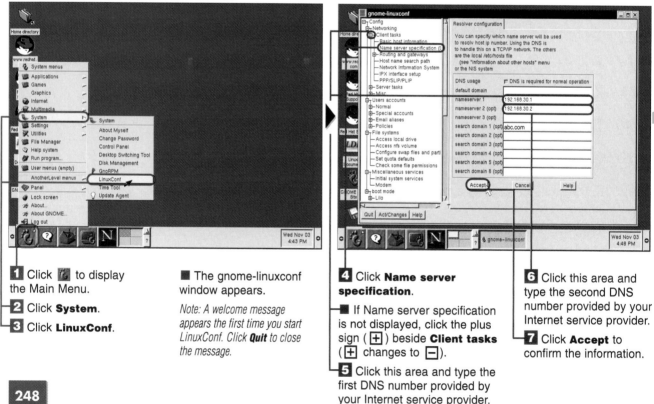

1 Click 🐾 to display the Main Menu.

2 Click **System**.

3 Click **LinuxConf**.

■ The gnome-linuxconf window appears.

*Note: A welcome message appears the first time you start LinuxConf. Click **Quit** to close the message.*

4 Click **Name server specification**.

■ If Name server specification is not displayed, click the plus sign (⊞) beside **Client tasks** (⊞ changes to ⊟).

5 Click this area and type the first DNS number provided by your Internet service provider.

6 Click this area and type the second DNS number provided by your Internet service provider.

7 Click **Accept** to confirm the information.

? Why would I need to enter DNS and gateway numbers?

You may need to enter DNS and gateway numbers to identify the Domain Name Server (DNS) and gateway used by your Internet service provider.

Domain Name Server (DNS)

A domain name server changes Web page addresses you type into IP numbers. IP numbers uniquely identify each computer that stores Web pages on the Internet. For example, when you type **www.maran.com**, a domain name server will change this address to 172.19.233.25.

Gateway

A gateway is a device that connects your computer to the Internet.

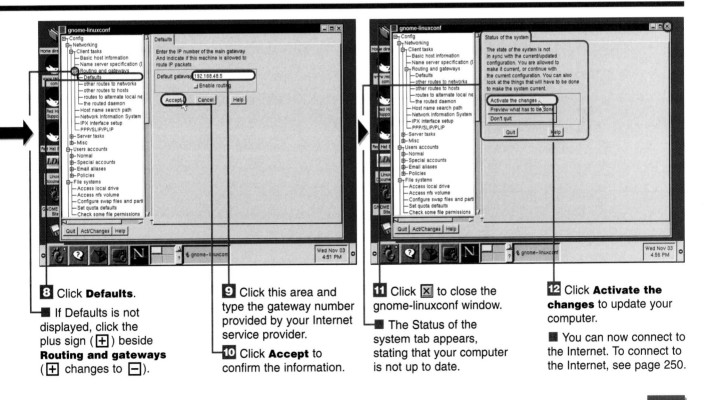

8 Click **Defaults**.

■ If Defaults is not displayed, click the plus sign (⊞) beside **Routing and gateways** (⊞ changes to ⊟).

9 Click this area and type the gateway number provided by your Internet service provider.

10 Click **Accept** to confirm the information.

11 Click ✕ to close the gnome-linuxconf window.

■ The Status of the system tab appears, stating that your computer is not up to date.

12 Click **Activate the changes** to update your computer.

■ You can now connect to the Internet. To connect to the Internet, see page 250.

CONNECT TO THE INTERNET

After you set up
a connection to
the Internet, you
can connect to
the Internet at
any time.

If you have an
external modem
that sits outside
of your computer,
make sure the
modem is turned on
before connecting
to the Internet.

CONNECT TO THE INTERNET

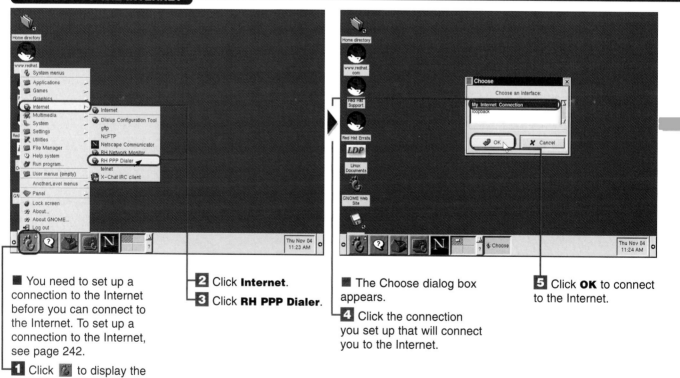

■ You need to set up a
connection to the Internet
before you can connect to
the Internet. To set up a
connection to the Internet,
see page 242.

1 Click 🖳 to display the
Main Menu.

2 Click **Internet**.

3 Click **RH PPP Dialer**.

■ The Choose dialog box
appears.

4 Click the connection
you set up that will connect
you to the Internet.

5 Click **OK** to connect
to the Internet.

Why am I having problems connecting to the Internet?

If you are having problems connecting to the Internet, the telephone lines at your Internet Service Provider (ISP) may be busy or your ISP may be experiencing computer problems. Try connecting to the Internet at a later time or contact your ISP to determine the cause of the problem.

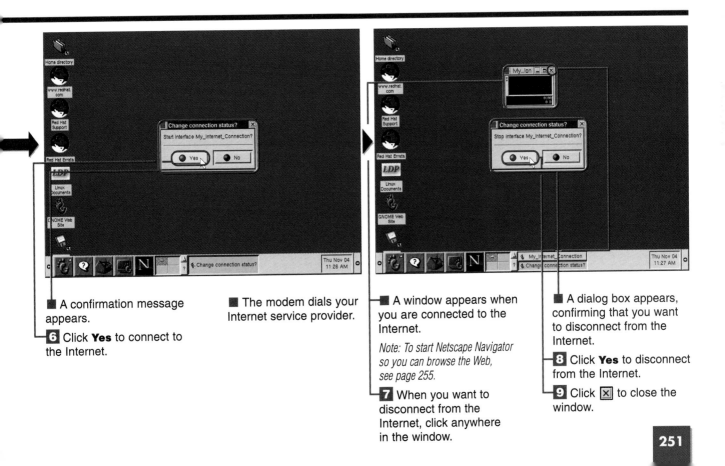

■ A confirmation message appears.

6 Click **Yes** to connect to the Internet.

■ The modem dials your Internet service provider.

■ A window appears when you are connected to the Internet.

Note: To start Netscape Navigator so you can browse the Web, see page 255.

7 When you want to disconnect from the Internet, click anywhere in the window.

■ A dialog box appears, confirming that you want to disconnect from the Internet.

8 Click **Yes** to disconnect from the Internet.

9 Click ⊠ to close the window.

CHAPTER 13

Browse the Web

This chapter introduces you to the World Wide Web and shows you how to transfer information from sites around the world.

INTRODUCTION TO THE WEB

The World Wide Web is part of the Internet and consists of a huge collection of documents stored on hundreds of thousands of computers around the world.

The World Wide Web is also called the Web.

Web Page

A Web page is a document on the Web. Web pages can include text, pictures, sound and video.

Web Site

A Web site is a collection of Web pages maintained by a college, university, government agency, company or individual.

Links

Web pages contain highlighted text or images, called links, that connect to other pages on the Web. You can select a link on a Web page to display another Web page located on the same computer or a computer across the city, country or world.

URL

Each Web page has a unique address, called a Uniform Resource Locator (URL). You can display any Web page if you know its URL.

Connecting to the Internet

Most people use an Internet Service Provider (ISP) to connect to the Internet. Once you pay your ISP to connect to the Internet, you can exchange information on the Internet free of charge.

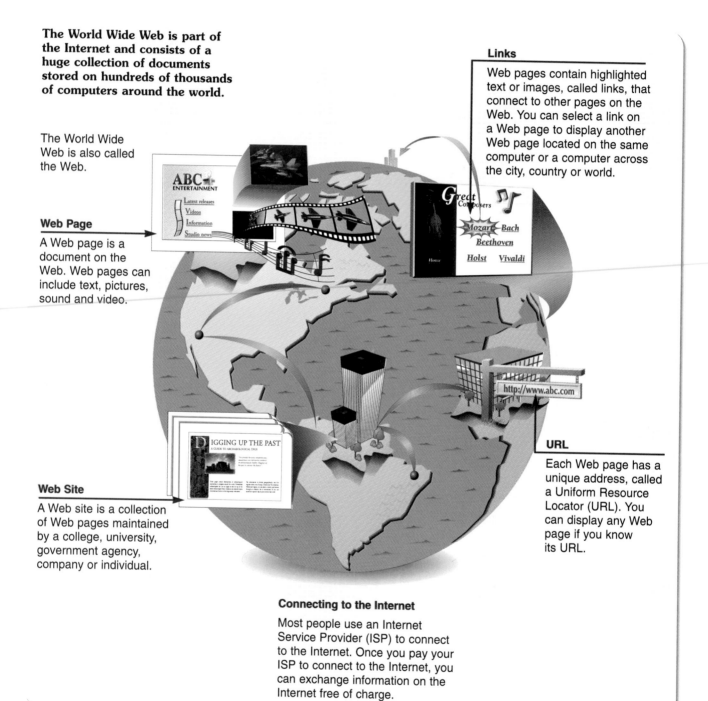

You can start Netscape Navigator to browse through the information on the Web.

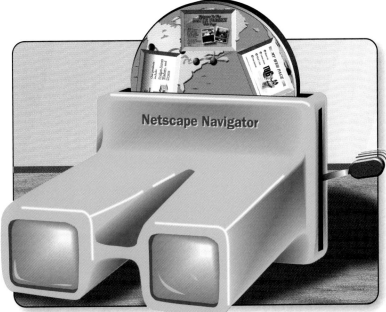

START NETSCAPE NAVIGATOR

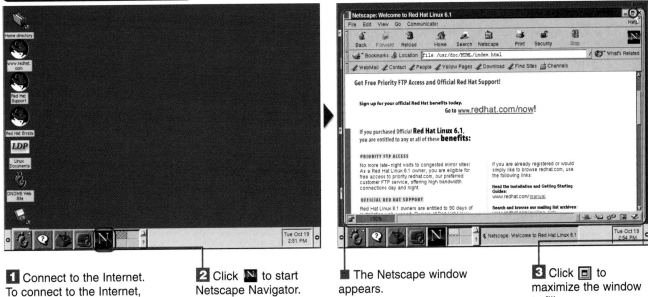

1 Connect to the Internet. To connect to the Internet, see page 250.

2 Click to start Netscape Navigator.

■ The Netscape window appears.

3 Click 🔲 to maximize the window to fill your screen.

DISPLAY A SPECIFIC WEB PAGE

You can display a page on the Web that you have heard or read about.

URL

http://www.flowerstop.com

You need to know the address of the Web page you want to view. Each page on the Web has a unique address, called a Uniform Resource Locator (URL).

DISPLAY A SPECIFIC WEB PAGE

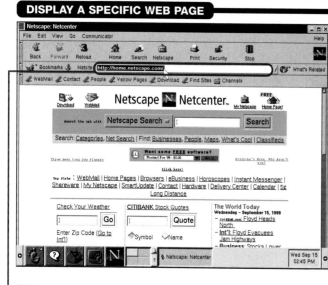

1 Double-click this area to highlight the current Web page address.

2 Type the address of the Web page you want to view and then press the **Enter** key.

*Note: You do not need to type **http://** when typing a Web page address.*

■ The Web page appears on your screen.

What are some popular Web pages that I can display?

Blue Mountain Arts	www.bluemountain.com
CBS SportsLine	www.sportsline.com
CNN.com	www.cnn.com
eBay	www.ebay.com
maranGraphics	www.maran.com
MSNBC	www.msnbc.com
MTV OnLINE	www.mtv.com
NASA	www.nasa.gov
Sony	www.sony.com
TIME.com	www.pathfinder.com

REDISPLAY A WEB PAGE

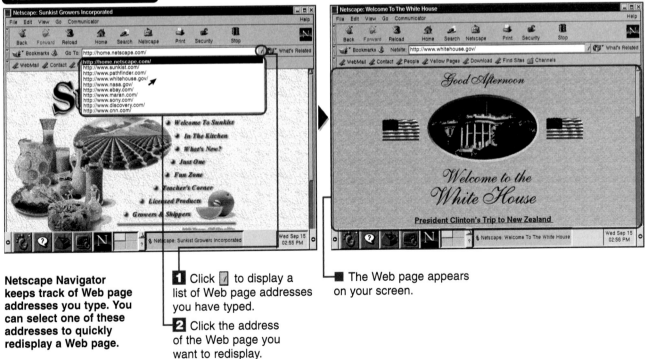

Netscape Navigator keeps track of Web page addresses you type. You can select one of these addresses to quickly redisplay a Web page.

1 Click 🔽 to display a list of Web page addresses you have typed.

2 Click the address of the Web page you want to redisplay.

■ The Web page appears on your screen.

SELECT A LINK

A link connects text or an image on one Web page to another Web page. When you select the text or image, the linked Web page appears.

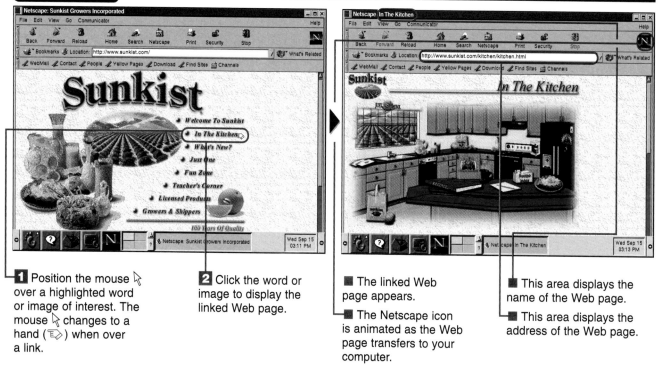

1 Position the mouse ▷ over a highlighted word or image of interest. The mouse ▷ changes to a hand (☜) when over a link.

2 Click the word or image to display the linked Web page.

■ The linked Web page appears.

■ The Netscape icon is animated as the Web page transfers to your computer.

■ This area displays the name of the Web page.

■ This area displays the address of the Web page.

If a Web page is taking
a long time to appear
on your screen, you
can stop the transfer
of the page and try
connecting again
later.

The best time to try connecting
to a Web page is during off-peak
hours, such as nights and
weekends, when fewer people
are using the Internet.

STOP TRANSFER OF INFORMATION

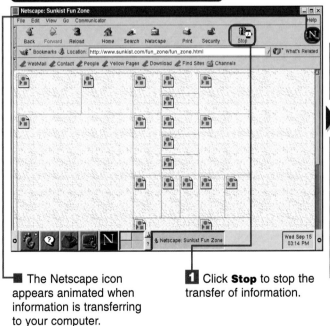

■ The Netscape icon
appears animated when
information is transferring
to your computer.

1 Click **Stop** to stop the
transfer of information.

■ The Stop button becomes
dimmed, indicating that
information is no longer
transferring to your computer.

RELOAD A WEB PAGE

You can reload a Web page to update the information displayed on your screen. Netscape Navigator will transfer a fresh copy of the Web page to your computer.

Reloading a Web page is useful for updating information such as the current news.

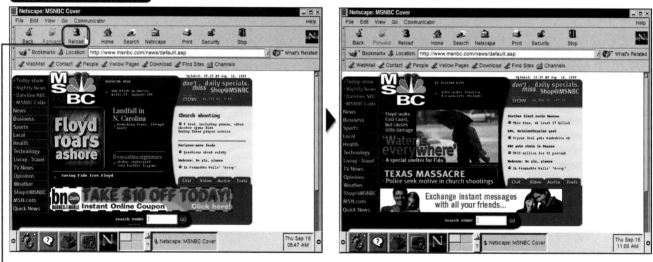

1 Click **Reload** to transfer a fresh copy of the displayed Web page to your computer.

■ A fresh copy of the Web page appears on your screen.

You can move back and
forth through the Web
pages you have viewed
since you last started
Netscape Navigator.

MOVE THROUGH WEB PAGES

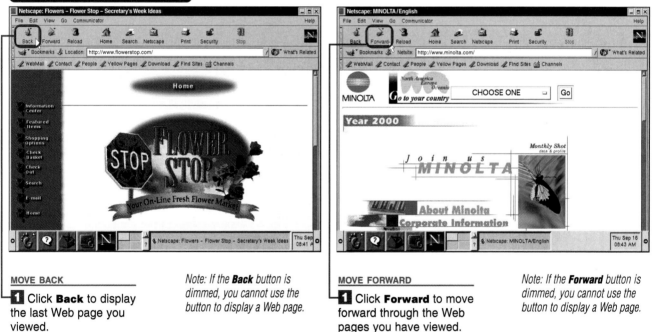

MOVE BACK

1 Click **Back** to display
the last Web page you
viewed.

*Note: If the **Back** button is
dimmed, you cannot use the
button to display a Web page.*

MOVE FORWARD

1 Click **Forward** to move
forward through the Web
pages you have viewed.

*Note: If the **Forward** button is
dimmed, you cannot use the
button to display a Web page.*

DISPLAY AND CHANGE YOUR HOME PAGE

You can specify which Web page you want to set as your home page. You can quickly display your home page at any time.

DISPLAY AND CHANGE YOUR HOME PAGE

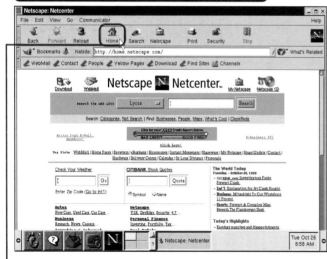

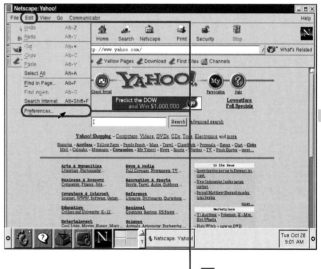

DISPLAY YOUR HOME PAGE

1 Click **Home** to display your home page.

■ Your home page appears.

Note: Your home page may be different than the home page shown here.

CHANGE YOUR HOME PAGE

1 Display the Web page you want to set as your home page.

2 Click **Edit**.

3 Click **Preferences**.

Which Web page should I set as my home page?

You can set any page on the Web as your home page. Your home page can be a Web page you frequently visit or a Web page that provides a good starting point for exploring the Web.

■ The Netscape: Preferences dialog box appears.

4 Click **Navigator**.

■ This area displays the address of your current home page.

5 Click **Use Current Page** to set the Web page displayed on your screen as your new home page.

■ This area displays the address of your new home page.

6 Click **OK** to confirm your change.

ADD A BOOKMARK

You can create bookmarks to store the addresses of your favorite Web pages. Bookmarks save you from having to remember and constantly retype Web page addresses.

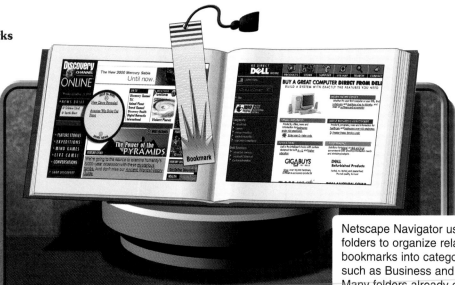

Netscape Navigator uses folders to organize related bookmarks into categories, such as Business and Finance. Many folders already contain bookmarks that let you quickly access popular Web pages.

ADD A BOOKMARK

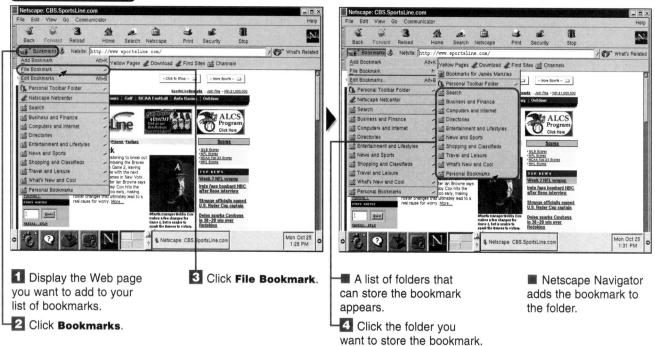

1 Display the Web page you want to add to your list of bookmarks.

2 Click **Bookmarks**.

3 Click **File Bookmark**.

■ A list of folders that can store the bookmark appears.

4 Click the folder you want to store the bookmark.

■ Netscape Navigator adds the bookmark to the folder.

Is there another way to quickly access useful Web pages?

The Personal toolbar gives you quick access to useful Web pages.

| WebMail | Contact | People | Yellow Pages | Download | Find Sites |

WebMail

Lets you access Netscape's free e-mail service.

Contact

Lets you access Netscape's contact management service, which includes a calendar and address book.

People

Lets you search for people.

Yellow Pages

Lets you search for people and businesses.

Download

Lets you obtain the latest versions of Netscape software.

Find Sites

Lets you search for Web pages.

SELECT A BOOKMARK

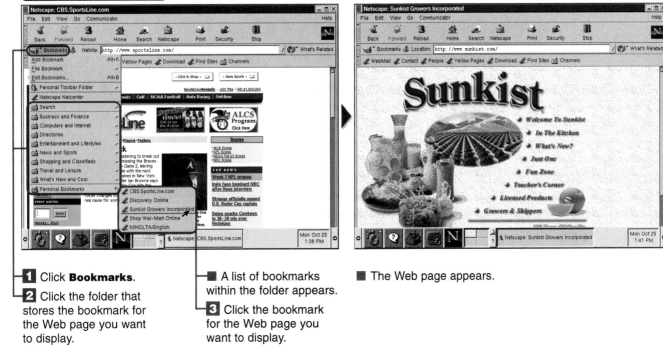

1 Click **Bookmarks**.

2 Click the folder that stores the bookmark for the Web page you want to display.

■ A list of bookmarks within the folder appears.

3 Click the bookmark for the Web page you want to display.

■ The Web page appears.

DELETE A BOOKMARK

You should delete
a bookmark you no
longer use. Deleting
bookmarks can help
keep your bookmark
list from becoming
cluttered.

DELETE A BOOKMARK

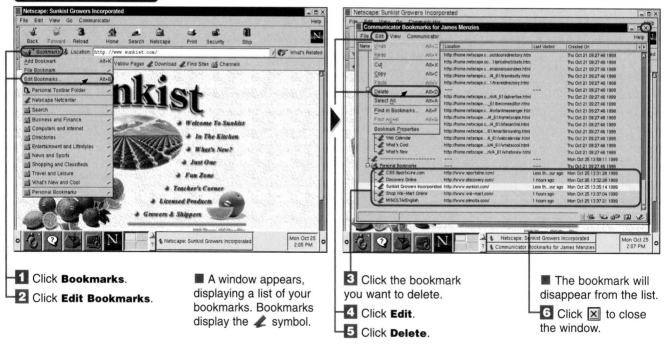

1 Click **Bookmarks**.

2 Click **Edit Bookmarks**.

■ A window appears,
displaying a list of your
bookmarks. Bookmarks
display the ✎ symbol.

3 Click the bookmark
you want to delete.

4 Click **Edit**.

5 Click **Delete**.

■ The bookmark will
disappear from the list.

6 Click ☒ to close
the window.

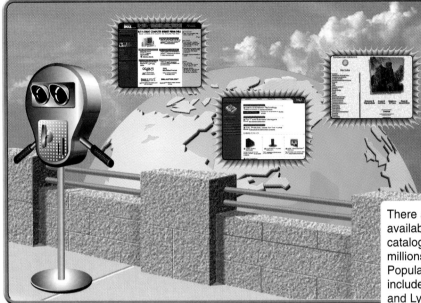

You can find pages on the Web that discuss topics of interest to you.

There are search tools available on the Web that catalog information about millions of Web pages. Popular search tools include Excite, HotBot and Lycos.

SEARCH THE WEB

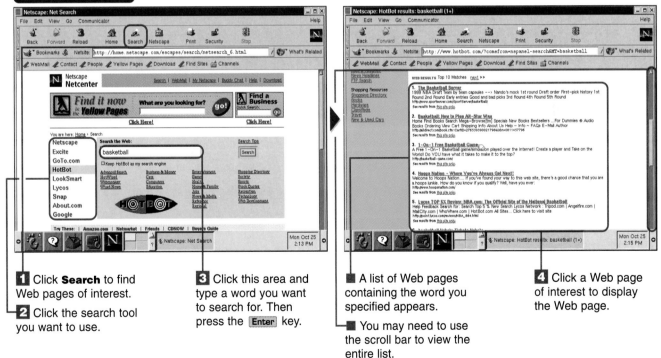

1 Click **Search** to find Web pages of interest.

2 Click the search tool you want to use.

3 Click this area and type a word you want to search for. Then press the Enter key.

■ A list of Web pages containing the word you specified appears.

■ You may need to use the scroll bar to view the entire list.

4 Click a Web page of interest to display the Web page.

CHAPTER 14

Exchange Electronic Mail

E-mail is a convenient way to exchange messages with family and colleagues worldwide. Learn how to set up an e-mail account and work with e-mail messages in this chapter.

SET UP AN E-MAIL ACCOUNT

You must set up
an e-mail account
before you can send
and receive e-mail
messages. You only
need to set up an
e-mail account once.

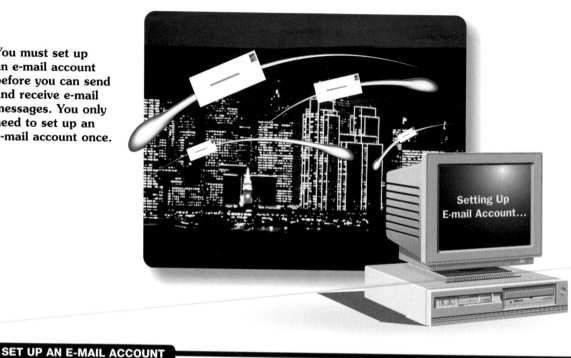

SET UP AN E-MAIL ACCOUNT

1 Click **N** to start Netscape Navigator.

2 Click **Edit**.

3 Click **Preferences**.

■ The Netscape: Preferences dialog box appears.

4 Click the arrow (▷) beside the **Mail & Newsgroups** category (▷ changes to ▽).

■ A list of items appears.

5 Click **Identity** to specify your name and e-mail address.

What information do I need to set up an e-mail account?

Before you can set up an e-mail account, you need the following information. If you do not know the information, ask your network administrator or Internet Service Provider (ISP).

| E-mail address | User name | Incoming mail server address | Outgoing mail server address |

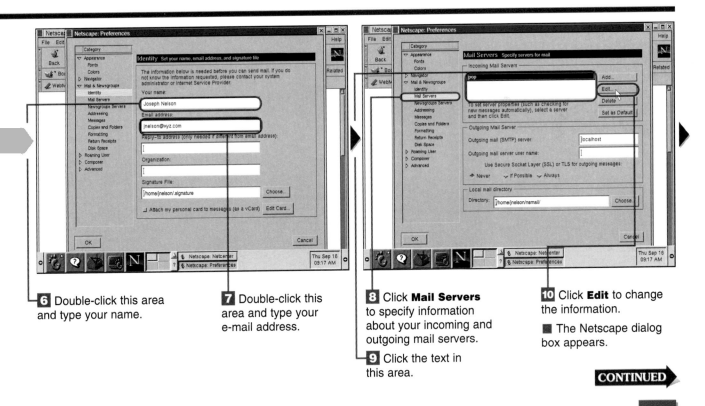

6 Double-click this area and type your name.

7 Double-click this area and type your e-mail address.

8 Click **Mail Servers** to specify information about your incoming and outgoing mail servers.

9 Click the text in this area.

10 Click **Edit** to change the information.

■ The Netscape dialog box appears.

CONTINUED

SET UP AN E-MAIL ACCOUNT

You can have Netscape Messenger remember your password so you do not need to enter the password each time you check your messages.

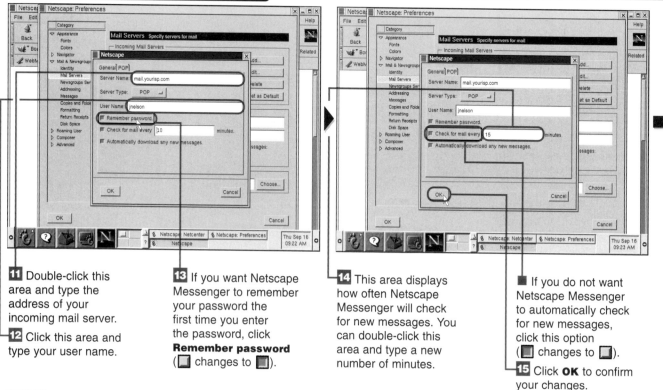

11 Double-click this area and type the address of your incoming mail server.

12 Click this area and type your user name.

13 If you want Netscape Messenger to remember your password the first time you enter the password, click **Remember password** (■ changes to ■).

14 This area displays how often Netscape Messenger will check for new messages. You can double-click this area and type a new number of minutes.

■ If you do not want Netscape Messenger to automatically check for new messages, click this option (■ changes to ■).

15 Click **OK** to confirm your changes.

When would I not want Netscape Messenger to automatically check for new messages?

You will not want Netscape Messenger to automatically check for new messages if you often read messages when you are not connected to the Internet. Each time Netscape Messenger checks for new messages, an error message will appear, indicating that you are not connected to the Internet. This can become distracting over time.

16 Double-click this area and type the address of your outgoing mail server.

Note: The addresses of the outgoing and incoming mail servers are usually the same.

17 If you need to provide a user name to send e-mail, click this area and type your user name.

18 Click **OK** to confirm your changes.

■ You can now send and receive e-mail messages.

START NETSCAPE MESSENGER
AND READ MESSAGES

You can start
Netscape Messenger
to exchange e-mail
messages with
people around
the world.

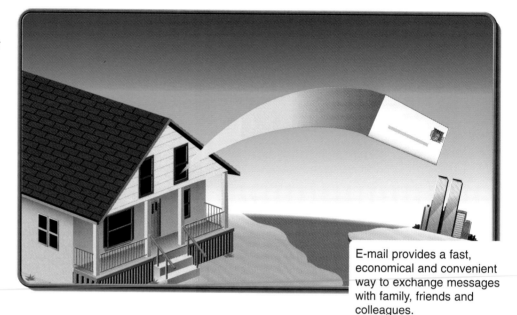

E-mail provides a fast,
economical and convenient
way to exchange messages
with family, friends and
colleagues.

START NETSCAPE MESSENGER

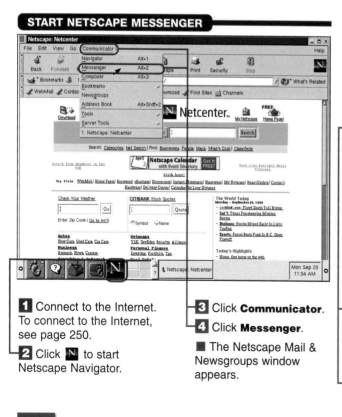

1 Connect to the Internet.
To connect to the Internet,
see page 250.

2 Click **N** to start
Netscape Navigator.

3 Click **Communicator**.

4 Click **Messenger**.

■ The Netscape Mail &
Newsgroups window
appears.

READ MESSAGES

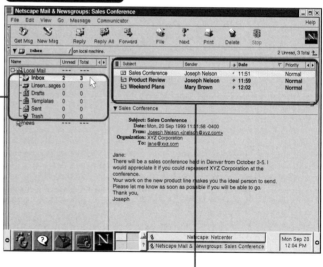

■ This area displays the
folders that store your
messages and the number
of unread and total number
of messages in each folder.

1 Click the folder
containing the messages
you want to read. The
folder is highlighted.

■ This area displays the
messages in the folder
you selected. Messages
you have not read
appear in **bold**.

What folders does Netscape Messenger use to store my messages?

Inbox
Stores messages you have received.

Unsent Messages
Stores messages you have not yet sent.

Drafts
Stores messages you have not yet completed.

Templates
Stores messages you have saved as templates so you can quickly send similar messages later.

Sent
Stores copies of messages you have sent.

Trash
Stores messages you have deleted.

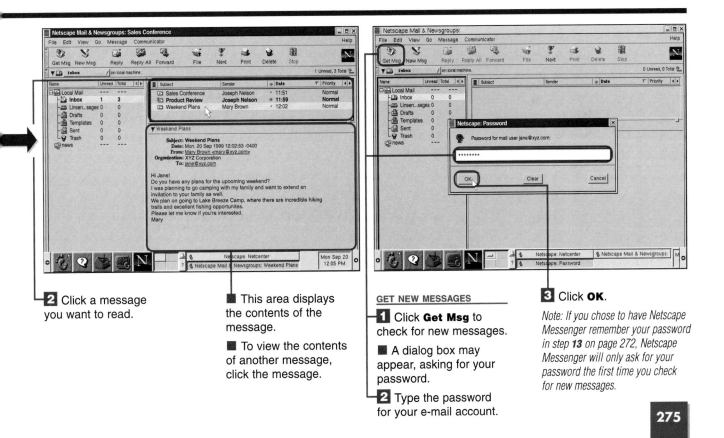

2 Click a message you want to read.

■ This area displays the contents of the message.

■ To view the contents of another message, click the message.

GET NEW MESSAGES

1 Click **Get Msg** to check for new messages.

■ A dialog box may appear, asking for your password.

2 Type the password for your e-mail account.

3 Click **OK**.

Note: If you chose to have Netscape Messenger remember your password in step **13** on page 272, Netscape Messenger will only ask for your password the first time you check for new messages.

SEND A MESSAGE

You can send a message to exchange ideas or request information.

SEND A MESSAGE

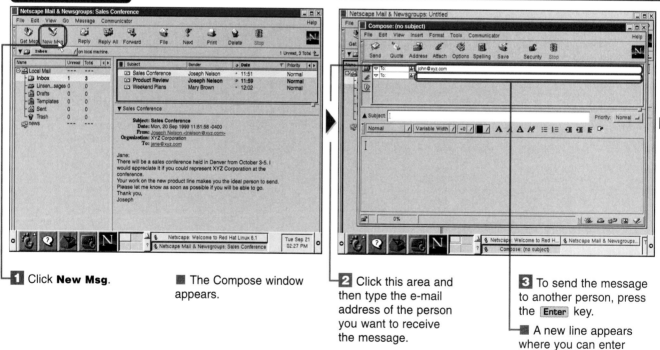

1 Click **New Msg**.

■ The Compose window appears.

2 Click this area and then type the e-mail address of the person you want to receive the message.

3 To send the message to another person, press the `Enter` key.

■ A new line appears where you can enter another e-mail address.

How can I address a message I want to send?

To

Sends the message to the person you specify.

Carbon Copy (Cc)

Sends an exact copy of the message to a person who is not directly involved, but would be interested in the message.

Blind Carbon Copy (Bcc)

Sends an exact copy of the message to a person without anyone else knowing that the person received the message.

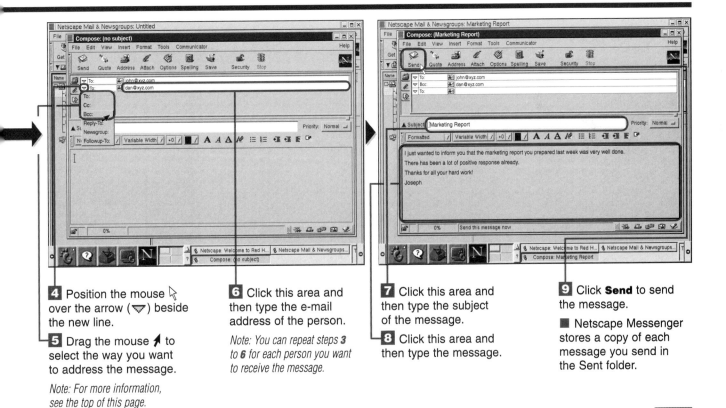

4 Position the mouse over the arrow (▽) beside the new line.

5 Drag the mouse to select the way you want to address the message.

Note: For more information, see the top of this page.

6 Click this area and then type the e-mail address of the person.

Note: You can repeat steps 3 to 6 for each person you want to receive the message.

7 Click this area and then type the subject of the message.

8 Click this area and then type the message.

9 Click **Send** to send the message.

■ Netscape Messenger stores a copy of each message you send in the Sent folder.

ATTACH A FILE TO A MESSAGE

You can attach a file to a message you are sending. Attaching a file is useful when you want to include additional information with a message.

ATTACH A FILE TO A MESSAGE

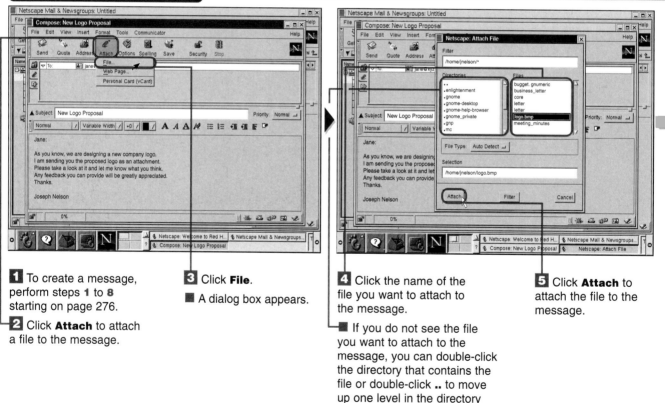

1 To create a message, perform steps **1** to **8** starting on page 276.

2 Click **Attach** to attach a file to the message.

3 Click **File**.

■ A dialog box appears.

4 Click the name of the file you want to attach to the message.

■ If you do not see the file you want to attach to the message, you can double-click the directory that contains the file or double-click **..** to move up one level in the directory structure.

5 Click **Attach** to attach the file to the message.

278

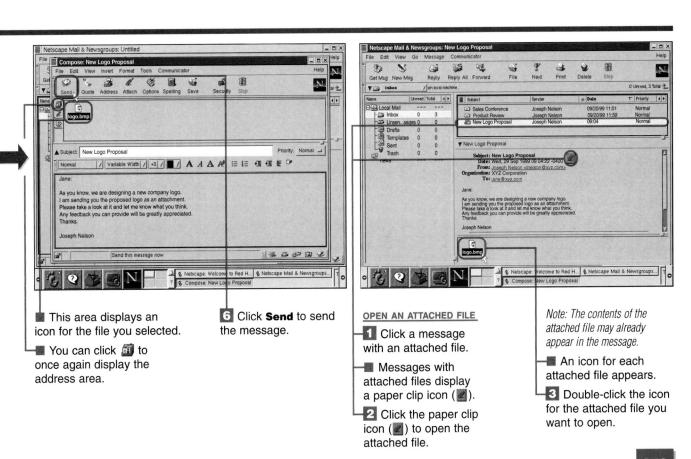

**What types of files can
I attach to a message?**

You can attach files such
as documents, pictures,
programs, sounds and videos
to a message. The computer
receiving the message must
have the necessary hardware
and software to display or
play the file.

■ This area displays an
icon for the file you selected.

■ You can click 📇 to
once again display the
address area.

6 Click **Send** to send
the message.

OPEN AN ATTACHED FILE

1 Click a message
with an attached file.

■ Messages with
attached files display
a paper clip icon (📎).

2 Click the paper clip
icon (📎) to open the
attached file.

*Note: The contents of the
attached file may already
appear in the message.*

■ An icon for each
attached file appears.

3 Double-click the icon
for the attached file you
want to open.

You can reply to a
message to answer a
question or comment
on the message.

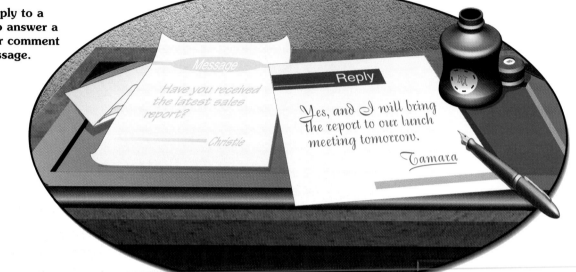

REPLY TO A MESSAGE

1 Click the message
you want to reply to.

2 Click the reply option
you want to use.

Reply

Sends a reply to the
author only.

Reply All

Sends a reply to the author
and everyone who received
the original message.

■ A window appears
for you to compose
the message.

■ Netscape Messenger
fills in the e-mail
address(es) for you.

■ Netscape Messenger
also fills in the subject,
starting the subject with **Re:**.

How can I express emotions in my e-mail messages?

You can use special characters, called smileys, to express emotions in e-mail messages. These characters resemble human faces if you turn them sideways.

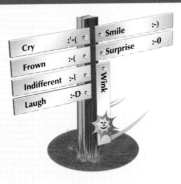

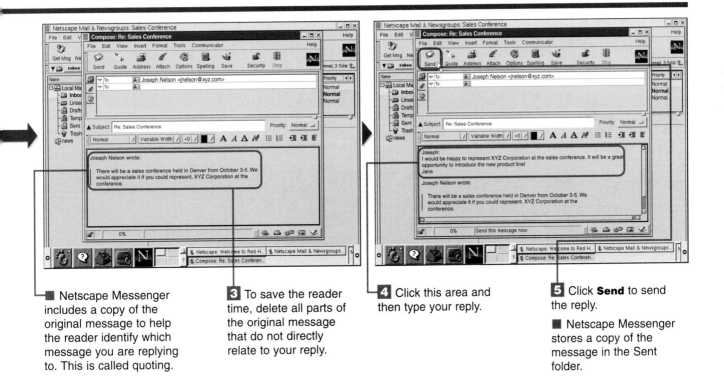

■ Netscape Messenger includes a copy of the original message to help the reader identify which message you are replying to. This is called quoting.

3 To save the reader time, delete all parts of the original message that do not directly relate to your reply.

4 Click this area and then type your reply.

5 Click **Send** to send the reply.

■ Netscape Messenger stores a copy of the message in the Sent folder.

FORWARD A MESSAGE

After reading a message, you can add comments and then forward the message to a friend or colleague.

Netscape Messenger sends a message you forward as an attached file.

FORWARD A MESSAGE

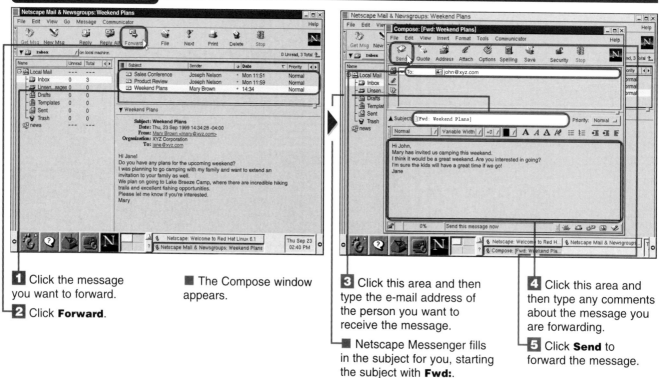

1 Click the message you want to forward.

2 Click **Forward**.

■ The Compose window appears.

3 Click this area and then type the e-mail address of the person you want to receive the message.

■ Netscape Messenger fills in the subject for you, starting the subject with **Fwd:**.

4 Click this area and then type any comments about the message you are forwarding.

5 Click **Send** to forward the message.

You can delete a
message you no
longer need. Deleting
messages prevents
your folders from
becoming cluttered
with messages.

DELETE A MESSAGE

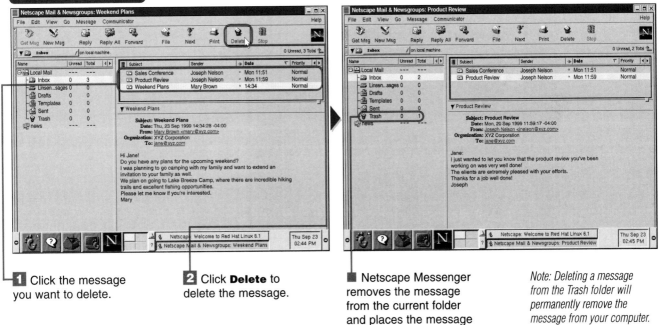

1 Click the message
you want to delete.

2 Click **Delete** to
delete the message.

■ Netscape Messenger
removes the message
from the current folder
and places the message
in the Trash folder.

*Note: Deleting a message
from the Trash folder will
permanently remove the
message from your computer.*

CHAPTER 15

Join Newsgroups

Newsgroups allow you to communicate with people who share your interests. In this chapter you will learn how to subscribe to newsgroups, read messages and more.

Music Lovers!

Join Now!

101 Great Karaoke Bars

Choosing a Partner

.music.karaoke

Sunday, August 22, 1999

How to Optimize Your Printing Speed

comp.laser-printers

SET UP NEWSGROUPS

You must set up
newsgroups before you
can join newsgroups.
Newsgroups are
discussion groups
that allow people with
common interests
to communicate. You
only need to set up
newsgroups once.

You must set up
an e-mail account
before you can join
newsgroups. To set
up an e-mail account,
see page 270.

SET UP NEWSGROUPS

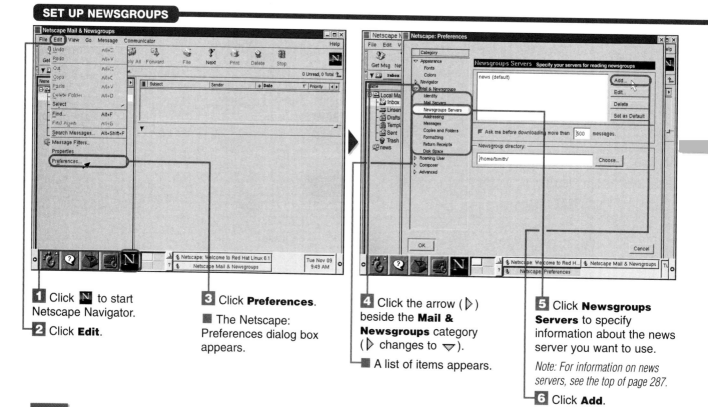

1 Click **N** to start
Netscape Navigator.

2 Click **Edit**.

3 Click **Preferences**.

■ The Netscape:
Preferences dialog box
appears.

4 Click the arrow (▷)
beside the **Mail &
Newsgroups** category
(▷ changes to ▽).

■ A list of items appears.

5 Click **Newsgroups
Servers** to specify
information about the news
server you want to use.

*Note: For information on news
servers, see the top of page 287.*

6 Click **Add**.

What is a news server?

A news server is a computer that stores newsgroup messages. News servers are usually maintained by Internet service providers.

When setting up newsgroups, you must specify the address of the news server you want to use. If you do not know the address, contact your Internet service provider. If you want to access newsgroups that can help you use Linux, you can specify the news.redhat.com address to use the Red Hat news server.

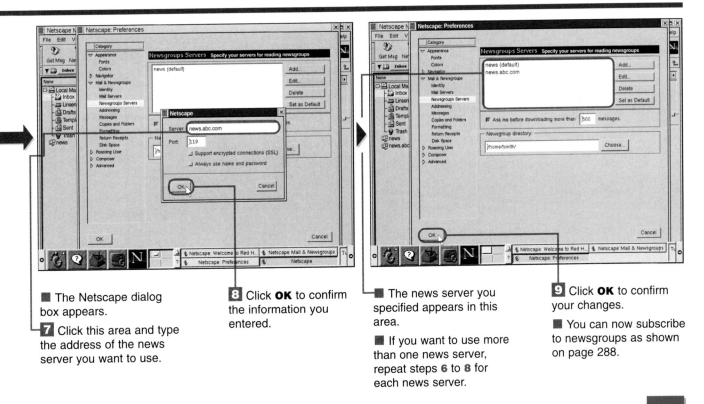

■ The Netscape dialog box appears.

7 Click this area and type the address of the news server you want to use.

8 Click **OK** to confirm the information you entered.

■ The news server you specified appears in this area.

■ If you want to use more than one news server, repeat steps **6** to **8** for each news server.

9 Click **OK** to confirm your changes.

■ You can now subscribe to newsgroups as shown on page 288.

SUBSCRIBE TO NEWSGROUPS

You must subscribe to newsgroups before you can read the messages in the newsgroups. Netscape Messenger can display a list of all the available newsgroups so you can find newsgroups of interest.

The available newsgroups depend on the news server you use.

SUBSCRIBE TO NEWSGROUPS

START NETSCAPE MESSENGER

1 Connect to the Internet. To connect to the Internet, see page 250.

2 Click **N** to start Netscape Navigator.

3 Click **Communicator**.

4 Click **Messenger**.

■ The Netscape Mail & Newsgroups window appears.

VIEW LIST OF NEWSGROUPS

5 Click the news server that offers newsgroups you want to subscribe to.

How are newsgroups named?

The name of a newsgroup describes the type of information discussed in the newsgroup. A newsgroup name consists of two or more words, separated by periods (.). The first word describes the main topic, such as alt (alternative), comp (computers), rec (recreation) or soc (social). Each of the following words narrows the topic.

Here are some examples of newsgroup names.

alt.fan.actors

comp.security.misc

rec.sport.football.pro

soc.culture.caribbean

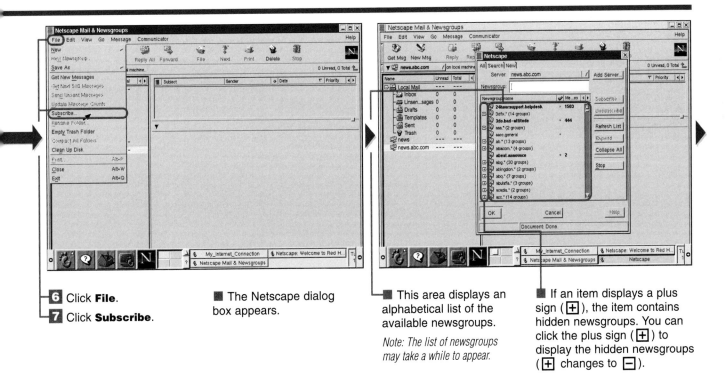

■ **6** Click **File**.

■ **7** Click **Subscribe**.

■ The Netscape dialog box appears.

■ This area displays an alphabetical list of the available newsgroups.

Note: The list of newsgroups may take a while to appear.

■ If an item displays a plus sign (⊞), the item contains hidden newsgroups. You can click the plus sign (⊞) to display the hidden newsgroups (⊞ changes to ⊟).

CONTINUED

SUBSCRIBE TO NEWSGROUPS

When subscribing to newsgroups, you can search for newsgroups that discuss topics of interest to you.

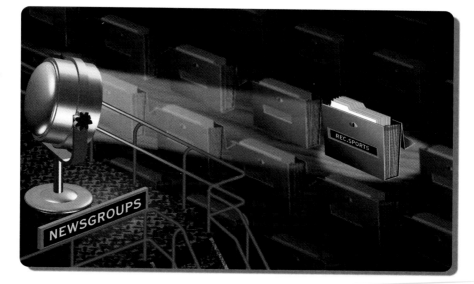

SUBSCRIBE TO NEWSGROUPS (CONTINUED)

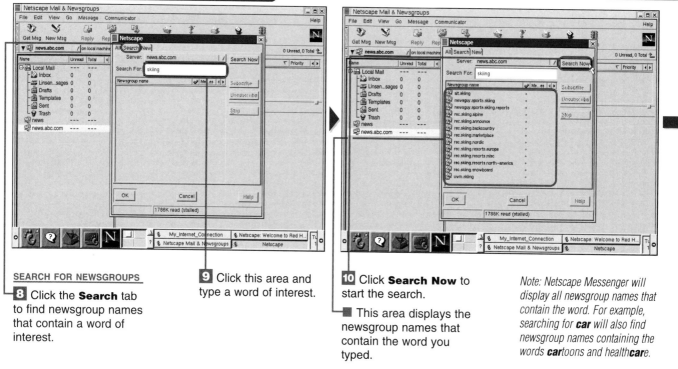

SEARCH FOR NEWSGROUPS

8 Click the **Search** tab to find newsgroup names that contain a word of interest.

9 Click this area and type a word of interest.

10 Click **Search Now** to start the search.

■ This area displays the newsgroup names that contain the word you typed.

*Note: Netscape Messenger will display all newsgroup names that contain the word. For example, searching for **car** will also find newsgroup names containing the words **car**toons and health**car**e.*

Where can I find information about a newsgroup?

You can read the FAQ (Frequently Asked Questions) for a newsgroup to learn about the newsgroup. A FAQ is a message in a newsgroup that contains a list of questions and answers that regularly appear in the newsgroup. A FAQ is designed to prevent new readers from asking questions that have already been answered. The news.answers newsgroup provides FAQs for a wide variety of newsgroups.

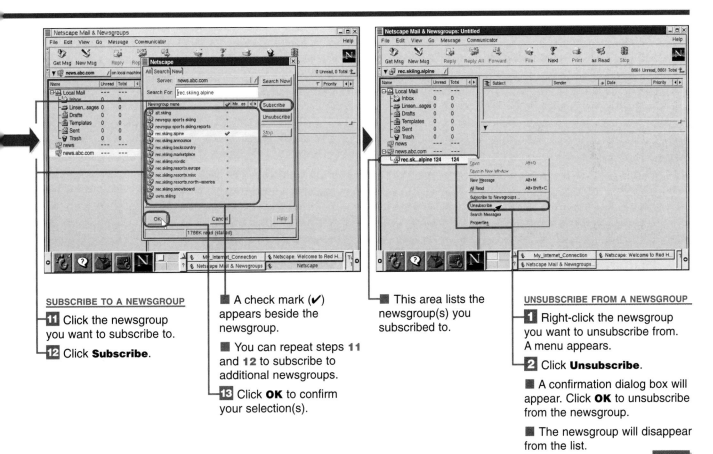

SUBSCRIBE TO A NEWSGROUP

11 Click the newsgroup you want to subscribe to.

12 Click **Subscribe**.

■ A check mark (✔) appears beside the newsgroup.

■ You can repeat steps **11** and **12** to subscribe to additional newsgroups.

13 Click **OK** to confirm your selection(s).

■ This area lists the newsgroup(s) you subscribed to.

UNSUBSCRIBE FROM A NEWSGROUP

1 Right-click the newsgroup you want to unsubscribe from. A menu appears.

2 Click **Unsubscribe**.

■ A confirmation dialog box will appear. Click **OK** to unsubscribe from the newsgroup.

■ The newsgroup will disappear from the list.

You can read the messages in a newsgroup to learn the opinions and ideas of thousands of people around the world.

Before you can read the messages in a newsgroup, you need to subscribe to the newsgroup. To subscribe to newsgroups, see page 288.

READ MESSAGES

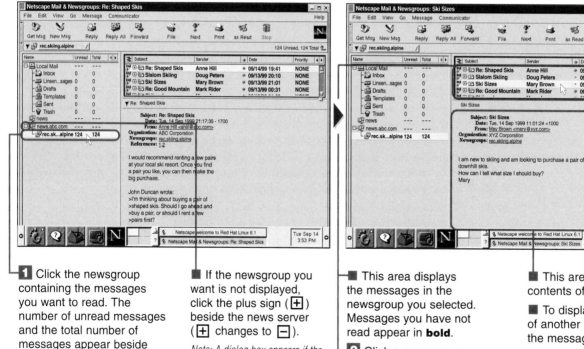

1 Click the newsgroup containing the messages you want to read. The number of unread messages and the total number of messages appear beside the newsgroup.

■ If the newsgroup you want is not displayed, click the plus sign (⊞) beside the news server (⊞ changes to ⊟).

Note: A dialog box appears if the newsgroup you selected contains more than 500 messages. Click OK to transfer all of the messages.

■ This area displays the messages in the newsgroup you selected. Messages you have not read appear in **bold**.

2 Click a message you want to read.

■ This area displays the contents of the message.

■ To display the contents of another message, click the message.

You can send a message to a newsgroup to ask a question or express your opinion.

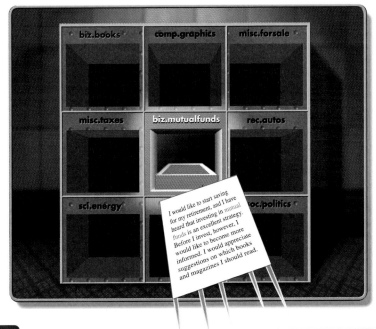

You should read the messages in a newsgroup for at least one week before sending a message. This helps you avoid sending information others have already read and is a great way to learn how people in the newsgroup communicate.

SEND A MESSAGE

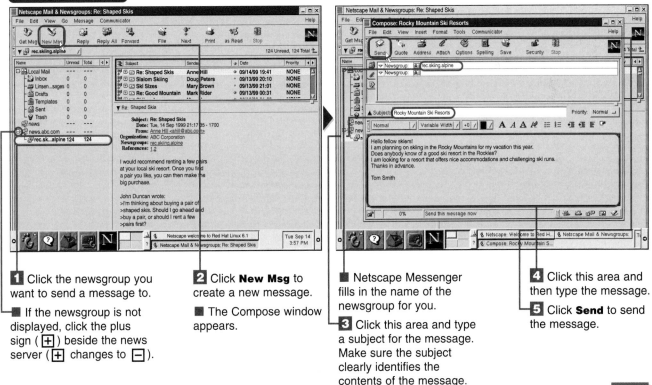

1 Click the newsgroup you want to send a message to.

■ If the newsgroup is not displayed, click the plus sign (⊞) beside the news server (⊞ changes to ⊟).

2 Click **New Msg** to create a new message.

■ The Compose window appears.

■ Netscape Messenger fills in the name of the newsgroup for you.

3 Click this area and type a subject for the message. Make sure the subject clearly identifies the contents of the message.

4 Click this area and then type the message.

5 Click **Send** to send the message.

INDEX

INDEX

INDEX

INDEX

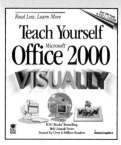

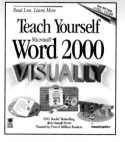

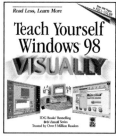

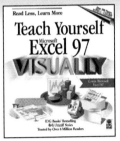

IDG BOOKS ®

TRADE & INDIVIDUAL ORDERS

Phone: **(800) 762-2974**
or **(317) 596-5200**
(8 a.m. – 6 p.m., CST, weekdays)
FAX : **(800) 550-2747**
or **(317) 596-5692**

EDUCATIONAL ORDERS & DISCOUNTS

Phone: **(800) 434-2086**
(8:30 a.m.–5:00 p.m., CST, weekdays)
FAX : **(317) 596-5499**

CORPORATE ORDERS FOR 3-D VISUAL™ SERIES

Phone: **(800) 469-6616**
(8 a.m.–5 p.m., EST, weekdays)
FAX : **(905) 890-9434**

Qty	ISBN	Title	Price	Total

Shipping & Handling Charges

	Description	First book	Each add'l. book	Total
Domestic	Normal	$4.50	$1.50	$
	Two Day Air	$8.50	$2.50	$
	Overnight	$18.00	$3.00	$
International	Surface	$8.00	$8.00	$
	Airmail	$16.00	$16.00	$
	DHL Air	$17.00	$17.00	$

Subtotal _____

CA residents add
applicable sales tax _____

IN, MA and MD
residents add
5% sales tax _____

IL residents add
6.25% sales tax _____

RI residents add
7% sales tax _____

TX residents add
8.25% sales tax _____

Shipping _____

Total _____

Ship to:

Name _____

Address _____

Company _____

City/State/Zip _____

Daytime Phone _____

Payment: ☐ Check to IDG Books (US Funds Only)
☐ Visa   ☐ Mastercard   ☐ American Express

Card # _____ Exp. _____ Signature _____

*maran*Graphics™